Augmented and Virtual Reality in Libraries

LIBRARY INFORMATION TECHNOLOGY ASSOCIATION (LITA) GUIDES

Marta Mestrovic Deyrup, Ph.D.
Acquisitions Editor, Library Information and Technology Association, a division of the American Library Association

The Library Information Technology Association (LITA) Guides provide information and guidance on topics related to cutting-edge technology for library and IT specialists.

Written by top professionals in the field of technology, the guides are sought after by librarians wishing to learn a new skill or to become current in today's best practices.

Each book in the series has been overseen editorially since conception by LITA and reviewed by LITA members with special expertise in the specialty area of the book.

Established in 1966, LITA is the division of the American Library Association (ALA) that provides its members and the library and information science community as a whole with a forum for discussion, an environment for learning, and a program for actions on the design, development, and implementation of automated and technological systems in the library and information science field.

Approximately 25 LITA Guides were published by Neal-Schuman and ALA between 2007 and 2015. Rowman & Littlefield took over publication of the series beginning in late 2015. Books in the series published by Rowman & Littlefield are:

Digitizing Flat Media: Principles and Practices
The Librarian's Introduction to Programming Languages
Library Service Design: A LITA Guide to Holistic Assessment, Insight, and Improvement
Data Visualization: A Guide to Visual Storytelling for Librarians
Mobile Technologies in Libraries: A LITA Guide
Innovative LibGuides Applications
Integrating LibGuides into Library Websites
Protecting Patron Privacy: A LITA Guide
The LITA Leadership Guide: The Librarian as Entrepreneur, Leader, and Technologist
Using Social Media to Build Library Communities: A LITA Guide
Managing Library Technology: A LITA Guide
The LITA Guide to No- or Low-Cost Technology Tools for Libraries
Big Data Shocks: An Introduction to Big Data for Librarians and Information Professionals
The Savvy Academic Librarian's Guide to Technology Innovation: Moving Beyond the Wow Factor
The LITA Guide to Augmented Reality in Libraries

Augmented and Virtual Reality in Libraries

Edited by
Jolanda-Pieta van Arnhem
Christine Elliott
Marie Rose

ROWMAN & LITTLEFIELD
Lanham • Boulder • New York • London

Published by Rowman & Littlefield
A wholly owned subsidiary of The Rowman & Littlefield Publishing Group, Inc.
4501 Forbes Boulevard, Suite 200, Lanham, Maryland 20706
www.rowman.com

Unit A, Whitacre Mews, 26-34 Stannary Street, London SE11 4AB

British Library Cataloguing in Publication Information Available

Library of Congress Cataloging-in-Publication Data

LCCN 2018001263 | ISBN 9781538102909 (cloth: alk. paper) | ISBN 9781538102916 (pbk. : alk. paper) | ISBN 9781538102923 (electronic)

∞™ The paper used in this publication meets the minimum requirements of American National Standard for Information Sciences—Permanence of Paper for Printed Library Materials, ANSI/NISO Z39.48-1992.

Printed in the United States of America

Contents

Illustrations

Preface

It is our opinion that libraries, archives, and museums are pretty good at what they do in the real, tangible world we all occupy. It is the intention of this book to expose those same institutions, and professionals within them, to the new world of augmented and virtual reality (AR/VR). In particular, this book is geared toward librarians, archivists, and other information professionals who are looking for inexpensive and nontechnical ways to incorporate AR/VR into their already existing endeavors. Some of the efforts explored in this guide include programming, instruction, information literacy, collections management, curation, and other initiatives.

While there is a healthy amount of literature written about AR/VR in general, this book covers new ground in that not a lot has been written about AR/VR in relation to libraries, archives, and museums. Starting in the introductory chapter, this book will identify what literature there is, and continue to build on that knowledge base throughout each chapter. It is our hope that the content within will provide a new perspective for those already familiar with AR/VR, as well as introduce AR/VR to those who have not explored its possibilities.

This book is divided into two main sections. Part I will introduce what augmented and virtual reality is, and provide a brief history, mostly because its history *is* brief. This section of the book will also introduce readers to some of the terminology surrounding this technology, as well as the hardware and software available at the time this guide was published. It will be no surprise to readers to find that the technical and social landscape of AR/VR is rapidly changing, with new innovations and incorporations occurring daily. Readers will also be made aware of possible accessibility challenges that will surface when utilizing these technologies and user-centered pedagogies. Because of the nearly daily evolution of AR/VR, new publications will continue to surface after the publication of this book, with its focus on accessibility. Some of the chapters in this book mention challenges related to location, user abilities or disabilities, technology, and other situations. For further studies on AR/VR, we recommend that readers explore the vast amount of literature referenced in each chapter's bibliography.

Part II will present a variety of case studies in which libraries and archives have implemented AR/VR into their institutional efforts. In "Augmenting Orientation," Hornick and Wade discuss the ways they used free AR/VR apps to introduce their new students to library services. For inspiration on incorporating augmentation into library instruction efforts, O'Dell and Gutierrez describe how the free application Blippar affected instruction at Emporia State University in "Blipping through Information Literacy." In the amusingly titled "Gotta Catch 'em All," Smith and Hottinger also wanted their orientation to appeal to new students, so they created a scavenger hunt using the free app Aurasma. Ovens and Mills describe how their digital media can still provide a multisensory experience for patrons in "That E-book Smell." Sutherland describes the basics of how to use AR for wayfinding purposes in "Wayfinding Narratives."

Two case studies follow the work of archivists and their incorporation of AR/VR. In "Augmented Archives," Calloway and Bishop discuss how Washington College Archives incorporated student work to increase visitor access to primary materials. Hibbert, Christa, Seeley, and Lee's "Dance Magic Dance" case study incorporated both AR elements and 360 Video hardware and software to enable patrons to be immersed in various dances held in their video archives through the use of headsets.

360-degree video applications and hardware are increasingly being used in conjunction with AR/VR initiatives to incorporate numerous senses when interacting with materials. In "VR, AR, and Video 360" Miltenoff outlines how St. Cloud State University uses both Video 360 and an augmented reality game to engage students during orientation and instruction. Moore and McAvoy utilized Video 360 in their Ethnic Studies 120 course to enable students to experience the stories of others in "Teaching through Experiencing."

Absent from this book are contributions from museums, schools, and public libraries. This is not meant to disparage their efforts. In fact, these types of institutions are where AR/VR has seen increased usage, particularly in museums where this type of technology has allowed users to experience exhibits and collections in entirely new ways.[1] Though this book focuses on higher education, it is our hope that the chapters and case studies presented here will provide inspiration for our own cultural and educational institutions. While the case studies are specific to higher education, the pedagogy used to engage physical materials and users with a wide range of technological expertise can be applied to individual situations. The heart of AR/VR is not just about the technology—it's the cultivation of innovative ways to make the learning process a two-way street. We think there is something here for everyone.

NOTE

1. Sophie Gilbert, "Please Turn On Your Phone in the Museum," *Atlantic Monthly* 318, no. 3 (2016): 32–33.

Part I

AR AND VR TECHNOLOGIES

1

AR U Ready for AR/VR?

An Overview of Augmented and Virtual Reality in Libraries

Jolanda-Pieta van Arnhem, Marie Rose, and Christine Elliott

With the advent of popular games like Pokémon GO, and the arrival of consumer devices such as the Oculus Rift, augmented reality (AR) and virtual reality (VR) have begun to creep into our everyday lives. But what do these terms really mean? Are they interchangeable? What does a busy librarian or educator need to know about AR/VR? Why are these technologies important in the context of libraries, and how can we leverage this technology within our institutions? What larger issues should libraries consider when adopting AR/VR, such as providing equal access to all?

This chapter will seek to define "augmented reality" and "virtual reality," and clarify what the terms mean and encompass. It will provide a short history as well as an overview of how AR/VR affects different spheres of life right now, particularly in higher education. Readers will also take away an understanding of the technical components common to most AR/VR hardware devices and software, while addressing issues related to safety and accessibility. Examples of consumer-level hardware and software will be covered, keeping smaller institutional budgets in mind. The chapter will conclude with the opportunities, potential considerations, and limitations afforded by AR/VR at the time this book was published.

WHAT ARE AUGMENTED AND VIRTUAL REALITY?

In its simplest form, marker AR uses printed markers and software/applications to recognize programmed objects when markers are viewed through a camera. When the marker is viewed through a camera lens, the software overlays a virtual object on top of the camera image, and the user can view the augmented image.[1] QR codes were an early form of marker AR, linking the physical and digital. If viewed through a mobile device connected to the Internet, users can interact with programmed content. The marker thus allows the augmented and real environments to work together.[2]

There are two perspectives for viewing AR. The magic mirror technique is often used to display augmentations via real-time video, which are displayed behind the area being captured using a projection screen. Viewers can stand in front of the display and watch as the augmentation is happening.[3] A few current iterations of the magic mirror technique can be found in the beauty industry. For example, Rimmel London created its "Get the Look" app in 2016 to let customers virtually try on makeup,[4] and the Charlotte Tilbury cosmetic line implemented an in-store magic mirror used during makeover sessions to enhance the in-store experience for customers.[5] In 2017, Rimmel London became an early adopter of Facebook's AR technology in an effort to increase the usage of its AR app by integrating into the new Facebook Camera Effects platform within the Facebook mobile app.[6] There are sure to be many more changes in this area of AR development in the near future as new platforms emerge, in particular the release of Apple's ARKit with iOS11, which will allow app developers to integrate the iPhone/iPad camera overlay in their own apps instead of the "walled garden" of the Facebook app.[7]

The magic lens view associated with augmented reality applications allows users to "see through to an image of the real world with added AR elements."[8] This is what users experience when they play Pokémon GO, the game that caused a major craze in 2016 and helped to bring AR into the mainstream.[9] The user can see the park, or museum, or street in front of them, but they are also interacting with digital objects on their display. Markerless AR is created without using markers, and instead uses distinctive features (edges, corners, textures) in real objects within the environment.[10] For example, Blippar requires users to upload photos of the object or location, which are then augmented via an online dashboard. Users can then simply point their phones or tablets at the object for interaction without using a QR code. Markerless AR technology has become more common and is increasingly available to the average user via mobile applications like Layar, Google Goggles, Wikitude, Aurasma, and Blippar. In recent years, many of these applications are also providing easy-to-use AR creation interfaces that allow users to create their own AR content.[11] There are many examples of librarians using augmented reality at their institutions in the following chapters.

In comparison, virtual reality technologies completely immerse the user in a synthetic environment in which the real environment cannot be perceived.[12] This immersion can be further heightened by adding visual, auditory, and haptic, or touch-based, simulation through means of headsets, earphones, and specially designed gloves or controllers. This is what happens when you put on a VR headset and play an immersive game: you cannot see anything but the virtual environment that the developer has intended for you. Another example of VR is 360-degree camera footage, if combined with a headset for viewing and interacting. VR can also be viewed on a computer or tablet without a headset, allowing viewers to explore the video using their mouse or touch screen.[13] At present, filmmakers are only beginning to explore the possibilities of immersive filmmaking,[14] and some have argued that 360-degree video is simply an adaptation of older technologies for a new delivery format.[15]

Are the terms AR and VR interchangeable? In short, no. They are related but distinct technologies. AR and VR share similarities in that they both use sensory simulations to create a virtual experience for the user. The user is seeing, feeling, and listening to something that does not exist in the real environment. In spite of these commonalities, AR and VR are distinctive technologies that exist within a virtuality continuum that ranges from the real environment to the virtual environment.[16] Along this continuum are the various forms of reality, often referred to as "mixed reality" (MR). Augmented reality is considered a subsection of mixed reality.[17] VR users experience only sensory simulations, whereas AR users experience simulations while also retaining their ability to experience real-environment sensations.

A SHORT HISTORY OF AR/VR

The history of AR/VR can be thought to start from a variety of places, whether you look to film, animation, computers, gaming, or the imaginings of writers, artists, and inventors. Consequently, no one person can lay claim to the invention of AR/VR, but there are many who have advanced it to its current state. This brief history is in no way complete, but calls attention to some of the more influential and pivotal moments in AR and VR.[18]

If we break down this history into the fundamentals of what AR/VR technology does, it could be argued that the stereoscope kicked things off. The stereoscope was invented over 180 years ago in 1838 by Sir Charles Wheatstone.[19] It allowed users to view three-dimensional objects using two photographs (one for the left eye, and one for the right eye) and two mirrors turned at a 45-degree angle. The result was that the images appeared as though they had three-dimensional depth (figure 1.1). The stereoscope was later adapted into a handheld version by David Brewster, who had also invented the kaleidoscope. He would go on to sell over 500,000 stereoscopes.[20]

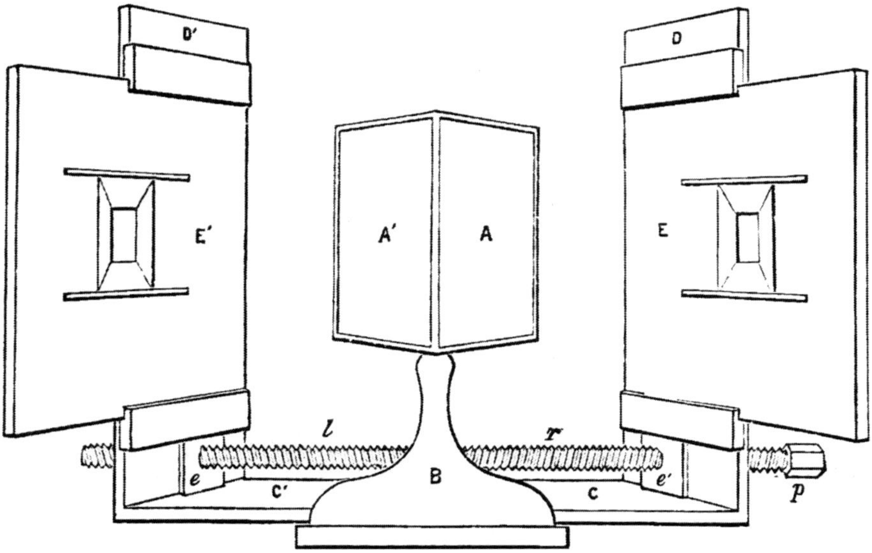

Figure 1.1. Stereoscope. ***commons.wikipedia.org.***

Fast forward to 1961, when cinematographer Morton Heilig filed his patent for a simulator prototype called the Stereoscopic Television Apparatus for individual use, which he built in 1962 and called the Sensorama (figure 1.2). The Sensorama encompassed multisensory technology for immersive film, and users were able to engage with visuals, vibrations, sounds, and smells. Heilig provided five short films for users to try out, including one that simulated a ride on a motorcycle in Brooklyn.[21] While this helped to further VR technology, the Sensorama ultimately met with little commercial success.

Ivan Sutherland, a computer scientist and pioneer of computer graphics, would follow shortly with the first AR/VR device, which he called the Sword of Damocles. Sutherland invented the device in 1968 while working with the Massachusetts Institute of Technology, Harvard University, and the University of Utah.[22] Users wore a head-mounted display (HMD) attached to a metal arm that was suspended from the ceiling, necessary because of the weight of the HMD and the need to track head movements. Users had a 40-degree field of view, and the first virtual object displayed was a cube floating in space.[23]

Sutherland's contemporary, Myron Krueger, an early pioneer of VR and a computer artist, invented the term "artificial reality" and explored this concept in a series of installations combining computer technology and interactive environments. Krueger was particularly interested in trying to get away from the need for wearable devices, such as the gloves and goggles that Sutherland depended on. He wanted the user to experience artificial reality in an immersive

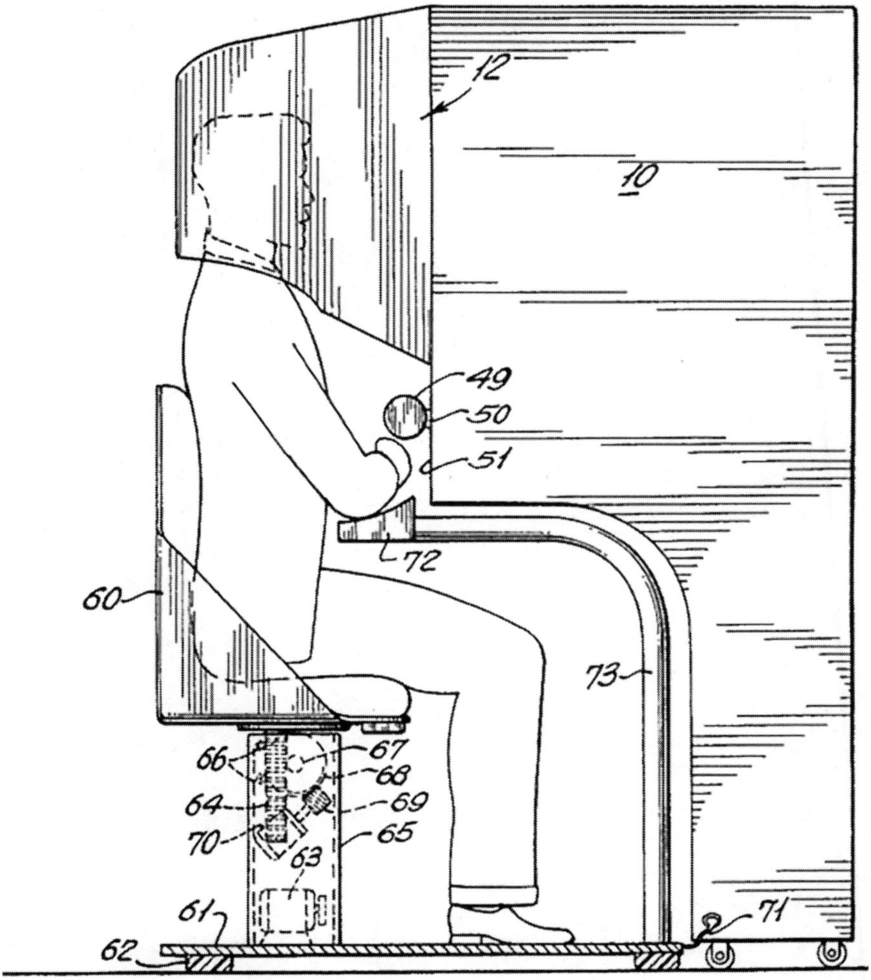

Figure 1.2. Sensorama Patent. ***commons.wikipedia.org.***

environment. His most notable project in 1975 was called "Videoplace." Videoplace relied on multiple rooms of video cameras, mixers, and projectors to create a responsive environment in which users could interact with one another through the use of silhouettes on the walls of the laboratory.[24]

In 1992, the term "augmented reality" was coined by two Boeing researchers, Tom Caudell and David Mizell.[25] Caudell and Mizell created software that showed manufacturers where cables were going to go by overlaying their positions on top of the real-world environment. A few years later in 1997, Ronald Azuma, another research pioneer in AR, defined AR as having three characteristics, which continue to guide AR technology today: (1) It combines real and virtual; (2) it is interactive in real time; and (3) it is registered in three dimensions (3D).[26]

The early 2000s saw a number of rapid developments in AR/VR technology as developers began to adapt the technology to a wide variety of uses. In gaming, one of the first AR games was created in 2000 by Bruce Thomas and the Wearable Computer Lab at the University of South Australia. It was an AR version of a game called Quake that was aptly named "ARQuake." Although users in the lab could play the game, it was not commercialized as the equipment was very expensive, costing over $10,000 at the time.[27]

In the field of government and defense, a system called Battlefield Augmented Reality System (BARS) was invented by Simon Julier and colleagues in collaboration with Columbia University in 2000. It allowed a soldier to use a portable computer and a head-mounted display to have augmented information displayed while in the field. It made use of four different modes: stealth, reconnaissance, route, and attack, depending on the needs of the soldier.[28]

AR/VR TODAY

To date, AR has primarily been used in the consumer sector for marketing, social engagement, amusement, or location-based information. This adoption parallels the trends noted in the 2013 New Media Consortium (NMC) *Horizon Report for Higher Education*, which projected an increase in the impact of these technologies in higher education as they "gain traction in the consumer market."[29] In the following year, augmented reality technologies were listed on the 2014 NMC Master List of Tracked Technologies,[30] and by 2015 the NMC noted augmented reality as an important development in educational technology for higher education[31] and posited the time to adoption at four to five years.[32]

By 2017, the *Horizon Report Library Edition* recommended incorporating new media and technologies (including VR) into library strategic planning in order to "match larger societal consumption trends favoring video, visualizations, virtual reality, and more,"[33] and projected that in order to facilitate the goal of providing services and resources to help patrons become creators, libraries should focus on the mid-term technology adoption of virtual reality and other emerging technologies over the next three to five years.[34] The report also notes a short-term need to keep apprised of virtual reality in relation to research data management over the next year or two.[35]

As discussed, there are many ways that AR/VR technology has begun to infiltrate our lives, or will in the near future. Everything from retail and shopping to public safety, medicine, education, and the military has the potential to be affected by the inclusion of AR/VR technology. Many books and articles have been dedicated to the current state, and not-so-distant future, of how AR/VR technology can enhance these realms of life. Suffice it to say, AR/VR is a technology with a long and storied past, and is not a fad that will fade away in the decades to come.

A few examples in the literature include a 2017 survey by Campus Technology, which found that 81 percent of the faculty in higher education institutions surveyed predict that augmented and virtual reality will be one of the top educational technologies to become important over the next decade.[36] The report also found that the number of faculty not using technology in their courses dropped to zero, from 9 percent from the previous year's survey.[37] The Center for Innovative Research in Cyberlearning recommends that educators and librarians focus on a ten-year educational horizon, using mature technologies in innovative ways and including emerging technologies like virtual reality in order to determine how these technologies can be used to help learners.[38]

Rogers's diffusion of innovation theory can be used to help inform a library's or librarians' decision to adopt augmented and virtual reality at their institution or in their services, activities, and instruction. The theory, developed in 1962, explains how an idea, product, or service gains momentum and spreads over time. Originally used in the field of communications, it has been used successfully in many fields of study to predict innovation adoption models over the years.[39] Rogers breaks down adopters into five categories: innovators (2.5 percent of the population), early adopters (13.5 percent of the population), early majority (34 percent of the population), late majority (34 percent of the population), and laggards (16 percent of the population). Rogers notes that the majority of the population falls in the middle categories, early and late majority, and that the four main elements of diffusion are the innovation, communication channels, time, and the social system.[40] He also notes that technology adoption provides additional considerations, including hardware and software requirements, and the understanding that technology innovations are not stand-alone events, but instead should be viewed as "technology clusters."[41] Rogers also notes that "[i]nnovations that are perceived . . . as having greater relative advantage, compatibility, trialability, and observability and less complexity will be adopted more rapidly than other innovations."[42] Based on the recent explosion of easily accessible AR and VR products and services in the past several years, it is feasible to conclude that both VR and AR technologies are moving from the realm of early adoption into the mainstream consumer market.

The American Library Association also points to this trend in its Center for the Future of Libraries, which identifies emerging trends and tools and provides information to libraries and librarians on why they matter. Trends are organized into seven categories: society, technology, education, the environment, politics (and government), economics, and demographics. According to the Center for the Future of Libraries, libraries play a key role in providing the public with exposure to new and emerging technologies. The center also provides information on a number of trends that could be considered educational "technology clusters," including Internet of Things, haptic technology, gamification, maker movement, robots, and virtual reality.[43] As the adoption of AR and VR increases, it is making its way into the everyday lives of individuals in the areas of education, entertainment, health care, architecture, construction, design, travel, and tourism.[44] As the uses of AR/VR technology grow, libraries and librarians must consider issues related to access, accessibility, information and digital literacy, privacy, and safety, as well as the need to include technology instruction and adoption on emerging technologies in library services, activities, and instruction. This sentiment is echoed by the Library and Information Technology Association's Top Tech Trends panel from the 2017 Midwinter Meeting, which provided Alison Marcotte from *American Libraries* magazine with recommendations for apps, devices, software, and best practices that libraries should consider adopting now and in the future. Top on the list were creating a virtual tour using 360-degree video, making Google Cardboard sets as a way of engaging and teaching students with VR, teaching with gamification, and introducing students to coding, making, and circuit technology.[45]

All of these resources provide considerations that run in tandem with the adoption of the 2015 ACRL Framework[46] geared toward metaliteracy,[47] and the recent revisions to the 2007 ACRL *Standards for Proficiencies for Instruction Librarians and Coordinators*. Currently revised as *Roles and Strengths of Teaching Librarians*, the document calls for librarians to express their roles in an "interconnected and flexible nature," which include advocate, coordinator, instructional designer, leader, lifelong learner, teacher, and teaching partner. Embracing emerging technologies such as AR and VR is one way for librarians to achieve these goals.[48]

AR/VR HARDWARE AND SOFTWARE

Hardware Components

As discussed earlier, Rogers notes that innovations, often synonymous with technology, generally require two components: hardware and software.[49] In the case of AR and VR, users rely on a reality system, or the hardware and its operating system, to experience the sensations of augmented and virtual reality.[50] The user and the system function together as a loop, with the user inputting information into the system, and the system displaying information to the user. Input, or tracking, includes the user telling the system where its eyes, hands, and body are located within the space. Output is what the system displays to the user, to include visuals, sounds, and haptic sensations.[51] This section will provide an overview of hardware devices that users currently rely on to engage with the AR/VR experience. These devices include visual displays, audio devices, and haptic devices.

Head-mounted displays (HMD) are one common way in which to experience AR/VR. As its name suggests, an HMD device is worn on the head. HMDs can be non-see-through, in which the user only sees the display. This allows for a virtual experience. They can also be optical see-through, in which the user can see his or her real environment and virtual elements. This allows for an augmented reality experience.[52]

HMD devices are screen fixed, but there are world-fixed displays as well. World-fixed displays exhibit graphics and audio onto a surface.[53] An example of this is a cave automatic virtual environment (CAVE) as shown in figure 1.3.[54]

Increasingly popular are hand-held displays. These devices, such as smartphones or tablets, are held in the user's hands and do not rely on user input

Figure 1.3. A cave automatic virtual environment (CAVE), University of Illinois at Chicago. *commons.wikipedia.org*.

in the same way as HMDs do.[55] Examples of hand-held displays will be discussed at length in this book, as this is often a low-cost way of incorporating AR/VR technology into library initiatives.

Whether a user is relying on displays built into an HMD or the display on a smartphone, what is the optical system that brings AR/VR to life? First, either type of display must have a high resolution, meaning that it should have a high number of pixels per inch (PPI), as well as a high pixel density, or pixels per degree (PPD).[56] Technology has a long way to go in this regard. For example, most devices hover around 25 PPD, while normal human vision sits around 120 PPD.[57] Also important for displays is the luminance and contrast of the screen. Luminance is the amount of light energy emitted from the screen, and contrast is the ratio of higher to lower luminance.[58]

A high-resolution screen, however, is not enough to make AR/VR an immersive experience, so the ability to track the user's position is also critical. Very few HMDs have the ability to track eye movement, but they do track the user's head position. This is typically done through a six degrees of freedom (6DOF) tracker or a three degrees of freedom (3DOF) tracker.[59]

In conjunction with visual displays, users also rely on audio to become immersed in AR/VR environments. Speakers or headphones are used to incorporate auditory sensations. To be most effective, auralization, or the rendering of sound to give it a location within the space, is needed.[60] For example, if you are experiencing a battlefield in a VR environment, it is much more effective to hear bullets whizzing by your ear, and explosions in the distance, than it would be to hear both sounds at the same volume and spatialization.

Lastly, haptics, or the feeling of touch and sensation, is another way to heighten the experience of AR/VR. There are four classifications of haptics: passive, active, tactile, and proprioceptive.[61] Passive haptics are real-world objects that match an object seen in a virtual environment. For example, as you touch something soft in a virtual environment, you also touch a piece of silk or velvet in your real environment. Active haptics are computer-controlled sensations. Tactile and proprioceptive haptics are both active, but tactile haptics are felt through the skin. Proprioceptive haptics give the user the feeling of limb movement. An example of this is haptic gloves rigged with an exoskeleton.

Today's Hardware

The consumer market for AR/VR hardware exploded in the early 2010s, taking shape in many formats and pushed ahead by some of the biggest names in technology, including Google, Microsoft, and Samsung. The solutions differ in their systematic approach. Some devices must be tethered to a PC, as is the case for the Oculus Rift,[62] or they can rely on mobile devices, such as Samsung's Gear VR headsets.[63] Microsoft's HoloLens is a mixture of the two, and is its own self-contained system, allowing users to tread into the world of mixed reality.[64] This section will examine tethered and self-contained devices first, followed by smartphone-based devices.

Propelling the world of VR forward, the Oculus Rift was first introduced on a crowdfunding website called Kickstarter in 2012. In total, it raised $2.4 million.[65] Oculus, the company, was quickly purchased by Facebook for $2 billion in 2014.[66] Oculus first sold two developer models, called the Oculus DK1 and DK2, in 2013 and 2014. Its consumer version, called the Rift, was released in 2016 for $600. Its pixel density hovers around 15 PPD, and its total pixel resolution is 2160 × 1200.[67] Users can also purchase the Rift with haptic technology, which works as a touch controller, aptly named Touch and costing around $100. For libraries thinking about purchasing this option, the total cost for both the HMD and controller stands at $399 at the time this chapter was written. Libraries will also need to consider the technical specifications needed for a computer to power the Rift, and may need to purchase a new computer or upgrade an existing one.

The HTC Vive launched on April 5, 2016, shortly after the Oculus Rift, and was more expensive at $800. The specs are similar to that of the Oculus Rift insofar as the headset goes, but Vive relies on haptic controllers and two base stations. The base stations use a laser and camera to track the user's movements in the room, allowing the playable space to be around 15" × 15".[68] The Vive VR system runs at $599 at this time, and libraries will again need to consider computer specs, as well as a space large enough to accommodate the Vive's base stations.

As previously mentioned, Microsoft's HoloLens does not rely on a computer to power the device. Instead, it is an HMD with see-through holographic lenses, capable of producing an AR, VR, and MR experience. For sensors, it relies on an inertial measurement unit (IMU) and built-in cameras that allow the user to record what Microsoft has dubbed "mixed reality capture" (MRC). With spatial sound, gaze tracking, and voice support, the HoloLens has a range of features that make it one of the more immersive systems currently available to consumers. It has two versions: the Development Edition for $3,000 and a Commercial Suite for $5,000, making it a pricey spend for libraries with small budgets.[69]

The following devices rely on a smartphone for the display, meaning that a user's experience will differ depending on their smartphone model. While there are many devices in this category, the Samsung Gear VR headset is one of the most popular.[70] The device was launched in 2015, and showed off the collaboration between Samsung and Oculus. Like other VR devices, users can also purchase the Gear VR controller to have a more immersive experience.[71] One downside to this device is that users must have a Samsung smartphone, limiting its usefulness to libraries where users are likely to have a variety of smartphones.

The most budget-friendly VR headset is the Google Cardboard, usually costing less than $15 per viewer. There are a variety of models to choose from, but the most basic is literally made of cardboard and constructed by the user. In each viewer are two curved lenses that allow the user to engage with the Google Cardboard app, which will be discussed later in this chapter.[72]

Google later came out with a second VR platform called the Google Daydream, which is comparable to the Samsung Gear VR. A downside of this platform is that users will need a newer Android-based phone, and only some models are "Daydream-ready."[73] Google recently announced that it would be creating a standalone VR headset in collaboration with HTC Vive and Lenovo, using a new technology called WorldSense that "understands your movement in space without the need to set up any external sensors."[74] No release date has been announced at the time of this writing.

Libraries have benefited from Google Cardboard's relatively low cost and its compatibility with Android and iOS smartphones. Many of the subsequent chapters in this book take advantage of this budget-friendly, easy-to-use platform. Libraries toying with the idea of incorporating AR/VR into their initiatives may want to start with this inexpensive device.

Today's Software

The development of both AR and VR experiences can be quite involved, but some tools are somewhat more welcoming to those willing to learn. These tend to follow one of two paths: tools with web interfaces, and more robust and involved tools for creating stand-alone applications. Both types can benefit from the integration of third-party 3D models. Quality 3D models typically require a serious amount of time to create, or money to purchase from experienced third parties, but numerous free resources exist from places like GrabCad, 3D Warehouse, Clara.io, and TurboSquid.[75]

Web tools for creation tend to focus on AR more than VR. This will likely change as groups like VR First push for the adoption of VR creation and standards for the web.[76] Popular web tools for AR include the previously mentioned Blippar, Layar, and Aurasma.[77] These tend to offer more specific, but limited, creation tools that work through their own apps on the user's end. Users generally scan markers in a mobile app to reveal the AR content. They may offer, as Blippar does, more extended functionality through an application programming interface (API) that web developers can use with

JavaScript.[78] Blippar's API is based on the Node.js framework, so making use of it requires a little more web knowledge than just basic HTML.

For coding stand-alone applications, such as iOS or Android apps, software development kits (SDKs) are available for a variety of AR and VR platforms. An SDK typically includes some form of code editor (or integrated development environment), libraries of reusable code, multimedia assets and other resources, debuggers, and compilers to create finished applications from source code. Considering the extensive time, skill, and effort required to create full-fledged AR and VR applications in high-level programming languages such as C++ or Java, interested libraries should make careful decisions about what platforms are best suited to their needs.

Platform-specific SDKs are available for Oculus and Samsung Gear,[79] HTC Vive,[80] HoloLens,[81] and Google Cardboard and Daydream.[82] More broad-based SDKs like Unity or Unreal, both robust and proven video game engines, offer somewhat more bang for the buck in terms of portability to different platforms.[83] Both of these engines offer graphical user interfaces (GUIs) and link new creators to helpful resources like 3D models and graphical textures right off the bat. Both are capable of creating apps for iOS, Android, Mac OS, Windows, and Linux, as well as for the Oculus Rift, HTC Vive, and a variety of more device-specific platforms.

Apple's ARKit is sure to be a game-changer in the area of mobile AR.[84] It promises markerless interactions beyond the "scan this code" model's limitations. Apple's 2017 WWDC featured live demonstrations of immersive ARKit experiences that were truly impressive, with real-time reading of surfaces and orientations that affected scores of complex 3D objects interacting in real space as a "real live" video game happening in front of the audience.[85] In beta testing when this chapter was written, developers familiar with the iOS SDK[86] can use ARKit's functionality to integrate AR into native iOS apps. Unity and Unreal have also announced support for ARKit.[87] It will be interesting to see how Google's new SDK ARCore, released in late August 2017, will compare. ARCore is built to work without any additional hardware, and will allow developers to create augmented reality for a wide range of Android devices. ARCore works with Java/Open GL, Unity, and Unreal.[88]

OPPORTUNITIES

AR/VR has many positive applications in higher education if used wisely.[89] Technology is transforming at the speed of days, and new gadgets are being widely accepted by people all over the world. With the wide popularity of Pokémon GO in 2016, the future of AR/VR is ripe with possibility, further proving that how we interact with content is forever changed.[90] These technologies are being used to supplement the daily functions of human beings, making teaching and learning information much more interactive. Libraries, for example, can use AR to meet the needs of students who deal with library anxiety[91] by allowing them to learn more about library services and resources on their own through an augmented reality app. Cabero and Barroso bring attention to programs that utilize immersive content in the sciences to increase student interest in STEM fields. AR/VR technology can be used as a cost-effective way to train students and employees in complicated engineering and architecture concepts.[92] Sharing experiences in new cultures is also within our grasp by using this technology, as Olalde and Guesalaga show with their augmented calendar that allows people to explore Japan's history and pop culture through augmented photographs.[93]

LIMITATIONS

In addition to considering the opportunities that AR and VR provide to higher education institutions, it is especially important to consider the literature focusing on existing and future challenges and limitations. Literature highlighting AR goes back as far as the 1990s, and the limitations back then are still relevant today. AR/VR technologies continue to improve every year, but there is progress to be made. In 1999, Azuma noted that the ultimate goal of AR displays was seamless usage in any environment, whether inside a building or out in the natural world. In 2017, as this book was written, new literature identifying the ongoing challenges of utilizing AR and VR can still be found.[94]

Some of the case studies collected in this book identify just a handful of limitations, referencing lighting issues, background interference with marker identification, user comfort with downloading unknown apps to their mobile devices, as well as privacy and accessibility issues. As AR companies step further away from physical markers, relying on invisible markers created within applications like Layar and Blippar, virtual data will not always properly align with the physical environment.[95] Ihsan and Sehat expound on other alignment challenges, such as portability, lag issues with real-time processing (latency), and accessibility.[96]

Libraries must consider safety issues related to participating with virtual reality, such as nausea and other side effects related to real-world simulation. These effects have been associated with AR/VR since its inception; however, wide-stream adoption of the technology has put these issues under further inspection.[97] One such cause for AR/VR–related illness is the negative effect of latency. Latency is the time difference between when a user sends information to the system, and the system is able to respond.[98] The user expects the visual environment or cues to correspond to the way that they would in a real environment, and the lag between the two experiences can cause the user to feel motion sickness. Latency can cause degraded performance, a less immersive experience, and even degraded vision.[99]

Stein, who considers himself "a seasoned VR veteran," mentions a few of the more practical considerations libraries may need to think about, including patrons slipping or tripping while using VR, the unpredictability of nausea while playing, and possible neurological effects such as fatigue and dizziness related to the simulated motion used in VR. Stein also mentions the real-world issues of using a VR headset that blocks vision and sound and involves motion and moving around a room, like running into inanimate objects and injury to the user or others.[100] It is worth noting that all VR devices come with manufacturer disclosures that should be reviewed closely by libraries considering implementing VR resources or services.[101] Of particular importance is the first study to be conducted by University of Leeds researchers regarding VR use for those aged eight to twelve. The researchers posit that the "use of VR sets could trigger eyesight and balance problems in this age group unless changes are made to VR devices."[102] This is not the first time Leeds researchers have commented on the health issues related to VR, and further investigation into these findings is certainly warranted.[103]

Apart from the functional challenges of AR/VR applications, a lot of work must go into the back end of creating these programs, especially if a company or institution is integrating original content.[104] Many publications, like the article by Siltanen and colleagues in *Computers in Entertainment*,[105] share popular resources like Blippar, Layar, Metaio, Aurasma, and ALVAR, which include a database of existing content that users can start with. Despite these assets, a lot of initial work is necessary to start an AR/VR program.

For libraries and educational institutions in particular, privacy concerns must be taken into serious consideration. Kotsios's 2015 publication on augmented reality and privacy compares the Google Glass concerns many consumers had with the initial release of Kodak cameras. Some users are hesitant to download an unknown application to their mobile devices to interact with AR/VR markers.[106] Taking away the safe buffer of a computer monitor, consumers "feel that their privacy is intruded by this new technology [AR/VR], since their image and other information can be captured . . . without their consent—many times without them even noticing that their information is being captured."[107]

ACCESSIBILITY

Of great importance to the discussion of AR/VR technologies is accessibility for those with physical and/or mental disabilities.[108] As already outlined, virtual environments rely on all human senses to provide an immersive experience. Therefore, an individual with a visual impairment would not benefit from many of the major features afforded by AR/VR. The core pedagogy of utilizing immersive technology like this is to provide a different venue or experience for a person to interact with new information. If the technology created for AR/VR is not applicable to a certain individual, it is still possible to use this to meet their needs in innovative ways.[109] If a library is aware that a group with diverse needs will be attending a learning session, for example, it is encouraged to use a mix of concurrent low-tech and high-tech activities so that everyone can contribute at their comfort level. Users who use an online application like Padlet can still participate in a conversation with those who use the "parking lot" method of sharing ideas with paper sticky notes.

Accessibility is a double-edged sword. AR/VR technology can create inaccessibility issues for those with physical and/or cognitive disabilities, but AR/VR can also be a tool to help. One such example is the creation of virtual environments for physically impaired people in order to test environmental modifications before costly renovations are undertaken.[110] This idea is applicable to libraries in that users could interact with their modified space or collections to generate meaningful feedback.

Much has also been written about how virtual environments also have an impact on those with intellectual or learning disabilities.[111] De Oliveira Malaquias and Malaquias highlighted the benefit that virtual environments bring to those who best learn from safe and repeated activities. They found that virtual environments have an impact on a variety of different types of learning outcomes, such as school activities, daily life situations, wayfinding behavior, and others. Cihak and colleagues also mention how effective picture prompts and focused guidance can be a useful way to teach basic skills to elementary students with autism.[112] If all these considerations are taken into account, it is possible that AR/VR technologies can provide libraries with an opportunity to connect to these specific populations in a new and beneficial way.

LOOKING AHEAD

The line between the virtual world and the "real world" will continue to blur as people, companies, and institutions continue to integrate AR/VR into their daily lives and operations in creative ways. This blurring has been called "mixed reality,"[113] but some scholars have argued that the mix has always been there. Humans have always added to their physical world with layers of shared social and cultural meaning. Digital tools that enable these annotations are not fundamentally different than physical tools or conceptual models that preceded them. Nathan Jurgenson has been a staunch critic of conceiving of the "real" physical world as separate from the layers people build on top of it. Of this, he wrote: "I am proposing an alternative view that states that our reality is both technological and organic, both digital and physical, all at once."[114] Jurgenson argues that "physical and material realities dialectically construct each other"[115] iteratively as digital interactions affect our behavior in physical spaces, and vice versa. Jurgenson's own definition of augmented reality assumes this blurred interdependence, with neither component being more "real" than the other: "I want to argue that the digital and physical are increasingly meshed, and want to call this opposite perspective that implodes atoms and bits rather than holding them conceptually separate *augmented reality*."[116] He echoes the thoughts of Manuel Castells, writing on the Arab Spring, on the failure of zero-sum thinking with regard to digital interactions: "Nobody who is on social networks everyday (and this is true for some 700 million of the 1,200 million social network users) is still the same person. It's an online/offline interaction, not an esoteric virtual world."[117]

Both VR and AR technologies are moving from the realm of early adoption into the mainstream consumer market.[118] For librarians, this means a rise in information needs from patrons who will require help navigating this space and becoming literate enough to make informed decisions about the opportunities and potential pitfalls of these technologies.[119] The library has a unique opportunity to start experimenting with these technologies now, regardless of their budgeting and staffing support. As immersive technology becomes more popular, new resources will continue to be available, and the library will firmly emerge as a strong player in Web 4.0.[120]

It's important to note that all the contributors in this volume have worked with AR or VR in their own institutions, and have done so with little to no budget. This book is full of pragmatic approaches from, in Rogers's terms, innovators and early adopters[121] who can help library professionals get started using these technologies with their patrons as AR and VR approach mainstream adoption.

NOTES

1. Stephen Cawood and Mark Fiala, "About Augmented Reality," 15; ARToolKit, "ARToolKit Documentation."

2. Greg Kipper and Joseph Rampolla, *Augmented Reality: An Emerging Technologies Guide to AR*.
3. Cawood and Fiala, "About Augmented Reality," 13.
4. Rachel Arthur, "Shazam for Beauty: Rimmel's New Augmented Reality App Lets Users Nab Real Life Make-Up Looks"; Coty, Inc., *Get the Look: Rimmel London*, Version 1.35.
5. Rachel Arthur, "Charlotte Tilbury's New Virtual 'Magic Mirror' Serves as Active Make-Up Selling Tool."
6. Ilyse Liffreing, "Rimmel London Uses Facebook's Camera Effects to Grow the Audience for Its AR 'Try-on' Concept"; Josh Constine, "Facebook Launches Augmented Reality Camera Effects Developer Platform"; Mike Isaac, "Mark Zuckerberg Sees Augmented Reality Ecosystem in Facebook"; Facebook, "Camera Effects Platform"; Facebook for Developers, *Camera Effects Platform*.
7. Josh Constine, "Apple Undercuts Facebook in the Augmented Reality Platform War"; Apple, "Build iOS 11 Apps for iPad"; Apple, "Introducing ARKit"; Jolanda-Pieta van Arnhem, "Mobile Apps for Libraries: App-titude," 60.
8. Cawood and Fiala, "About Augmented Reality," 14.
9. Georgia Perry, "Imagination in the Augmented-Reality Age"; Wharton University of Pennsylvania, "How 'Pokemon Go' Took Augmented Reality Mainstream"; Tim Merel, "The Reality of VR/AR Growth."
10. Cawood and Fiala, "About Augmented Reality," 16.
11. Jolanda Pieta van Arnhem and Jerry M. Spiller, "Augmented Reality (AR) for Discovery and Instruction"; van Arnhem and Spiller, "Using Augmented Reality (AR) as a Discovery Tool"; Layar, "Products"; Jolanda-Pieta van Arnhem, "Mobile Apps for Libraries: Exploring Blippar for Education"; Blippar, "Augmented Reality in Education"; Jolanda-Pieta van Arnhem, "Mobile Apps for Libraries: Exploring Aurasma Studio 2.0"; Aurasma, "Aurasma Studio"; Jolanda-Pieta van Arnhem, "Mobile Apps for Libraries: Checking Out Interactive Print."
12. Jason Jerald, *The VR Book: Human-Centered Design for Virtual Reality*, 9.
13. Creator Academy, "360-Degree Video and Virtual Reality on YouTube"; Alex Balladares, "Virtual Reality vs Augmented Reality—What's the Difference?"; Sophie Charara and Husain Sumra, "Virtual Reality v Augmented Reality: Which Is the Future?"
14. Lanre Bakare, "Virtual Reality: The Immersive Film-Making Wowing Sundance."
15. Will Smith, "Stop Calling Google Cardboard's 360-Degree Videos 'VR.'"
16. Paul Milgram and Fumio Kishino, "Taxonomy of Mixed Reality Visual Displays," 1321.
17. Jerald, *The VR Book*, 30.
18. Brian Crecente, "VR's Long, Weird History"; Markus Wust, "Augmented Reality"; Frank Steinicke, *Being Really Virtual: Immersive Natives and the Future of Virtual Reality*.
19. Charles Wheatstone, "Contributions to the Physiology of Vision. Part the First."

20. David Brewster, *The Stereoscope: Its History, Theory, and Construction*; Jerald, *The VR Book*, 15.
21. Morton Heilig, Sensorama Simulator, US Patent US003050870; Howard Rheingold, *Virtual Reality*, 49–67.
22. Rheingold, *Virtual Reality*, 104–13; Steinicke, *Being Really Virtual*, 27–30.
23. Ivan Sutherland, "A Head-Mounted Three-Dimensional Display," 759.
24. Myron Krueger, *Artificial Reality* and *Artificial Reality 2*; Myron Krueger, "Videoplace"; Rheingold, *Virtual Reality*, 113–28.
25. Kipper and Rampolla, *Augmented Reality*, 8.
26. Ronald Azuma, "A Survey of Augmented Reality," 2.
27. Bruce Thomas et al., "ARQuake: An Outdoor/Indoor Augmented Reality First Person Application."
28. Simon Julier et al., "BARS: Battlefield Augmented Reality System."
29. L. Johnson et al., *NMC Horizon Report: 2013 Higher Education Edition*, 6.
30. L. Johnson et al., *NMC Horizon Report: 2014 Higher Education Edition*, 35.
31. L. Johnson et al., *NMC Horizon Report: 2015 Higher Education Edition*, 34.
32. Ibid., 46.
33. S. Adams Becker et al., *NMC Horizon Report: 2017 Library Edition*, 2.
34. Ibid., 18.
35. Ibid., 22.
36. Rhea Kelly, "2017 Teaching with Technology Survey," 37.
37. Ibid., 30.
38. J. Roschelle et al., eds., *Cyberlearning Community Report: The State of Cyberlearning and the Future of Learning with Technology*, 7.
39. Everett M. Rogers, *Diffusion of Innovations*.
40. Ibid., 11.
41. Ibid., 15.
42. Ibid., 16.
43. American Library Association, "Trends."
44. American Library Association, "Virtual Reality."
45. Alison Marcotte, "Top Library Tech Trends."
46. Association of College and Research Libraries, *Framework for Information Literacy for Higher Education*.
47. T. P. Mackey and T. E. Jacobson, "Reframing Information Literacy as Metaliteracy."
48. Association of College and Research Libraries, *Roles and Strengths of Teaching Librarians*.
49. Rogers, *Diffusion of Innovations*, 13.
50. Jerald, *The VR Book*, 30.
51. Ibid., 31.
52. Ibid., 32–33.
53. Ibid., 33.
54. C. Demiralp et al., "CAVE and Fishtank Virtual-Reality Displays: A Qualitative and Quantitative Comparison."

55. Jerald, *The VR Book*, 34.
56. Philippe Fuchs, *Virtual Reality Headsets: A Theoretical and Pragmatic Approach*, 60.
57. Ibid., 80.
58. Ibid., 61.
59. Ibid., 55–56.
60. Jerald, *The VR Book*, 240.
61. Ibid., 36–39.
62. Oculus VR, "Oculus Rift."
63. Samsung, "Samsung Gear VR."
64. Microsoft, "Microsoft HoloLens."
65. Oculus VR, "Oculus Rift: Step into the Game."
66. Mark Zuckerberg, "I'm Excited to Announce . . . "
67. Olivier Hugues, "Function and Technical Characteristics of VR Headsets," 86.
68. HTC, "HTC Vive."
69. Microsoft, "Microsoft HoloLens."
70. Matt Kamen, "Samsung Gear VR Shipped More Devices than Oculus, HTC Vive, and PSVR Combined."
71. Samsung. "Samsung Gear VR."
72. Google, "Google Cardboard."
73. Google, "Google Daydream."
74. Google, "Daydream Standalone VR Headsets."
75. GrabCad Community, "Library"; Clara.io, "3D Model Library."
76. Sri Ravipati, "Global Initiative to Open 50 Virtual and Augmented Reality Labs"; VR First, "Democratizing VR/AR Innovation"; WebVR, "About."
77. van Arnhem, "Mobile Apps for Libraries: Exploring Blippar for Education"; Blippar, "Augmented Reality in Education"; van Arnhem, "Mobile Apps for Libraries: Checking Out Interactive Print"; Layar, "Products"; van Arnhem, "Mobile Apps for Libraries: Exploring Aurasma Studio 2.0"; Aurasma, "Aurasma Studio."
78. Blippar, "Blippbuilder Script."
79. Oculus VR, "Experiences"; Oculus VR, "Developers."
80. HTC, "Introducing Viveport for Developers."
81. Microsoft, "Install the Tools."
82. Google, "Google Cardboard"; Google, "Google Cardboard Developers Site."
83. Unity, "Unity 2017: The World-Leading Creation Engine for Gaming"; Epic Games, "Unreal Engine."
84. Apple, "Introducing ARKit."
85. Apple, "Apple WWDC 2017."
86. Apple, "Build iOS 11Apps for iPad."
87. Apple, "Apple WWDC 2017."
88. David Burke, "ARCore: Augmented Reality at Android Scale."
89. "Complete Guide to Virtual Reality."
90. Eric Martin, "Virtual, Augmented, and Mixed Reality: Opens Up a World of Possibilities for Publishers."

91. Elizabeth Zak, "Do You Believe in Magic? Exploring the Conceptualization of Augmented Reality and Its Implications for the User in the Field of Library and Information Science."

92. Julio Cabero and Julio Barroso, "The Educational Possibilities of Augmented Reality"; Xiangyu Wang and Phillip S. Dunston, "Design, Strategies, and Issues Towards an Augmented Reality-based Construction Training Platform."

93. Karle Olalde and Imanol Guesalaga, "The New Dimension in a Calendar: The Use of Different Sense and Augmented Reality Apps."

94. Rabbi Ihsan and Ullah Sehat, "A Survey on Augmented Reality Challenges and Tracking Authors."

95. Reshma Kamble et al., "Knowledge Based Augmented Reality."

96. Ihsan and Sehat, "A Survey on Augmented Reality Challenges."

97. Clare Regan, "An Investigation into Nausea and Other Side-effects of Head-coupled Immersive Virtual Reality"; Stephanie Pappas, "Why Does Virtual Reality Make Some People Sick?"

98. Jerald, *The VR Book*, 183.

99. Ibid., 183–84.

100. Scott Stein, "The Dangers of Virtual Reality."

101. Oculus VR, "Legal Documents"; FreeFly VR, "Safety"; Samsung, "Gear VR: Safety and Health Precautions."

102. Robin McKie, "Virtual Reality Headsets Could Put Children's Health at Risk."

103. University of Leeds, "Is Virtual Reality Bad for Our Health? The Risks and Opportunities of a Technology Revolution"; Brendan Sinclair, "A Word of Warning on VR."

104. Kamble et al., "Knowledge Based Augmented Reality."

105. Sanni Siltanen et al., "Augmented Reality Enriches Print Media and Revitalizes Media Business."

106. Andreas Kotsios, "Privacy in an Augmented Reality," 158; Siltanen et al., "Augmented Reality."

107. Kotsios, "Privacy in an Augmented Reality," 158.

108. Joav Merrick and Paul M. Sharkey, *Virtual Reality: People with Special Needs*.

109. Deborah Price, "Pedagogies for Inclusion of Students with Disabilities in a National Curriculum."

110. Abdelhak Moussaoui, Alain Pruski, and Choubeila Maaoui, "Virtual Reality for Accessibility Assessment of a Built Environment for a Wheelchair User."

111. Fernanda Francielle de Oliveira Malaquias and Rodrigo Fernandes Malaquias, "The Role of Virtual Reality in the Learning Process of Individuals with Intellectual Disabilities."

112. David Cihak et al., "Evaluating Augmented Reality to Complete a Chain Task for Elementary Students with Autism," 101.

113. Martin, "Virtual, Augmented, and Mixed Reality," 18–22.

114. Nathan Jurgenson, "Digital Dualism versus Augmented Reality."

115. Nathan Jurgenson, "Towards Theorizing an Augmented Reality."

116. Jurgenson, "Digital Dualism."

117. Manuel Castells, "The Popular Uprisings in the Arab World Perhaps Constitute the Most Important Internet-Led and Facilitated Change," quoted in Jurgenson, "Digital Dualism."

118. Rogers, *Diffusion of Innovations*, 22.

119. Gartner, "Gartner Hype Cycle."

120. Younghee Noh, "Imagining Library 4.0: Creating a Model for Future Libraries."

121. Rogers, *Diffusion of Innovations*, 22.

BIBLIOGRAPHY

Adams Becker, S., M. Cummings, A. Davis, A. Freeman, C. Giesinger Hall, V. Ananthanarayanan, K. Langley, and N. Wolfson. *NMC Horizon Report: 2017 Library Edition*. Austin, TX: The New Media Consortium, 2017.

American Library Association. "Trends." Accessed November 21, 2017. http://www.ala.org/tools/future/trends.

———. "Virtual Reality." Library of the Future. Accessed November 21, 2017. http://www.ala.org/tools/future/trends/virtualreality.

Apple. "Apple WWDC 2017." YouTube, 2017. Accessed August 29, 2017. https://youtu.be/oaqHdULqet0.

———. "Build iOS 11Apps for iPad." Apple Developer. Accessed August 15, 2017. https://developer.apple.com/ipad/.

———. "Introducing ARKit." Apple Developer. Accessed August 15, 2017. https://developer.apple.com/arkit/.

Arthur, Rachel. "Charlotte Tilbury's New Virtual 'Magic Mirror' Serves as Active Make-Up Selling Tool." *Forbes*, October 21, 2016. https://www.forbes.com/sites/rachelarthur/2016/10/21/charlotte-tilburys-new-virtual-magic-mirror-serves-as-active-make-up-selling-tool/#59e11def5a59.

———. "Shazam for Beauty: Rimmel's New Augmented Reality App Lets Users Nab Real Life Make-Up Looks." *Forbes*, July 4, 2016. https://www.forbes.com/sites/rachelarthur/2016/07/04/shazam-for-beauty-rimmels-new-augmented-reality-app-lets-users-nab-real-life-make-up-looks/#75533707a4a6.

ARToolkit. "ARToolKit Documentation." Accessed August 15, 2017. https://archive.artoolkit.org/documentation/.

Association of College and Research Libraries. *Framework for Information Literacy for Higher Education*. 2015. American Library Association. http://www.ala.org/acrl/standards/ilframework.

———. *Roles and Strengths of Teaching Librarians*. 2017. American Library Association. http://www.ala.org/acrl/standards/teachinglibrarians.

Aurasma. "Aurasma Studio." Accessed August 29, 2017. https://aurasma.zendesk.com/hc/en-us/categories/200402879-Aurasma-Studio.

Azuma, Ronald. "The Challenge of Making Augmented Reality Work Outdoors." In *Mixed Reality: Merging*, edited by Yuichi Ohta and Hideyuki Tamura, 379–90. Secaucus, NJ: Springer, 1999.

———. “A Survey of Augmented Reality.” *Presence: Teleoperators and Virtual Environments* 6, no. 4 (1997): 355–85.

Bakare, Lanre. “Virtual Reality: The Immersive Film-Making Wowing Sundance.” *Guardian*, January 11, 2016. https://www.theguardian.com/film/2016/jan/28/virtual-reality-immersive-film-making-wowing-sundance.

Balladares, Alex. “Virtual Reality vs Augmented Reality—What’s the Difference?” Virtual Reality Pop, April 25, 2017. https://virtualrealitypop.com/virtual-reality-vs-augmented-reality-whats-the-difference-a650a4b3895f.

Blippar. “Augmented Reality in Education.” Accessed August 29, 2017. https://blippar.com/en/solutions/blippar-for-education/.

———. “Blippbuilder Script.” Accessed August 29, 2017. https://blippar.com/en/products/blippbuilder-script/.

Brewster, David. *The Stereoscope: Its History, Theory, and Construction, with Its Application to the Fine and Useful Arts and to Education*. London: John Murray, 1868. https://archive.org/details/stereoscopeitshi00brewrich.

Burke, David. “ARCore: Augmented Reality at Android Scale.” *The Keyword* (blog), August 29, 2017. https://www.blog.google/products/google-vr/arcore-augmented-reality-android-scale/.

Cabero, Julio, and Julio Barroso. “The Educational Possibilities of Augmented Reality.” *Journal of New Approaches in Educational Research* 5, no. 1 (2016): 44–50.

Cawood, Stephen, and Mark Fiala. “About Augmented Reality.” In *Augmented Reality: A Practical Guide*, edited by Daniel H. Steinberg, 11–26. Raleigh, NC: Pragmatic Bookshelf, 2008.

Charara, Sophie, and Husain Sumra. “Virtual Reality v Augmented Reality: Which Is the Future?” Wareable. Accessed July 12, 2017. https://www.wareable.com/vr/virtual-reality-vs-augmented-reality-which-is-the-future.

Cihak, David, Eric Moore, Rachel Wright, Don McMahon, Melinda Gibbons, and Cate Smith. “Evaluating Augmented Reality to Complete a Chain Task for Elementary Students with Autism.” *Journal of Special Education Technology* 31, no. 2 (June 2016): 99–108.

Clara.io. “3D Model Library.” Accessed August 29, 2017. https://clara.io/library.

“Complete Guide to Virtual Reality.” *Campus Technology*, June 2017. https://digital.1105media.com/CampusTech/2017/CAM_1706/SY_1706Q1_701923778.html#p=1.

Constine, Josh. “Apple Undercuts Facebook in the Augmented Reality Platform War.” TechCrunch, June 13, 2017. https://techcrunch.com/2017/06/13/augmented–reality-platform-wars/.

———. “Facebook Launches Augmented Reality Camera Effects Developer Platform.” TechCrunch, April 18, 2017. https://techcrunch.com/2017/04/18/facebook-camera-effects-platform/.

Coty, Inc. *Get the Look: Rimmel London*, Version 1.35. 2017. iTunes. Accessed August 15, 2017. https://itunes.apple.com/us/app/get-the-look-rimmel-london/id1120244830?mt=8.

Creator Academy. "360-Degree Video and Virtual Reality on YouTube." YouTube. Accessed August 27, 2017. https://creatoracademy.youtube.com/page/course/360video?hl=en.

Crecente, Brian. "VR's Long, Weird History." Polygon, October 26, 2016. https://www.polygon.com/2016/10/26/13401128/25-vr-greatest-innovators.

de Oliveira Malaquias, Fernanda Francielle, and Rodrigo Fernandes Malaquias. "The Role of Virtual Reality in the Learning Process of Individuals with Intellectual Disabilities." *Technology and Disability* 28, no. 4 (2016): 133–38.

Demiralp, C., C. D. Jackson, D. B. Karelitz, S. Zhang, and D. H. Laidlaw. "CAVE and Fishtank Virtual-Reality Displays: A Qualitative and Quantitative Comparison." *IEEE Transactions on Visualization and Computer Graphics* 12, no. 3 (May/June 2006): 323–30.

Epic Games. "Unreal Engine." Accessed August 29, 2017. https://www.unrealengine.com/en-US/what-is-unreal-engine-4.

Facebook. "Camera Effects Platform." Accessed August 15, 2017. https://www.facebook.com/fbcameraeffects/home/.

Facebook for Developers. *Camera Effects Platform.* 2017. https://developers.facebook.com/docs/camera-effects.

FreeFly VR. "Safety." Accessed August 29, 2017. https://freeflyvr.com/safety/.

Fuchs, Philippe. *Virtual Reality Headsets: A Theoretical and Pragmatic Approach.* Leiden, The Netherlands: CRC Press, 2017.

Gartner. "Gartner Hype Cycle." Accessed August 29, 2017. http://www.gartner.com/technology/research/methodologies/hype-cycle.jsp.

Google. "Daydream Standalone VR Headsets." Google VR. Accessed August 27, 2017. https://vr.google.com/daydream/standalonevr/.

———. "Google Cardboard." Google VR. Accessed August 27, 2017. https://vr.google.com/cardboard/.

———. "Google Cardboard Developers Site." Google VR. Accessed August 29, 2017. https://vr.google.com/cardboard/developers/.

———. "Google Daydream." Google VR. Accessed August 27, 2017. https://vr.google.com/daydream/.

GrabCad Community. "Library." Accessed August 29, 2017. https://grabcad.com/library.

Heilig, Morton. Sensorama Simulator. US Patent US003050870, filed Jan. 10, 1961. Accessed August 27, 2017. http://pdfpiw.uspto.gov/.

Henneberg, Susan. *Virtual Reality.* New York: Greenhaven Publishing, 2017.

HTC. "HTC Vive." Vive. Accessed August 27, 2017. https://www.vive.com/us/.

———. "Introducing Viveport for Developers." Vive. Accessed August 29, 2017. https://developer.viveport.com/us/develop_portal/.

Hughes, Raymond. *Augmented Reality: Developments, Technologies and Applications.* Hauppauge, NY: Nova Science Publishers, 2014.

Hugues, Olivier. "Function and Technical Characteristics of VR Headsets." In *Virtual Reality Headsets: A Theoretical and Pragmatic Approach*, edited by Philippe Fuchs, 79–94. Leiden, The Netherlands: CRC Press, 2017.

Ihsan, Rabbi, and Ullah Sehat. "A Survey on Augmented Reality Challenges and Tracking Authors." *ACTA Graphica* 24 (2013): 29–46.

Isaac, Mike. "Mark Zuckerberg Sees Augmented Reality Ecosystem in Facebook." *New York Times*, April 18, 2017. https://www.nytimes.com/2017/04/18/technology/mark-zuckerberg-sees-augmented-reality-ecosystem-in-facebook.html.

Jerald, Jason. *The VR Book: Human-Centered Design for Virtual Reality*. Williston, VT: Morgan and Claypool Publishers, 2016.

Johnson, L., S. Adams Becker, M. Cummins, V. Estrada, A. Freeman, and H. Ludgate. *NMC Horizon Report: 2013 Higher Education Edition*. Austin, TX: The New Media Consortium, 2013.

Johnson, L., S. Adams Becker, V. Estrada, and A. Freeman. *NMC Horizon Report: 2014 Higher Education Edition*. Austin, TX: The New Media Consortium, 2014.

———. *NMC Horizon Report: 2015 Higher Education Edition*. Austin, TX: The New Media Consortium, 2015.

Julier, Simon, Yohan Baillot, Marco Lanzagorta, Dennis Brown, and Lawrence Rosenblum. "BARS: Battlefield Augmented Reality System." *NATO Symposium on Information Processing Techniques for Military Systems*, 2000. http://citeseerx.ist.psu.edu/viewdoc/download;jsessionid=1476E02D2B3C5F80F48D958EFC5A98E0?doi=10.1.1.1.5064&rep=rep1&type=pdf.

Jurgenson, Nathan. "Digital Dualism versus Augmented Reality." *Cyborgology* (blog), February 24, 2011. https://thesocietypages.org/cyborgology/2011/02/24/digital-dualism-versus-augmented-reality/.

———. "Towards Theorizing an Augmented Reality." *Nathan Jurgenson: A Social Theory and Culture Blog*, October 5, 2009. https://nathanjurgenson.wordpress.com/2009/10/05/towards-theorizing-an-augmented-reality/.

Kamble, Reshma, Swati Kadam, Pushpa Bagul, Priyanka Lokhande, and M. K. Kodmelwar. "Knowledge Based Augmented Reality." *International Journal of Computer Science and Management Research* 3, no. 3 (2014): 4012–17.

Kamen, Matt. "Samsung Gear VR Shipped More Devices than Oculus, HTC Vive, and PSVR Combined." *Wired*, February 6, 2017. http://www.wired.co.uk/article/samsung-vr-outships-psvr-htc-vive-and-oculus.

Kelly, Rhea. "2017 Teaching with Technology Survey." *Campus Technology* 30, no. 7 (July 2017): 25–43. https://campustechnology.com/.

Kipper, Greg, and Joseph Rampolla. *Augmented Reality: An Emerging Technologies Guide to AR*. Rockland, MA: Syngress, 2012.

Kotsios, Andreas. "Privacy in an Augmented Reality." *International Journal of Law and Information Technology* 23, no. 2 (2015): 157–85.

Krueger, Myron. *Artificial Reality*. Boston: Addison-Wesley, 1983.

———. *Artificial Reality 2*. 2nd ed. Boston: Addison-Wesley Professional, 1991.

———. "Videoplace." Ars Electronica Archive: Picture Archive. Accessed August 27, 2017. https://www.aec.at/about/en/archiv/.

Layar. "Products." Accessed August 29, 2017. https://www.layar.com/products/.

Liffreing, Ilyse. "Rimmel London Uses Facebook's Camera Effects to Grow the Audience for Its AR 'Try-on' Concept." Digiday, August 4, 2017. https://digiday.com/marketing/rimmel-london-uses-facebooks-camera-effects-get-scale-ar-technology/.

Mackey, T. P., and T. E. Jacobson. "Reframing Information Literacy as Metaliteracy." *College and Research Libraries* 72, no. 1 (2011): 62–78.

Marcotte, Alison. "Top Library Tech Trends," *American Libraries*, May 1, 2017. https://americanlibrariesmagazine.org/2017/05/01/top-library-tech-trends/.

Martin, Eric. "Virtual, Augmented, and Mixed Reality: Opens Up a World of Possibilities for Publishers." *Econtent Magazine* 40, no. 3 (2017): 18–22.

McKie, Robin. "Virtual Reality Headsets Could Put Children's Health at Risk." *Guardian*, October 28, 2017. https://www.theguardian.com/technology/2017/oct/28/virtual-reality-headset-children-cognitive-problems.

Merel, Tim. "The Reality of VR/AR Growth." TechCrunch, January 11, 2017. https://techcrunch.com/2017/01/11/the-reality-of-vrar-growth/.

Merrick, Joav, and Paul M. Sharkey. *Virtual Reality: People with Special Needs*. Hauppauge, NY: Nova Science Publishers, 2014.

Microsoft. "Install the Tools." Windows Dev Center. Accessed August 29, 2017. https://developer.microsoft.com/en-us/windows/mixed-reality/install_the_tools.

———. "Microsoft HoloLens." Accessed August 27, 2017. https://www.microsoft.com/en-us/hololens/hardware.

Milgram, Paul, and Fumio Kishino. "Taxonomy of Mixed Reality Visual Displays." *IEICE Transactions on Information and Systems* E-77D, no. 12 (1994): 1321–29.

Moussaoui, Abdelhak, Alain Pruski, and Choubeila Maaoui. "Virtual Reality for Accessibility Assessment of a Built Environment for a Wheelchair User." *Technology and Disability* 24, no. 2 (2012): 129–37.

Noh, Younghee. "Imagining Library 4.0: Creating a Model for Future Libraries." *Journal of Academic Librarianship* 41, no. 6 (2015): 786–97.

Oculus VR. "Developers." Accessed August 29, 2017. https://developer.oculus.com/.

———. "Experiences." Accessed August 29, 2017. https://www.oculus.com/experiences/rift/.

———. "Legal Documents." Accessed August 29, 2017. https://www.oculus.com/legal/health-and-safety-warnings/.

———. "Oculus Rift." Accessed August 27, 2017. https://www.oculus.com/rift/.

———. "Oculus Rift: Step into the Game." Kickstarter. Accessed August 27, 2017. https://www.kickstarter.com/projects/1523379957/oculus-rift-step-into-the-game.

Olalde, Karle, and Imanol Guesalaga. "The New Dimension in a Calendar: The Use of Different Sense and Augmented Reality Apps." *Procedia Computer Science* 25 (2013): 322–29.

Pappas, Stephanie. "Why Does Virtual Reality Make Some People Sick?" Live Science, April 20, 2016. https://www.livescience.com/54478-why-vr-makes-you-sick.html.

Perry, Georgia. "Imagination in the Augmented-Reality Age." *Atlantic*, August 4, 2016. https://www.theatlantic.com/education/archive/2016/08/play-in-the-augmented-reality-age/494597/.

Price, Deborah. "Pedagogies for Inclusion of Students with Disabilities in a National Curriculum: A Central Human Capabilities Approach." *Journal of Educational Enquiry* 14, no. 2 (2015): 18–32.

Ravipati, Sri. "Global Initiative to Open 50 Virtual and Augmented Reality Labs." *Campus Technology*, April 17, 2017. https://campustechnology.com/articles/2017/04/17/global-initiative-to-open-50-vr-ar-labs.aspx.

Regan, Clare. "An Investigation into Nausea and Other Side-effects of Head-coupled Immersive Virtual Reality." *Virtual Reality* 1, no. 1 (1995): 17.

Rheingold, Howard. *Virtual Reality*. New York: Simon and Schuster, 1991.

Rogers, Everett M. *Diffusion of Innovations*. 5th ed. New York: Free Press, 2003.

Roschelle, J., W. Martin, J. Ahn, and P. Schank, eds. *Cyberlearning Community Report: The State of Cyberlearning and the Future of Learning with Technology*. October 2017. http://circlcenter.org/resources/community-report/.

Samsung. "Gear VR: Safety and Health Precautions," June 30, 2017. Accessed August 29, 2017. http://www.samsung.com/au/support/skp/faq/1105625.

———. "Samsung Gear VR." Accessed August 27, 2017. http://www.samsung.com/global/galaxy/gear-vr/.

Siltanen, Sanni, Maiju Aikala, Sari Jarvinen, and Ville Valjus. "Augmented Reality Enriches Print Media and Revitalizes Media Business." *Computers in Entertainment* 15, no. 3 (2017): 1–15.

Sinclair, Brendan. "A Word of Warning on VR." GamesIndustry.biz, November 8, 2017. http://www.gamesindustry.biz/articles/2017-11-08-a-word-of-warning-on-vr.

Smith, Will. "Stop Calling Google Cardboard's 360-Degree Videos 'VR.'" *Wired*, November 16, 2015. https://www.wired.com/2015/11/360-video-isnt-virtual-reality/.

Stein, Scott. "The Dangers of Virtual Reality." *CNET*, March 29, 2016. https://www.cnet.com/news/the-dangers-of-virtual-reality/.

Steinicke, Frank. *Being Really Virtual: Immersive Natives and the Future of Virtual Reality*. New York: Springer, 2016.

Sutherland, Ivan. "A Head-Mounted Three-Dimensional Display." *Proceedings of the AFIPS Fall Joint Computer Conference* (1968): 757–64.

Thomas, Bruce, Benjamin Close, John Donoghue, John Squires, Phillip De Bondi, Michael Morris, and Wayne Piekarski. "ARQuake: An Outdoor/Indoor Augmented Reality First Person Application." *4th International Symposium on Wearable Computers*, Atlanta (2000): 139–46.

Unity. "Unity 2017: The World-Leading Creation Engine for Gaming." Accessed August 29, 2017. https://unity3d.com/unity.

University of Leeds. "Is Virtual Reality Bad for Our Health? The Risks and Opportunities of a Technology Revolution." *Medium,* September 14, 2017. https://medium.com/university-of-leeds/is-virtual-reality-bad-for-our-health-the-risks-and-opportunities-of-a-technology-revolution-31520e50820a.

van Arnhem, Jolanda-Pieta. "Mobile Apps for Libraries: App-titude." *Charleston Advisor* 14, no. 1 (July 2012): 60–62. doi:10.5260/chara.14.1.60.

———. "Mobile Apps for Libraries: Checking Out Interactive Print." *Charleston Advisor* 16, no. 1 (January 2015): 62–64. doi:10.5260/chara.16.3.46.

———. "Mobile Apps for Libraries: Exploring Aurasma Studio 2.0." *Charleston Advisor* 17, no. 3 (January 2016): 50–54. doi:10.5260/chara.17.3.50.

———. "Mobile Apps for Libraries: Exploring Blippar for Education." *Charleston Advisor* 17, no. 4 (April 2016): 53–57. doi:10.5260/chara.17.4.53.

van Arnhem, Jolanda-Pieta, and Jerry M. Spiller. "Augmented Reality (AR) for Discovery and Instruction." *Journal of Web Librarianship* 8, no. 2 (May 2014): 214–30. doi:10.1080/19322909.2014.904208.

———. "Using Augmented Reality (AR) as a Discovery Tool." *Proceedings of the Charleston Library Conference*, November 2013, 584–91. doi:10.5703/1288284315328.

VR First. "Democratizing VR/AR Innovation." Accessed August 29, 2017. https://www.vrfirst.com/.

Wang, Xiangyu, and Phillip S. Dunston. "Design, Strategies, and Issues Towards an Augmented Reality-based Construction Training Platform." *Journal of Information Technology in Construction* 12 (2007): 363–80.

WebVR. "About." Accessed August 29, 2017. https://webvr.info/.

Wharton University of Pennsylvania. "How 'Pokemon Go' Took Augmented Reality Mainstream." Knowledge@Wharton: Technology, July 21, 2016. http://knowledge.wharton.upenn.edu/article/how-pokemon-go-took-augmented-reality-mainstream/.

Wheatstone, Charles. "Contributions to the Physiology of Vision. Part the First. On Some Remarkable, and Hitherto Unobserved, Phenomena of Binocular Vision." *Philosophical Transactions: The Royal Society of Publishing* 128 (January 1838): 371–94. doi:10.1098/rstl.1838.0019.

Wust, Markus. "Augmented Reality." In *Doing Digital Humanities: Practice, Training, Research*, edited by Constance Crompton, Richard J. Lane, and Ray Siemens, 303–10. New York: Routledge, 2016.

Zak, Elizabeth. "Do You Believe in Magic? Exploring the Conceptualization of Augmented Reality and Its Implications for the User in the Field of Library and Information Science." *Information Technology and Libraries* 33, no. 4 (2014): 23–50.

Zuckerberg, Mark. "I'm Excited to Announce . . ." Facebook, March 25, 2014. https://www.facebook.com/zuck/posts/10101319050523971.

2

Augmented Reality

What It Is and How It Came About

Markus Wust

In his 1901 novel, *The Master Key: An Electrical Fairy Tale Founded Upon the Mysteries of Electricity and the Optimism of its Devotees*, L. Frank Baum describes a series of curious devices gifted to his protagonist, Rob, by a "Demon of Electricity." One of them, the "Character Marker," is designed to help the one wearing it judge "all your fellow-creatures truly, and know upon whom to depend." It is described by the demon as a pair of spectacles that will display a letter on the forehead of every person Rob meets and thus indicate the person's character.[1] This description bears more than a passing resemblance to augmented reality (AR) devices such as Google Glass or the Microsoft HoloLens that, like Baum's Character Marker, have the ability to visually augment physical objects in the user's environment with additional information.[2] AR has also been present in popular culture, such as movies—*Robocop* (1987) and *Terminator 2: Judgment Day* (1991) include scenes filmed from the protagonist's point of view that showed textual data layered on top of the real-world display—or sports broadcasts on TV (for example, the yellow first-down line shown during professional football games). However, it was only recently that AR has begun to truly capture the imagination and interest of the general public and spurred larger financial and intellectual investment toward the development of consumer-ready hardware and software.

This chapter tells the story of the emergence of AR from relative obscurity, and delineates its history, variety of technical approaches, and its affordances for libraries. However, in order to understand AR, it is also important to comprehend how it differs from virtual reality, a related concept that has attracted even greater attention. Thus, the chapter begins with an attempt to define AR and explain the difference between augmented and virtual reality.

This section is followed by a history of AR that shows how recent developments in mobile technology and years of academic and commercial research have finally enabled the emergence of viable AR consumer products. The final part describes the most common technical approaches to implementing AR, and provides suggestions as to how each technology could be used to support library projects.

DEFINING AUGMENTED REALITY

In 1994, Paul Milgram and colleagues published several papers[3] in which they presented the "Reality-Virtuality Continuum" to describe the various ways "real" and "virtual" content can be mixed in a display. At one end, this continuum is bounded by "reality," in which the display shows an unaltered image of a real-world environment that is captured by a camera. At the opposite end sits "virtuality," that is, a completely computer-generated image is displayed on the screen (as is the case with most virtual reality applications). The zone between both borders is called "mixed reality" and can include anything from minimal augmentations, such as the aforementioned first-down line, to heavily augmented environments with just small real-world elements. This mixed character is reflected in most definitions of AR, like the one provided by Carmigniani and Furht, who describe AR as "a real-time direct or indirect view of a physical real-world environment that has been enhanced/*augmented* by adding virtual computer-generated information to it" (emphasis in original).[4] In an early survey of AR, Azuma added two more characteristics to these definitions. In addition to the combination of real-world and virtual elements, for him AR also required real-time interactivity, and the augmented objects needed to be registered in three-dimensional (3D) space.[5]

When Wellner, Mackay, and Gold contrasted virtual and augmented reality, they emphasized AR's ability to let users engage simultaneously with the physical world and virtual objects instead of enclosing them in a virtual environment, as would be the case with virtual reality:

> Another view of the future of computing is emerging, taking the opposite approach from VR. Instead of using computers to enclose people in an artificial world, we can use computers to augment objects in the real world. . . . With see-through displays and projectors, we can create spaces in which everyday objects gain electronic properties without losing their familiar physical properties. *Computer-augmented environments* merge electronic systems into the physical world instead of attempting to replace them. Our everyday environment is an integral part of these systems; it continues to work as expected, but with new integrated computer functionality. (emphasis in original)[6]

Wendy Mackay expanded this idea of AR; for her, it was not just the user who was "augmented" through head-worn displays. Instead, she allowed for augmented objects where "the physical object is changed by embedding input, output or computational devices on or within it," thus turning regular objects into "smart" objects.[7] Also, there are augmentations to the user's and the object's environment—as in the case of interactive paper—that allow users to "see and interact with electronic information without wearing special devices or modifying the objects they interact with."[8] As Barba, MacIntyre, and Mynatt put it, Mackay's vision of AR "was understood to connote technologies that took everyday objects and activities and enhanced them in some way. Making activities more collaborative or more personalized, and giving objects memory or awareness, were all ways of 'augmenting' user experiences."[9] Mackay herself emphasized the enhanced user experiences that augmented objects could provide, particularly in comparison to virtual reality: "The future we envision is not a strange world in which we are immersed in 'virtual reality.' Instead, we see our familiar world, enhanced in numerous, often invisible ways."[10]

AUGMENTED REALITY: A BRIEF LONG HISTORY[11]

As described in the previous section, AR refers to the addition of (most commonly visual) data to a real-world scene in order to provide additional information on an object, landscape, or person. While viable digital devices and applications—which we would normally associate with the term augmented reality—have only recently entered our day-to-day environment, humans have been augmenting their environment for thousands of years. Waymarkers, for example, can be understood as (non-electronic) augmented reality devices. Another example are historic markers that augment historically relevant buildings with textual data. Even electronic augmented reality devices go back several decades. During World War II, the British military built the first aircraft heads-up display for its Mark VIII Airborne Interception Radar that could project data onto a plane's windshield, thus creating a precursor of modern military heads-up displays.[12] In 1968, Ivan Sutherland—then a computer scientist at Harvard University—developed what is now considered to be the first augmented reality head-mounted display (HMD). His application "used half-silvered mirrors as optical combiners that allowed the user to see both the computer-generated images reflected from cathode ray tubes (CRT) and objects in the room, simultaneously."[13] Two trackers followed the display's motions; based on this data, the computer superimposed the simple wire frame of a three-dimensional room onto the user's view. Given the physical size of the device—which had to be suspended from the ceiling—it was rather appropriately named "Sword of Damocles." In 1992, two Boeing researchers, Tom Caudell and David Mizell, coined the term "augmented reality" for a system they developed to help workers assemble and install complex airplane parts without having to resort to multiple editions of printed manuals. Their goal was to provide "a 'see-thru' virtual reality goggle to the factory worker, and to use this device to augment the worker's visual field of view with useful and dynamically changing information."[14] One year later, the Global Positioning System (GPS) became operational, thus providing a critical infrastructural component for future location-based augmented reality applications. In 1997, Steven Feiner, Blair MacIntyre, Tobias Höllerer, and Anthony Webster developed an early mobile AR system. Unlike later smartphone-based systems, it consisted of several bulky components: "a see-through head-worn display with integral orientation tracker; a backpack holding a computer, differential GPS, and digital radio for wireless web access; and a hand-held computer with stylus and touchpad interface."[15] It functioned as a mobile guide to the campus of Columbia University a decade before advances in mobile hardware and software technologies made it possible that such tools could become commonplace on campuses.[16] In 1999, Hirokazu Kato and Mark Billinghurst released ARToolKit, a video-tracking library that allowed developers to correctly align digital objects with fiducial markers. By handling crucial tracking tasks, it made it easier for developers to build AR applications, and the library has since been used in a variety of AR projects. A first AR browser was developed in 2001 by Rob Kooper and Blair MacIntyre, and provided a user with contextualized information drawn from what they described as the Real-World Wide Web:

> This work is based on a vision of an enhanced WWW in which each information object (i.e., "Web page," containing two-dimensional [2D] and 3D visual and auditory information) may have contextual meta-data associated with it, such as a location, person, or activity. This meta-data could be used to decide when and where to present the information objects to users. We refer to such a space as the *Real-World Wide Web* (RWWW) and interfaces to it as *RWWW browsers*. In an RWWW browser, Web pages would be registered with real-world locations and presented to the user at the appropriate place and time.[17]

The RWWW browser was still dependent on cumbersome hardware; although mobile phone–based augmented reality applications were first demonstrated in 2004, they were limited by the devices on which they ran. Mobile phones at that time "were difficult to develop for, had slow processing and graphics power, and limited sensors."[18] It was not until 2007 that Apple released the first version of its iPhone and thus launched a revolution in mobile computing. The device finally offered a technology platform that provided the necessary processing capabilities and development environment for a satisfying AR

experience in a single device. A year later, HTC released the first smartphone running the Android operating system. Unlike the original iPhone, the device also had GPS and inertial compass sensors and thus could be used as a platform for outdoor AR applications. That same year, Wikitude, an AR browser for Android devices, became available. The application overlaid location-based data on real-time video captured by a phone's camera. In 2009, SPRX Mobile published a similar application named Layar, another AR browser that organized data into separate "layers" that users could select and then serendipitously discover content based on their current location (figure 2.1).

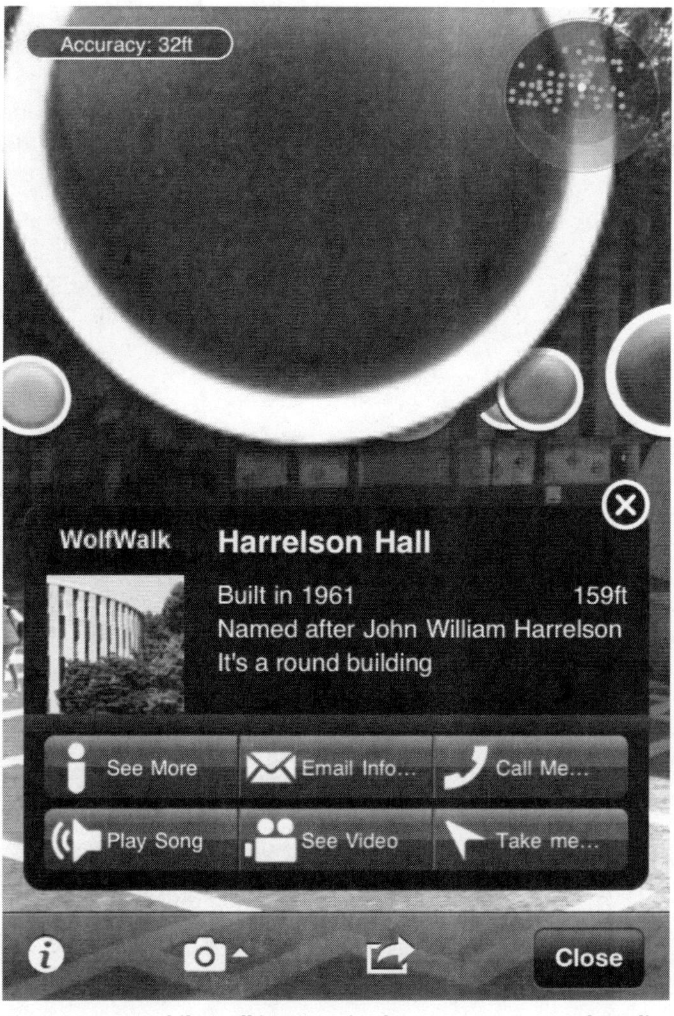

Figure 2.1. Mobile walking tour in the Layar Augmented Reality Browser. ***North Carolina State University Libraries.***

Initially, applications like Wikitude and Layar relied on a mobile device's screen to display content to their users. Head-mounted displays—which up to this point had primarily been used in research projects and by industry and the military—had not been successful in the consumer market. Google attempted to change this with the launch of Google Glass, first to select customers and developers in 2013 and, one year later, to the general public. Unlike previous bulky headsets, Google Glass resembled a pair of glasses with a single small display; users controlled the device via a touch sensor or through voice commands (figure 2.2). However, instead of bringing AR to a wider audience, Google Glass caused considerable backlash from a public that, among others, brought up several privacy concerns. For example, users could use the device's integrated video camera to videotape others without their knowledge, or use facial recognition software to identify strangers in the street.[19] Also, as is the case with other mobile devices, Google Glass could potentially be used to track and surveil its wearer. In the end, Google stopped distributing

Figure 2.2. Google Glass. ***North Carolina State University Libraries.***

the product to the public in 2015, although it later began to find traction in the manufacturing industry.[20]

In 2016—which also saw the release of several VR head-mounted displays such as the Oculus Rift, HTC Vive, and Playstation VR—two products were launched that, to differing degrees, brought more positive attention to AR than Google Glass was able to achieve. Developer Niantic released Pokémon GO, a mobile game app that included location-based augmented reality. The game quickly became the year's most popular app, and revenue from app sales, in-app purchases, and fees from businesses that used the app to attract customers reached around $950 million by the end of 2016.[21] On the hardware side, Microsoft began to make early versions of its HoloLens head-mounted display available to developers; like the Google Glass, the HoloLens incorporated all required components into a single device, but offered stereoscopic viewing and greater processing power (figure 2.3).

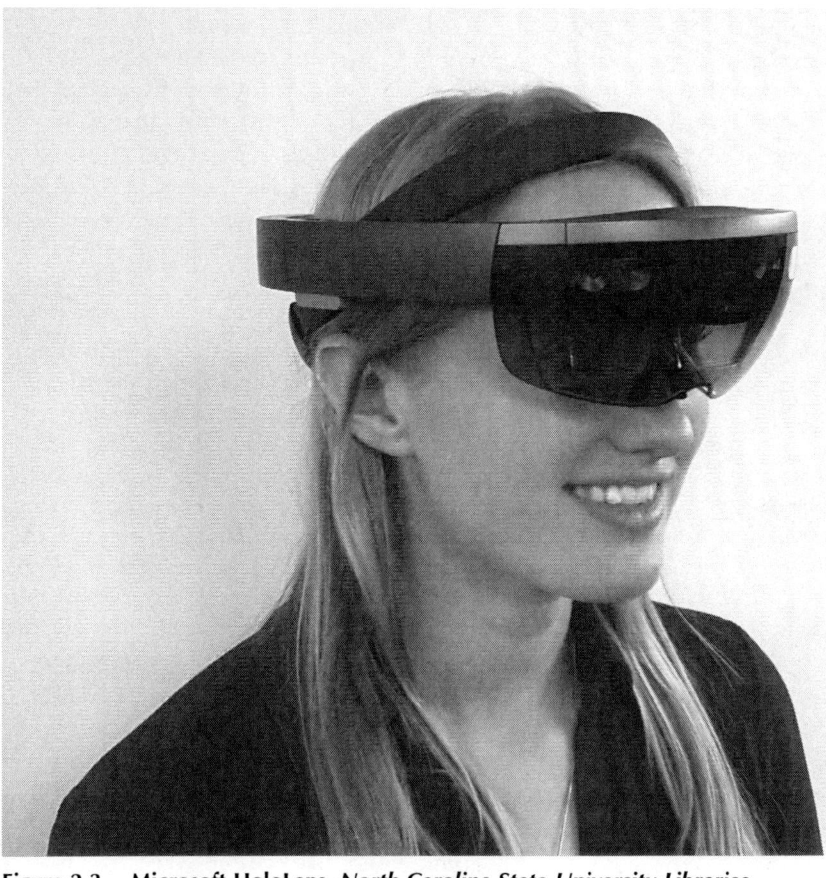

Figure 2.3. Microsoft HoloLens. ***North Carolina State University Libraries.***

At the same time the HoloLens was released, several other AR head-mounted displays were set to launch, and it remains to be seen whether they and other future devices will be successful in helping AR reach its full potential.

TECHNOLOGIES[22]

AR systems can employ a wide variety of technologies, and also modes of augmentation. Most common are visual augmentations that function by overlaying virtual elements on physical objects or video captures of such objects. In order to accomplish this, the application needs to know where to place these elements on the display, and how to size and orient them; this process is also referred to as registration. One way of classifying such applications is based on how they locate and register virtual content, that is, into location-based and image-based AR. In the first case, each virtual element is associated with a physical location. If the application's user is in the vicinity of this location, the item is shown on the display. Based on the relative position of the user's device, and its orientation and tilt, the application calculates the correct location of the virtual element on the display. An example of such an application is a mobile walking tour where markers are placed in a geographically limited region, such as a city or campus. Users moving through this area can see then see these markers and any associated information on their display.

Image-based AR, on the other hand,

> requires specific labels to register the position of 3D objects on the real-world image. . . . [An] AR book with basic equipment such as a webcam and marker labels is one of the typical marker-based applications and has been employed in several studies. . . . A marker label in typical marker-based applications is commonly presented as an iconic coded image. . . . By detecting a marker label on a book through a webcam capture, a virtual element is then generated by the AR software. This virtual element would be shown upon the book and recovered on the computer screen that can be manipulated by tilting or rotating the book.[23]

While the above-mentioned marker labels initially had to be very distinctive graphical elements, such as Quick Response (QR) codes, advances in image recognition algorithms as well as improving performance of mobile platforms now make it possible to augment any sufficiently distinctive image, for example, magazine covers. Although images without specialized markers allow for greater flexibility as they can be retroactively augmented, they need to somehow indicate to users that augmented content is available, whereas QR codes have become common and users generally know how to use them.[24] While browsers like Wikitude and Layar initially only provided location-based AR, later versions and competing services, such as Aurasma, added powerful image-based AR capabilities.

Another way of differentiating AR systems is based on the type of display that is used. The first kind, head-mounted displays (HMDs), are usually implemented as optical see-through displays, such as the Microsoft HoloLens, which allow the user to see the physical world through a transparent screen that serves as the projection surface for any virtual augmentations. When implemented as an HMD, the second variant, video see-through displays, have mostly been used in research laboratories. One or more attached cameras would capture the user's point of view and then merge it with virtual elements, basically functioning like a virtual reality HMD with an attached camera; the combined scene is then shown on one or two small displays located before the user's eyes. As Billinghurst, Clark, and Lee point out, both approaches have clear advantages and disadvantages. Optical see-through systems can provide a real-life, real-time image of the physical environment. These also require fewer graphics computing resources, as they only need to generate and place the augmentations into the user's field of view instead of creating the complete scene. Their main drawback compared to video see-through displays is often a less accurate registration:

> In many cases, optical see-through displays require [a] manual calibration process which ends up with relatively poor quality of registration compared to automated computer vision based approach in video based AR displays. Since the calibration parameters are dependent on the spatial relationship between the user's eyes and the display's image plane, there is a higher chance of parameters changing over time (e.g., wearable displays sliding off from the original position) and eventually causing misalignment between the real and virtual view images. Hence, accurate 3D eye tracking (relative to the display) becomes more important to visualize a correctly aligned AR scene with optical see-through displays.[25]

A second display category are hand-held devices, such as smartphones and tablets that combine display, sensory, and processing technologies into a single, portable device; here, video see-through displays are far more common. These solutions are also better suited for users who are wearing glasses, as head-mounted displays often do not offer enough space to accommodate those. However, their portability is at the same time their main drawback: as the augmented environment is limited to the relatively small screen, they provide a less immersive experience than could be achieved with head-mounted displays. This is further aggravated by the fact that users need to point their devices at an augmented object instead of just turning their heads.

Despite these limitations, hand-held devices can deliver a wide variety of AR services for libraries and other institutions. For example, augmented posters or flyers can be used to better promote events and services. Exhibits can be augmented with additional media, such as video, audio, or 3D models, to provide information that could not be sufficiently conveyed through physical objects or printed text. And while the visual focus of most AR applications can create accessibility barriers, appropriately designed software and experiences can also help overcome those barriers by using a platform that has become almost ubiquitous. Audio augmentations, for example, have been used for many years in museums in the form of audio guides; in the case of usually heavily visual AR applications, audio can be used to make an experience more immersive, and more accessible to users with visual impairments by adding spoken descriptions and instructions.

Finally, there are spatial displays that project augmentations directly onto physical objects such as statues or landscape models using one or more projectors. This approach makes it easy for multiple users to simultaneously experience the same augmentation without having to actually handle or wear a device.[26] Perhaps the best-known applications of this technology can be found in theme parks such as those opened by the Walt Disney Company where video recordings of human faces are projected on busts with relatively simple features, giving the impression that the viewer sees a three-dimensional face instead of a flat projection. Another interesting example is Tangible Landscapes, an interactive spatial display developed at North Carolina State University (figure 2.4). Tangible Landscapes allows users to project augmentations onto surfaces made from deformable materials such as sand. A Microsoft Kinect 3D sensor placed above the projection surface senses any modifications, and the system modifies the augmentations accordingly. This can be used, for example, for real-time modeling and visualization of the impact of dams or other obstructions on waterways.[27]

As for what the future will hold for AR, predictions are, as always, difficult to make when it comes to technology and the ways people adopt and interact with it. Baum's Character Marker was science fiction for his contemporaries, just like today's smartphones would have seemed like science fiction at the time Ivan Sutherland built his Sword of Damocles. At the time this chapter was written, researchers were working on AR contact lenses that may at some point replace current-generation head-mounted displays.[28] They may look like science fiction right now, but, as the past has shown, many technologies that used to be science fiction can eventually turn into (augmented) reality.

Figure 2.4. Users working with the Tangible Landscapes project. *North Carolina State University Libraries.*

NOTES

An earlier version of this chapter was previously published under the title "Augmented Humanities: Augmented Reality and the Digital Humanities," in *Doing Digital Humanities: Practice, Training, Research*, edited by Constance Crompton, Richard J. Lane, and Ray Siemens, 303–12 (London: Routledge, 2016).

1. L. Frank Baum, *The Master Key: An Electrical Fairy Tale Founded Upon the Mysteries of Electricity and the Optimism of Its Devotees*, 93–94.
2. David Grover, "Augmented Reality History, Background and Philosophy."
3. Paul Milgram et al., "Augmented Reality: A Class of Displays on the Reality-Virtuality Continuum"; Paul Milgram and Fumio Kishino, "A Taxonomy of Mixed Reality Visual Displays."
4. Julie Carmigniani and Borko Furht, "Augmented Reality: An Overview," 3.
5. Ronald T. Azuma, "A Survey of Augmented Reality."

6. Pierre Wellner, Wendy E. Mackay, and Rich Gold, "Computer-Augmented Environments: Back to the Real World," 26.

7. Wendy Mackay, "Augmented Reality: Linking Real and Virtual Worlds: A New Paradigm for Interacting with Computers," 13; Evan Barba, Blair MacIntyre, and Elizabeth D. Mynatt, "Here We Are! Where Are We? Locating Mixed Reality in the Age of the Smartphone," 930.

8. Mackay, "Augmented Reality," 15.

9. Barba, MacIntyre, and Mynatt, "Here We Are!" 930.

10. Mackay, "Augmented Reality," 20.

11. Unless noted otherwise, this section draws on Clemens Arth et al., *The History of Mobile Augmented Reality: Developments in Mobile AR over the Last Almost 50 Years.*

12. Steven J. Vaughan-Nichols, "Augmented Reality: No Longer a Novelty?" 19.

13. Oliver Bimber and Ramesh Raskar, *Spatial Augmented Reality: Merging Real and Virtual Worlds*, 4.

14. Thomas P. Caudell and David W. Mizell, "Augmented Reality: An Application of Heads-Up Display Technology to Manual Manufacturing Processes," 660.

15. Arth et al., *History of Mobile Augmented Reality*, 7; Steven Feiner et al., "A Touring Machine: Prototyping 3D Mobile Augmented Reality Systems for Exploring the Urban Environment."

16. Feiner et al., "A Touring Machine."

17. Rob Kooper and Blair MacIntyre, "Browsing the Real-World Wide Web: Maintaining Awareness of Virtual Information in an AR Information Space," 427.

18. Mark Billinghurst, Adrian Clark, and Gun Lee, *A Survey of Augmented Reality*, 28.

19. Claire Cain Miller, "Google Searches for Style."

20. Tasnim Shamma, "Google Glass Didn't Disappear: You Can Find It on the Factory Floor."

21. Nathaniel Mott, "App Anne: 'Pokemon Go' Made Almost $1B in 2016."

22. For an extensive discussion of augmented reality technologies, see Dieter Schmalstieg and Tobias Höllerer, *Augmented Reality: Principles and Practice.*

23. Kun-Hung Cheng and Chin-Chung Tsai, "Affordances of Augmented Reality in Science Learning: Suggestions for Future Research," 451–52.

24. Frederic P. A. Vogt and Luke J. Shingles, "Augmented Reality in Astrophysics."

25. Billinghurst, Clark, and Lee, *A Survey of Augmented Reality*, 65–66.

26. Mark Mine et al., "Projection-Based Augmented Reality in Disney Theme Parks."

27. NCSU GeoForAll Lab, "Tangible Landscape: An Open Source Tangible Interface for Grass GIS."

28. Woodrow Barfield, "Wearable Computers and Augmented Reality: Musings and Future Directions."

BIBLIOGRAPHY

Arth, Clemens, Raphael Grasset, Lukas Gruber, Tobias Langlotz, Alessandro Mulloni, Dieter Schmalstieg, and Daniel Wagner. *The History of Mobile Augmented Reality: Developments in Mobile AR over the Last Almost 50 Years*. Technical report ICG-TR-2015-001. Institution for Computer Graphics and Vision, Graz University of Technology, 2015. http://citeseerx.ist.psu.edu/viewdoc/download?doi=10.1.1.697.3463&rep=rep1&type=pdf.

Azuma, Ronald T. "A Survey of Augmented Reality." *Presence: Teleoperators and Virtual Environments* 6, no. 4 (1997): 355–85.

Azuma, Ronald, Yohan Baillot, Reinhold Behringer, Steven Feiner, Simon Julier, and Blair MacIntyre. "Recent Advances in Augmented Reality." *IEEE Computer Graphics and Applications* 21, no. 6 (2001): 34–47. doi:10.1109/38.963459.

Barba, Evan, Blair MacIntyre, and Elizabeth D. Mynatt. "Here We Are! Where Are We? Locating Mixed Reality in the Age of the Smartphone." *Proceedings of the IEEE* 100, no. 4 (2012): 929–36.

Barfield, Woodrow. "Wearable Computers and Augmented Reality: Musings and Future Directions." In *Fundamentals of Wearable Computers and Augmented Reality*, 2nd edition, edited by Woodrow Barfield, 3–11. Boca Raton, FL: CRC Press, 2015.

Baum, L. Frank. *The Master Key: An Electrical Fairy Tale Founded Upon the Mysteries of Electricity and the Optimism of Its Devotees. It Was Written for Boys, But Others May Read It*. Indianapolis: Bowen-Merrill, 1901.

Billinghurst, Mark, Adrian Clark, and Gun Lee. *A Survey of Augmented Reality*. Foundations and Trends in Human–Computer Interaction series, vol. 8. Boston: Now Publishers, 2015.

Bimber, Oliver, and Ramesh Raskar. *Spatial Augmented Reality: Merging Real and Virtual Worlds*. Boca Raton, FL: CRC Press, 2005.

Carmigniani, Julie, and Borko Furht. "Augmented Reality: An Overview." In *Handbook of Augmented Reality*, edited by Borko Furht, 3–46. New York: Springer, 2011.

Caudell, Thomas P., and David W. Mizell. "Augmented Reality: An Application of Heads-Up Display Technology to Manual Manufacturing Processes." *Proceedings of the Twenty-Fifth Hawaii International Conference on System Sciences* 2 (1992): 659–69.

Cheng, Kun-Hung, and Chin-Chung Tsai. "Affordances of Augmented Reality in Science Learning: Suggestions for Future Research." *Journal of Science Education and Technology* 22, no. 4 (2013): 449–62.

Feiner, Steven, Blair MacIntyre, Tobias Höllerer, and Anthony Webster. "A Touring Machine: Prototyping 3D Mobile Augmented Reality Systems for Exploring the Urban Environment." *Personal and Ubiquitous Computing* 1, no. 4 (1997): 208–17.

Grover, David. "Augmented Reality History, Background and Philosophy." Macquarie University. Last modified February 24, 2014. https://wiki.mq.edu.au/display/ar/Augmented+reality+history,+background+and+philosophy.

Kooper, Rob, and Blair MacIntyre. "Browsing the Real-World Wide Web: Maintaining Awareness of Virtual Information in an AR Information Space." *International*

Journal of Human–Computer Interaction 16, no. 3 (2003): 425–46. doi:10.1207/S15327590IJHC16033.
Mackay, Wendy. "Augmented Reality: Linking Real and Virtual Worlds: A New Paradigm for Interacting with Computers." In *Proceedings of the Workshop on Advanced Visual Interfaces AVI*, 13–21. N.p., 1998.
Milgram, Paul, and Fumio Kishino. "A Taxonomy of Mixed Reality Visual Displays." *IEICE Transactions on Information Systems* E77-D, no. 12 (1994): 1321–29.
Milgram, Paul, Haruo Takemura, Akira Utsumi, and Fumio Kishino. "Augmented Reality: A Class of Displays on the Reality-Virtuality Continuum." *Telemanipulator and Telepresence Technologies* 2351 (1994): 282–92.
Miller, Claire Cain. "Google Searches for Style." *New York Times*, February 20, 2013. http://www.nytimes.com/2013/02/21/technology/google-looks-to-make-its-computer-glasses-stylish.html.
Mine, Mark, David Rose, Bei Yang, Jeroen van Baar, and Anslem Grundhoefer. "Projection-Based Augmented Reality in Disney Theme Parks." *Computer* 45, no. 7 (2012): 32–40. doi:10.1109/MC.2012.154.
Mott, Nathaniel. "App Anne: 'Pokemon Go' Made Almost $1B in 2016." Tom's Hardware, January 17, 2017. http://www.tomshardware.com/news/pokemon-go-billion-revenue-2016,33435.html.
NCSU GeoForAll Lab. "Tangible Landscape: An Open Source Tangible Interface for Grass GIS." Tangible Landscape, 2016. https://tangible-landscape.github.io/.
Schmalstieg, Dieter, and Tobias Höllerer. *Augmented Reality: Principles and Practice.* Boston: Addison-Wesley, 2016.
Shamma, Tasnim. "Google Glass Didn't Disappear: You Can Find It on the Factory Floor." NPR, All Tech Considered, March 18, 2017. http://www.npr.org/sections/alltechconsidered/2017/03/18/514299682/google-glass-didnt-disappear-you-can-find-it-on-the-factory-floor.
Vaughan-Nichols, Steven J. "Augmented Reality: No Longer a Novelty?" *Computer* 42, no. 1 (2009): 19–22. doi:10.1109/MC.2009.380.
Vogt, Frederic P. A., and Luke J. Shingles. "Augmented Reality in Astrophysics." *Astrophysics and Space Science* 347, no. 1 (2013): 47–60. doi:10.1007/s10509-013-1499-x.
Wellner, Pierre, Wendy E. Mackay, and Rich Gold. "Computer-Augmented Environments: Back to the Real World." *Communications of the ACM* 36, no. 7 (1993): 24–26.

3

Hardware and Software for AR/VR Development

Phillip Ballo

Augmented reality (AR) and virtual reality (VR) together present a new and emerging field in libraries where patrons can interact with information through digital objects. This chapter is not about AR/VR projects currently being used in libraries or educational institutions. Rather, it is meant to discuss the tools and software used in AR/VR *development* to encourage people who work in or with libraries to become AR/VR developers. With enough passion, time, and devotion, you can create amazing virtual worlds or blended reality. Individuals with game development experience may find this chapter easier to understand, as the skills and software used in game development are the same for AR/VR development. By the end of this chapter, once you have decided on the hardware and software that fit the requirements of your project, you will be able to start building AR/VR projects on your own.

Before starting with AR/VR, new developers will need to take into consideration the aspects and characteristics of each visual style, as they are fundamentally different from each other. VR is best used for creating an entire virtual world to interact with, while AR is meant to blend virtual objects with reality.

For example, within the library you could use AR for logistics by displaying a graphical heads-up display containing information on the surrounding environment for those walking through the library. You could also create an interactive educational project that uses 3D historical objects accompanied by digital information about each piece, and have the entire learning experience triggered by physical posters within the library.

On the other hand, an example of a VR project would be to reimagine existing space, such as an entire classroom or library, and rearrange the furniture without actually doing so. Or, you could create a training simulator, such as a shelving simulator, without needing to purchase additional training material or claimed work equipment. By designing around the user, you can make your library more accessible and inclusive for everyone. As you plan out your project, keeping these examples in mind, choose the path that is the best use for your project.

An additional consideration to make prior to undertaking an AR/VR project is money. For libraries with small budgets, a combination of common smart devices and open source or free software would be best, while libraries with larger budgets could use AR-dedicated hardware and proprietary software. With more expensive equipment, please note that lending out AR equipment to patrons without firmly established policies may put the library at financial risk. A more lightweight and far less expensive version of AR would be the option of using smart devices, such as smartphones or tablets. While VR technology is slightly cheaper, the technology requires a dedicated space for use, as well as powerful gaming computers or smart devices. Staff may need to keep watch for accidents, as VR fully obscures vision and hearing. When matching your budget with equipment, take note of the risks and additional equipment needed to showcase a product.

Technology is rapidly changing and, at the time of this writing, several companies have recently debuted or announced new AR and VR hardware. Qualcomm recently came out with the new Snapdragon processor, supposedly optimized for AR/VR experiences strictly for mobile devices.[1] During CES 2017, a tradeshow that specifically deals with innovative technologies, companies announced several new AR/VR product enhancements, for example, new 360-degree cameras, VR controllers that perfectly map hands, and room-scale wireless VR, as well as newer editions of their products. Be forewarned that investing in a future product will be risky, as the technology may evolve quickly over time. As such, products mentioned in this chapter will include direct links to the company website rather than provide information on price or exact features (see Appendixes A through C).

The final and most important point to consider is that development is not easy, as AR/VR development requires different skill sets. Not only will an AR/VR project require programming, it may also need 3D modeling, 2D artwork, image manipulation, and sound effects. Successfully implementing an AR/VR project may require a team of skilled individuals to develop an AR/VR program that is customized to the mission, vision, and values of a library.

Although not recommended, single-person development is possible, depending on skill set and available time. Ready-made digital assets may reduce development time, as some institutions, such as the Smithsonian and the British Museum, provide high-definition models of their pieces through Sketchfab or through their own sites.[2] Finally, for individuals with little or

Figure 3.1. Microsoft HoloLens. ***Phillip Ballo.***

no experience with AR/VR hardware, it is strongly suggested that any new developer, prior to purchasing any product, should borrow the hardware from another institution or individual, or use emulators (like the Microsoft HoloLens, figure 3.1) and practice AR/VR development at home first to understand the costs and work effort needed to develop software.

This chapter is divided into three parts: the first part details the hardware of AR glasses and smart devices, the second part explains the hardware requirements for VR, and the final part goes in depth about the software tools needed to develop both AR and VR.

AUGMENTED REALITY HARDWARE

Most current AR devices should be capable of layering virtual 2D images onto the real world through the display of smart devices or AR glasses. If the AR project relies heavily on high-resolution 3D models, voice recognition, sound, hand gestures, and information processing, then something like the HoloLens, ODG's R series, or other expensive high-end smart glasses would have the capability. However, if the AR project does not require immense processing power, such as simple 2D animations with low-polygon 3D models, it may be best to go the cheaper route. Smart devices, such as smartphones and tablets, would possess the necessary hardware requirements to produce high-quality AR projects. For the new developer, it is recommended to start with a smart device. See Appendix A for a list of AR devices.

There are several sensors in AR devices that can be used to display environmental information in AR projects. One of the standard sensors is a gyroscope, which helps determine orientation, and is a requirement for both AR and VR apps such as Pokémon GO and Google Cardboard. A similar sensor, the accelerometer, can be used to calculate orientation as well as velocity, and is commonly used in sports-related applications. Altimeter and altitude sensors measure position from sea level. AR devices may also contain weather sensors, such as a barometer or a humidity sensor. A GPS tracker is also necessary if the AR project requires information about location. A microphone is required for voice commands or audio recording. This is not a comprehensive list, but they are all used for gathering environmental data that could then be applied to a feature in an AR project.

For AR glasses, be sure to check the display and video capture resolution. Many should be capable of high-resolution images or video (at least 720 progressive scan, or 720p). Be sure to check whether or not the display is capable of color, as there are smart glasses that incorporate a monochromatic heads-up display (HUD). Although advertisements often portray AR glasses that place solid virtual objects on top of real surfaces, the digital objects are in fact translucent. Using AR glasses in the daytime or in extremely bright areas will cause the digital objects to be more translucent and, for some glasses, might make digital objects almost transparent. Furthermore, many video demonstrations of AR glasses are recorded through the camera, or recorded while the camera is completely stationary. If the camera was moving via natural human motions, motion-tracked digital objects within the scene would be jittery. Therefore, video demonstrations are not necessarily an accurate visual representation of what the user will see. Translucency can easily be rectified by using the glasses in low light or by increasing the brightness on the glasses, but this may still not work in bright areas. Jittery movement can be rectified by moving the smart device camera slowly. Be sure to look for the field of view for AR glasses as well, as this will determine the observable area in which digital objects are displayed (figure 3.2).

All AR devices should be capable of recognizing markers,[3] which allows the camera to recognize specific objects in the real world. Developers should use markers to place digital objects on top of markers, or have a digital object interact with the marker. In order to recognize objects/trackers within the environment, it is necessary to have a camera that can clearly identify small details. Cameras in AR glasses are assumed to be optimized for the device and, as such, are not a primary concern. However, a good display comes down to multiple factors: the brightness of the environment, the details of the marker itself, and the device's hardware. In this case, it is best to stick with modern

Figure 3.2. Field of view. ***Phillip Ballo.***

smart devices, which can support the minimum OS version suggested by the AR plugin being used to develop the project.

In regard to battery life, look for the mAh (milliampere-hour) capacity, as this indicates the battery life. The more processing power an AR project has, the more power it will drain. Screencasting, Internet use, or wireless computer accessories will require Bluetooth and wireless connection capabilities on the AR device. Finally, look for expandable storage, as storage capacity listed for smart devices are misleading. In addition to the operating system, AR-capable devices may come with bloatware (unnecessary pre-installed applications) that can take up a significant amount of space.

AR development can be a difficult and expensive field to enter. For new developers, it is highly recommended to start developing with smart devices, as they are commonplace and cheap. The benefit of using smart devices is that most newer models, including off-brand phones, should possess several environmental sensors and the processing power to handle augmented reality. The downside is that the user is only watching a live-action video with virtual objects integrated with the scene, which is a different experience from using AR glasses. However, due to the more cost-effective availability of smart devices, new developers can begin developing AR projects right away.

VIRTUAL REALITY HARDWARE

Virtual reality project development may require more powerful computer hardware than do augmented reality projects. The minimum requirements for VR headsets are listed on their official sites, but with the new VR headsets announced recently, hardware requirements may change. Some VR headsets advertise a "mixed reality" experience, which is a combination of both virtual and augmented reality capabilities. However, most of the hardware requirements for a VR project depend on the quality of the digital assets, and how well the project was optimized. Throughout this section, there will be references to a development computer, as well as a computer that will deploy a VR project. These two conceptual computers can be the same computer, but if patrons can access the original project files, it is recommended that the original project files be stored on a separate computer.

Computer-dependent VR headsets, such as the HTC Vive or Oculus Rift (figure 3.3), will need to connect to a graphics card via DisplayPort or HDMI, so be sure the graphics card possesses the necessary connections. Within recent years, these graphics cards are often marketed as "VR Ready" or "Oculus Ready," but connectivity is as simple as looking for a graphics card with multiple ports. For desktop computers, it is possible to connect the computer monitor to the DVI or VGA port, but the visual experience might

Figure 3.3. HTC Vive. *Phillip Ballo.*

be diminished if the VR development process requires heavy graphics editing while testing. If developing for a mobile device, such as Samsung's Gear VR or Google Cardboard, please be aware of the capabilities of the device, as VR is a resource-heavy software.

Prior to purchasing any computer, always compare the actual hardware requirements of the VR device with the computer's internal hardware and its requirements for VR. NVIDIA, for example, recommends a GTX 1060 or above for VR, 8GB RAM, and at least an i5-4590 processor for desktop (i5-7300HQ for laptops).[4] The Oculus Rift, on the other hand, has a lower threshold. The minimum requirements for the Oculus Rift can be as low as an NVIDIA GTX 1050 Ti/AMD Radeon RX 470 (Alternative: GTX 960 4GB/ AMD Radeon R9 290), 8GB RAM, and an Intel i3-6100/AMD FX4350.[5] While less powerful hardware might be capable of running VR hardware, quality could drop for more hardware-intensive games. See Appendix B for a list of virtual reality hardware.

DEVELOPMENT CONSIDERATIONS

The intent of this chapter assumes that the new developer will use existing equipment. The minimum requirements are only indications that the software and hardware will work on a computer. The final VR project may require more powerful hardware and, as such, it is necessary to test the development computer, as well as the computer that will deploy the VR project. Prior to purchasing a brand-new computer for either development or playing a VR game or project, use the SteamVR performance test, Oculus Rift Compatibility Check Tool, GeForce Experience, or other hardware tools to test performance and hardware compatibilities. For the development computer, download the development software, located in Appendix C (such as Unity), and run it. Try adding a few models from a trusted 3D model repository (such as Sketchfab) within the scene, and try to move it around.

Depending on the hardware and software, virtual reality projects may require a dedicated space for movement and equipment. When looking for VR software, check the game details as to whether or not the patron will be moving around a room or sitting down. The HTC Vive and the Oculus Rift are more equipment-heavy VR options and may take more physical space than a smaller VR headset, such as Gear VR.

Finally, be aware of motion sickness. VR creates a disconnect between the mind and body, and those not accustomed to VR might injure themselves. Be sure to test your games or software for any sudden movements, in-game camera desynchronization, and frame rate drops. If you are designing for inclusiveness and accessibility, try designing VR software that only requires the user to sit down, without rotation. Additionally, you can design around a single controller, an Xbox or PC controller, or if you have the budget, implement motion-tracking gloves. Avoid flashing lights and the sudden appearance of digital objects.

Software

Prior to the start of development, you must check the operating system of the AR/VR hardware. Some of the more popular AR glasses, such as the Sony SmartEyeglass, use Android OS, while smart devices can use either Android OS or iOS.[6] Android uses Java as the main development language, and uses the Android Development Studio as its official integrated development environment (IDE). Microsoft HoloLens runs Windows 10 and uses Visual Studio as its recommended IDE. Apple products run iOS, and their primary development language is Objective-C or Swift.

For multisystem development, using middleware development software such as Unity or Unreal is highly recommended. This software can export to different platforms, including iOS, Android, Linux, and Windows. AR glasses, such as Meta, Moverio, and Microsoft HoloLens, and VR hardware, such as Oculus and HTC Vive, advertise the use of Unity for augmented reality projects. Unreal is also highly recommended for VR and AR projects. The Unity game engine supports C# and JavaScript/Unity Script, while the Unreal game engine uses C++. For the new developer who does not wish to learn programming, Unity has a paid visual scripting plugin called Playmaker, but this may require an additional plugin to access VR development content for the HTC Vive or Oculus. The Unreal engine also has an internal visual scripting program called Blueprints that could make development easier, but this, like Unity, may require additional plugins to access AR/VR content.

Be wary of toolkits when developing for AR, as many toolkits are hardware dependent. Unless the AR glass advertises a specific toolkit, the software may or may not work. For example, ARToolKit, as great as it is on smart devices and on PCs, is unfortunately not available for many smart glasses. Gesture recognition[7] in AR devices is the ability to recognize hand movements in order to communicate with the device, which many toolkits do not support. Devices like the HoloLens may come with gestures programmed into the device. There are some hand-gesture software libraries, such as OpenCV and FastCV, but these require heavy technical programming knowledge. For the new developer, hand-gesture tracking should be programmed with the gestures provided by the hardware, and workarounds should be implemented.

For drag-and-drop AR development, Aurasma is a for-pay software development kit that individuals with no AR experience find easier to use. At the time of this writing, Aurasma has a free "starter subscription" feature. To develop AR applications with smart devices, iOS has a toolkit called ARKit, and Android has ARCore. See Appendix C for a list of software for both VR and AR.

License Agreements

Many software programs mentioned in this chapter may be free for individuals and most kinds of developers. Unity, for example, offers a subscription package for educational institutions teaching Unity. Unfortunately, institutions will need to pay a subscription fee. License agreements are constantly changing, so it is best to research the product prior to implementing a project.

CONCLUSION

New developers, especially those who work with smaller budgets or have fewer technological skills, should start with what they can afford. Most likely, the new developer will not be able to develop an enterprise-level experience on his or her first try. Assuming that that the new AR/VR developer is learning independent of an institution, the following hardware and software for AR is suggested: a smartphone, Unity, Vuforia, or ARToolKit. Likewise, for VR, use the Google Cardboard viewer with a compatible smartphone and Unity. The total cost, assuming that the developer already owns a smart device and a computer capable of game development, should be zero or minimal at most. Start with something simple, such as creating an empty virtual room (for VR) with some furniture or making an historical digital artifact appear on a piece of paper (for AR). AR/VR development can be difficult, and may not be a task for beginners, but learning about the technology now will benefit librarians and information professionals in the future.

Once you have practiced enough, think about AR and VR within the scope of education, inclusiveness, and skill development. Because AR allows for a mix of digital and real environments, it enables students to learn a subject in different ways.[8] For example, if students who are visual learners have a digital model to work with, they can conceptualize math and engineering problems. Combining AR technology with book inventory practices (such as book location) can help individuals with disabilities retrieve information about the books they need.[9] Virtual reality can assist with socioeconomic issues, such as providing the general public with work and safety skills by immersing individuals in a world customized to their needs. After all, companies are now integrating AR and VR systems into their training and work programs.[10]

When designing VR training systems, note that procedural skills work better in 2D environments, and that the user may become dependent on visual cues.[11] As your development skills improve, begin imagining AR and VR in isolation in outer space. VR can be used to train astronauts in simulated environments without using expensive space equipment. In fact, NASA already does this.[12] Keeping this in mind, develop AR and VR applications as tools, and you will be on your way to becoming a successful developer.

APPENDIX A: AUGMENTED REALITY HARDWARE

Popular AR Hardware	*URL*
Microsoft Hololens	https://www.microsoft.com/microsoft-hololens/en-us
Epson BT (Series)	https://epson.com/moverio-augmented-reality
Sony SmartEyeGlass	http://developer.sonymobile.com/products/smarteyeglass/
ODG's R (Series) Glasses	http://www.osterhoutgroup.com/home
Meta (Series)	https://www.metavision.com/
Vuzix M (Series)	https://www.vuzix.com/
Atheer Air	http://www.atheerair.com/smartglasses
Recon Jet	http://www.reconinstruments.com/products/jet/
Intel RealSense Cameras	https://software.intel.com/en-us/realsense/
Recommended Hardware for Practice Development	
Any smart device supporting the minimum system requirements recommended by an AR plugin	
Any modern webcam attached to a PC supporting the minimum system requirements recommended by an AR plugin	

APPENDIX B: VIRTUAL/MIXED REALITY HARDWARE

VR Hardware	*URL*
Oculus Rift	https://www.oculus.com/
HTC Vive	https://www.vive.com/us/
Leap Motion	https://www.leapmotion.com/
Samsung GearVR	http://www.samsung.com/global/galaxy/gear-vr/
PSVR	https://www.playstation.com/en-us/explore/playstation-vr/
Google Cardboard (platform consists of case, software, and phone)	https://vr.google.com/cardboard/
Google Daydream (platform consists of case, software, and phone)	https://vr.google.com/daydream/
Windows Mixed Reality Headsets (various brands)	https://www.microsoft.com/en-us/windows/windows-mixed-reality

APPENDIX C: RECOMMENDED SOFTWARE

Recommended Development Software

Software	*Type*	*Free or Paid*	*URL*
Unity	Game engine	Free with paid features	https://unity3d.com/
Unreal	Game engine	Free with paid features	https://www.unrealengine.com/
CryEngine	Game engine	Free with paid services	https://www.cryengine.com/
Xenko	Game engine	Free with paid features	https://xenko.com/
Android Development Studio	IDE	Free	https://developer.android.com/studio/index.html
Visual Studio	IDE	Free with paid features	https://www.visualstudio.com/
Aurasma	Drag and drop	Free/paid features	https://www.aurasma.com/

Recommended Toolkits/Plugins for Augmented Reality Only

Name	*Free or Paid*	*URL*
Vuforia	Free to develop, paid features	https://www.vuforia.com/
Wikitude	Free to develop, paid features	http://www.wikitude.com/
ARToolKit	Free	http://artoolkit.org/
Augumenta	Free trial	http://augumenta.com/
Unreal4AR	Free/paid features	http://www.unreal4ar.com/
ARKit (iOS)	Free	https://developer.apple.com/arkit/
ARCore (Android)	Free	https://developers.google.com/ar/

NOTES

1. Qualcomm, "Qualcomm Snapdragon 835 Mobile Platform to Power Next-Generation Immersive Experiences."
2. Some sites include the British Museum's Sketchfab account (https://sketchfab.com/britishmuseum) and the Smithsonian's 3D Digitization website (https://3d.si.edu/).
3. Also called fiduciary markers.
4. NVIDIA, "System Requirements for VR."
5. Oculus, "What Are the Minimum and Recommended System Specifications Needed to Power Oculus Rift?"
6. Epsom Moverio BT-300 (https://epson.com/moverio-augmented-reality-smart-glasses-for-drone-flying), Sony SmartEyeglass (https://developer.sony.com/

develop/wearables/smarteyeglass-sdk/), ODG R series (https://www.osterhoutgroup.com/r-7-glasses-system.html), Vuzix M Series (https://www.vuzix.com/Products/m300-smart-glasses), and Atheer AiR (http://atheerair.com/2016/10/18/8-ways-ar-is-used-for-business/).

7. Similar terms include hand-gesture and hand-tracking recognition.

8. Teresa Coimbra, Teresa Cardoso, and Artur Mateus, "Augmented Reality: An Enhancer for Higher Education Students in Math's Learning?"

9. Zulqarnain Rashid et al., "Using Augmented Reality and Internet of Things to Improve Accessibility of People with Motor Disabilities in the Context of Smart Cities."

10. Vincent Higgins, "Augmented & Virtual Reality: The Future of Work, Not Just Play," 86.

11. Yaiza Vélaz et al., "The Influence of Interaction Technology on the Learning of Assembly Tasks Using Virtual Reality."

12. NASA, "Mars Immersion: NASA Concepts Bring Precision to New Virtual Reality Experience."

BIBLIOGRAPHY

Coimbra, Teresa, Teresa Cardoso, and Artur Mateus. "Augmented Reality: An Enhancer for Higher Education Students in Math's Learning?" *Procedia Computer Science* 67 (2015): 332–39.

Higgins, Vincent. "Augmented & Virtual Reality: The Future of Work, Not Just Play." *Professional Safety* 62, no. 6 (2017): 86.

NASA. "Mars Immersion: NASA Concepts Bring Precision to New Virtual Reality Experience." December 16, 2015. https://www.nasa.gov/feature/nasa-concepts-bring-precision-mars-to-virtual-reality.

NVIDIA. "System Requirements for VR." Accessed November 11, 2017. http://www.geforce.com/hardware/technology/vr/system-requirements.

Oculus. "What Are the Minimum and Recommended System Specifications Needed to Power Oculus Rift?" Accessed November 11, 2017. https://support.oculus.com/help/oculus/170128916778795/.

Qualcomm. "Qualcomm Snapdragon 835 Mobile Platform to Power Next-Generation Immersive Experiences." January 3, 2017. https://www.qualcomm.com/news/releases/2017/01/03/qualcomm-snapdragon-835-mobile-platform-power-next-generation-immersive.

Rashid, Zulqarnain, Joan Melià-Seguí, Rafael Pous, and Enric Peig. "Using Augmented Reality and Internet of Things to Improve Accessibility of People with Motor Disabilities in the Context of Smart Cities." *Future Generation Computer Systems* 76 (2017): 248–61.

Vélaz, Yaiza, Jorge Rodríguez Arce, Teresa Gutiérrez, Alberto Lozano-Rodero, and Angel Suescun. "The Influence of Interaction Technology on the Learning of Assembly Tasks Using Virtual Reality." *Journal of Computing and Information Science in Engineering* 14, no. 4 (2014): 041007.

4

Presence versus Utility

Similarities and Differences between Virtual Reality and Augmented Reality

Cynthia Hart

It's been a long time since augmented reality (AR) and virtual reality (VR) were first conceptualized in the 1950s and began the slow transition from ideas to the consumer products of today. Debuted in 1968, the Sword of Damocles, brainchild of computer scientist Ivan Sutherland, is often credited as the first VR and AR head-mounted display system.[1] However, Morton Heilig beat Sutherland to it by eight years with his 1960 patent for the Telesphere Mask.[2] The 1960s was a busy decade for this prolific inventor. In 1962, he also patented the Sensorama Machine, an early example of technology that works to create alternative realities. Myron Krueger's VR research in the 1970s contributed greatly to VR systems and responsive virtual rooms.[3] While Heilig, Krueger, and Sutherland envisioned reality technologies early on, it was not until the success of Pokémon GO in 2016 that these emerging technologies gained hype in popular news outlets.

Now, hope and hype for the success of these technologies stretches beyond researchers and computer scientists into many types of businesses. Advancements in exponential technologies and investments by large corporations are behind the breakout success of these technologies. For example, industry giants are helping VR become a household word. Known for splashy product launches, in 2016 Samsung gave away Gear VR headsets with the purchase of Galaxy S7 and S Edge smartphones. They also partnered with the NBC television network to bring the world 85 hours of VR coverage during the 2016 Summer Olympics.[4] It's no surprise, then, that Gartner's 2016 Hype Cycle for Emerging Technologies lists AR and VR as high-priority trends for businesses over the next few years.

These are the technologies that Gartner anticipates will greatly accelerate innovation and competitive advantages for businesses.[5] Libraries are key components of lifelong education and workforce development. Our customers expect more than books when they visit. Imagine the hue and cry if the library did not have free Wi-Fi, public computers, or 3D printers.[6] Our customers need access to emerging technologies such as AR and VR today in order to succeed tomorrow. For libraries, understanding the similarities and differences between AR and VR is an essential aspect of leveraging both technologies in meaningful ways to meet the needs of our customers. This chapter seeks to help libraries determine if the presence of VR or utility of AR are appropriate experiences for their institutional or customer needs.

DEFINING CHARACTERISTICS

Definitions are fundamental to understanding these technologies. Augmented reality has several defining characteristics. It combines real and virtual images that can be seen simultaneously by the user. These virtual objects appear in 3D and are fixed in space.[7] The data or objects, such as characters in the popular game Pokémon GO, are generated through an AR application and appear on top of the user's real-world view though a device such as a smartphone. It's this useful real-time layering of digital objects over a user's real-world view that makes AR a utility. Through the resulting composite view of the real world, users have new and expanded interactions and experiences. It's easy, though, for the user to break the illusion of the computer-generated objects because they are in the real world, not a simulated one.[8]

Virtual reality, in contrast, creates a simulated world or environment for the user.[9] In 1992, David Zelter plotted three variables—autonomy, interaction, and presence—on a three-axis coordinate system to create the AIP Cube, a model of a virtual reality system. Zelter's model shows that presence, or the sense of being in an environment, is key to defining VR in terms of experience. Telepresence is the experience of presence in an environment by means of a communication medium. VR is defined as a real or simulated environment in which a perceiver experiences telepresence.[10] Remember those Gear VR headsets that Samsung gave away in 2016 with the purchase of new smartphones? They stimulated the human senses to draw viewers in, take them to Barcelona, and keep them present in the moment.[11] Or, in other words, they created presence through a communication medium.

PRESENCE: VIRTUAL REALITY

VR's ultimate goal is to create presence in a real or imagined world through vibrant visuals, accurate sounds, and intuitive interactions. Presence, or the fact or condition of being present, is created through trickery.[12] It requires multiple sensory inputs and user-controlled or manipulated components. Illusions fool the user's brain into believing the visual data that the eyes provide and pass along. The user's brain interprets the data without the contextual information needed to determine whether or not it's a visual anomaly. Combined with appropriate sounds and interactions, the user's brain response is immersion into the reality.[13]

Furthermore, the combination of low latency and high frame rate in VR display devices, together with exact position tracking inputs, places the user in the world—at full-scale view. It changes how the user interacts with the world by giving him or her a sense of presence. Immersive VR takes over the two senses that we need most—vision and hearing—and tricks the brain into thinking that the user is somewhere else.[14] VR presence is usually equated with immersion, or the perception of being physically present in a non-physical world. Comparing immersive, semi-immersive, and non-immersive VR is also helpful in understanding presence.

Immersive VR is that sweet spot when everything comes together for the user. It starts with a creative concept that sparks the user's imagination. It is made believable through fully developed graphics and subtle rendering. Lastly, it offers powerful storytelling that leaves the user wanting more. The Blue Marble experience is an early yet powerful example of immersive VR. As they jettison into space with their favorite soundtrack playing in the background, users of the Blue Marble VR experience move into a weightless environment with breathtaking, realistically detailed views of the Earth and beyond. As they pass a satellite, they can reach out and touch it. The Blue Marble VR experience is believable because it immerses users into the environment.[15]

As expected, semi-immersive VR differs from immersive VR in that it partly immerses the user into the virtual environment. Examples of semi-immersive VR include a flight simulator and a first-person shooter arcade game. Each employs a large concave screen with a projector system and, generally, a comfortable chair. They allow for easy but limited interactions and assumptions of a new identity for the user.[16] Since non-immersive VR was originally accessible with a desktop computer, early developers categorized it as "desktop" VR. The user's sense of situational awareness and immersion were low in comparison to semi-immersive or immersive VR.[17] Today, non-immersive VR takes advantage of advances in and widespread ownership of smartphone technology. Non-immersive VR is one of the forces moving the technology toward mainstream consumer adoption. Google Cardboard is an example of non-immersive VR.

Downloaded more than 160 million times, the free Google Cardboard app works with the inexpensive Google Cardboard VR headset and YouTube

360, Google's VR channel.[18] With millions of active subscribers, it offers a growing content collection. Visit the electronics section of any superstore and you will find a collection of VR headsets with a price range designed to fit any budget. They are all non-immersive VR devices requiring a smartphone and an app for a VR experience. Mental and emotional immersion still takes place with non-immersive VR, contributing to presence.[19]

Researchers exploring VR further explain the concept of VR presence by dividing it into three subcategories: personal, social, and environmental. Personal presence refers to the user's perception of physically existing within a virtual world. One key to creating personal presence is offering a virtual identity that is similar to the user's real-world physically identity. VR personal presence can help us understand one another, too. BeAnotherLab, a group focusing on promoting empathy, offers Gender Swap, a VR experience with the Oculus Rift. In this VR experience, a man and a woman swap physical entities in a virtual environment.[20]

Social presence is defined by the user's ability to interact with simulated or real entities within a virtual world. vTime, a VR social network, is an example of social presence in VR. After creating an account and an avatar, users can chat with friends in 19 different settings with full 3D sound, 360-degree images, and familiar gestures such as clapping. Lastly, environmental presence occurs when the virtual world is aware of the VR user and reacts to his or her presence. Research shows that there is a direct correlation between environmental presence and VR immersion.[21] Owlchemy Lab's Job Simulator is a fun example of how a VR user can explore the environmental presence of VR. In this VR experience, a user can undertake hundreds of actions on the job, from drinking coffee to working on a computer.[22] VR is distinguished by the level of immersion it promises the user. It stands out as a medium for learning, playing, and communicating by creating believable presence in a virtual environment. Experts agree that VR will also have a growing presence in the market for years to come. By 2025, Goldman Sachs Research predicts that the combined AR/VR market will be worth $25 billion, or roughly the size of today's desktop computer market. It expects AR/VR to be the next-generation computing platform.[23]

VR in Libraries

VR offers powerful experiences in many ways. Imagine the possibilities if libraries provide opportunities for our customers to create immersive VR experiences themselves. Prince George County Libraries' VR Roadshow, coordinated by FutureMakers and Seven Hills Games, provided resources, expert know-how, and technology so that kids could learn how to create VR games with the Unity game engine, software, and developers kit, as well as experience VR firsthand. The skills they learned are valuable now as well as into the future. While the games can be classified as semi-immersive VR, the libraries gave the kids the opportunity to use and create virtual environments with VR.[24] Google Cardboard provides libraries with an inexpensive and easy way to implement VR for educational programs or personal experiences.

VR is a natural storytelling medium for people to experience other times and places without leaving the library. It's not too hard to imagine virtual reality labs, tours, and workshops as the next step for libraries.[25] On the exhibit floor at the American Library Association (ALA) Midwinter 2017, Booth 838, otherwise known as the "Innovation Pavilion," showcased eight technologies with potential for libraries. VR was one of those technologies with the inclusion of VARlibraries.[26] Started in 2016, this group functions as a clearinghouse for libraries. It directs the sharing of best practices for the installation and use of virtual and augmented reality technologies in libraries, and also works as the project coordinator for the California Virtual Reality Experience.[27] In this new opportunity, California's public libraries can apply for a VR-enabled computer with pre-loaded educational programs, plus the Oculus Rift VR headgear. The libraries also receive installation assistance, training, and access to VR programming resources.[28] Libraries as trusted community centers are in a unique position to offer emerging technologies as learning resources.

UTILITY: AUGMENTED REALITY

It's not far-fetched to imagine augmented reality (AR) as part of the next-generation computing platform. AR is a utility; it's a useful real-time, real-world technology that layers digital objects over a user's real-world view. Through the resulting composite view of the world, users have new and expanded interactions and experiences. AR has been in the public eye for almost two decades. Whether they realize it or not, every National Football League fan has seen it in use. It's the technology behind the "first and ten line" on televised football games. The yellow virtual first-down marker is displayed on-screen during live NFL games twice a week during the regular season.[29] Other sports see AR as useful technology as well.

The National Basketball Association, Major League Baseball, and the National Hockey League are all experimenting with AR.[30] With the NBA's Cleveland Cavaliers app, "Deep in the Q," fans can scan an image on the scoreboard and shoot hoops from their seat in the team's Cleveland Quicken Loans Arena during games. Fans can move their smartphone around the arena to shoot baskets from believable angles. From home, fans can scan the Bud Light logo for the same interactions.[31] Cleveland's new app is a fun and potentially addicting example of how major league sports anticipate AR changing how audiences watch and experience live gameplay. AR is also showing up in other public places, including museums.

AR in Museums

Museums are not new to the business of creating interactions between visitors and displays through technology. Remember audio and video guides? Over the last few years, museums have embraced digital storytelling as a means of educating and engaging visitors. Noteworthy is the British Museum's app, A Gift for Athena. Through this app and a dedicated tablet, AR technology transforms a child's museum experience into a story puzzle. The app rewards the user for finding certain statues by telling them more about the exhibit and directing them into the next stage of the game.[32] Until recently, museums did not fully tap the digital storytelling power of AR with full museum tours encompassing all collections.

Visitors to the Detroit Institute of Arts (DIA) can experience and interact with the collections in new ways thanks to Lumin, the museum's AR-powered mobile tour. Built with Google's Tango technology and GuidiGO's AR composer, the tour integrates 3D mapping with smartphone AR. Using the Android smartphone Lenovo Phab 2 Pro, visitors engage with the collection through AR overlays including videos, photographs, sounds, and animation that add to contextual information and enhance visitors' experiences. Imagine a user moving along the halls in the Egyptian Galley, then gasping as the Lumin app reveals an X-ray view of the skeleton inside the museum's 2,000-year-old mummy.[33] The technology elevates the user's experience through new dimensions of interaction. The museum is no longer a passive collection of works, each with its own story waiting to be read. While not quite the same experience, AR is bringing stories to life in users' homes as well.

Stories are narratives that can enrich our lives. AR is a medium of expression that enriches user experiences. For British start-up Mardles, combining the two is good business. Mardles first used AR as a means to engage with kids through stickers. Now, they have turned to books. Using an app and the camera on their phone or tablet, users bring stories to life. After scanning a book page, the user sees a 3D representation of the illustrations on the page. On his or her device screen, the user can interact with the new 3D environment by tapping on any part of it. The book characters will interact or react as part of the story.[34] Libraries, like museums, are excellent choices for the application of useful technology. With AR, customers can marvel and interact with library spaces and collections in exciting new ways. AR expands on what a user can learn, see, and do. Imagine a library user opening the pages of a book and seeing a 3D image of the galaxy through a smartphone.

More on AR in Libraries

In 2011, the Virginia Beach Public Library (VBPL) partnered with Tagwhat, an AR-based mobile app, to bring their local history collection to life. As a result, VBPL became the first library in the nation to use AR for rich, location-based storytelling to showcase library collections.[35] The Tagwhat stories are organized into subject channels, including heritage, movies, music, sports, art, food, and nature. Users can tap on a story tag to read, watch videos, view photos, or listen to audio. They can even share a "digital postcard" through social media sites such as Facebook or Twitter, and through email. App users view the local scenery through their smartphones. Stories about the locations appear on the screen, enhancing users' experiences.

Reader's Delight

AR enhances the user experience. Young readers can especially benefit from AR-enhanced books and lessons. Interactive books such as *The Fantastic Flying of Morris Lessmore* transform the reader from passive to active, as they feel like they are part of the book. AR-based books such as Daqri's *Elements 4D* or *Anatomy 4D* bring science to life.[36] During the past few years, many different developers have experimented with creating a variety of AR experiences. Sony's Playstation 3 Wonderbook, released in 2012, uses Playstation's Move Motion controller and the Playstation Eye Camera to create virtual games for users. The user holds a physical book-like object, and the stories come to life as the system displays AR content on the Playstation 3 screen.[37] For AR to truly add dimensions for the reader, AR-powered books need to be readable on their own; the interactions need to enhance rather than detract from the overall user experience. Add-ons or peripherals such as Playstation's Move Motion controller can detract from AR's optimal usefulness. As a consumer product, the success of augmented reality relies heavily on untethered usefulness to create a seamless user experience. Smartphone AR technology is fully integrated into the device and is invisible to the user.

Exponential Technologies

AR and non-immersive VR both require a smartphone and an app. For non-immersive VR, a smartphone must be mounted inside a VR headset for VR content to display correctly to the user. Both AR and VR use most of the same exponential technologies, which are advancing with unprecedented speed. The huge shift in development of exponential technologies in almost every category from sensors to thermal efficiencies is behind the breakout success of AR and VR. These include both hardware and software components.

AR and VR share common sensors, including accelerometers, gyroscopes, magnetometers, and proximity sensors. There are some differences in sensors, though. AR requires additional sensors, including Global Positioning System (GPS) and 3D depth. VR uses an image sensor as well. Both have semiconductor components, including controllers and processors, integrated circuits, and displays. The AR market can be categorized by four unique types of displays: head-mounted (HMD), heads-up (HUD), hand-held, and spatial. The VR market can be described by device type, including head-mounted displays, gesture-control devices and projectors, and display walls.[38]

Whether it's a huge display wall or a small screen, AR hardware is striding forward as the winner of the day. However, software development is lagging. Noah Falstein, Google's chief game designer, thinks that we're still in the very early days of AR and VR development, and the two might even end up as a mixed medium.[39] Both technologies are part of what Price Waterhouse refers to as the "tech breakthroughs" megatrend. For business, AR improves the user experience for a task or a product. The augmentation is rendered and displayed through a device that provides countless everyday opportunities for user experience enrichment. VR is designed and used to recreate reality within a confined experience. Price Waterhouse sees AR and VR as technologies to apply to product design and assembly as well as to promote collaboration and engagement.[40] AR, like VR, is a medium of expression, providing users with new ways to interact with and experience the world around them.

CONCLUSION

Augmented reality, by layering digital objects over a user's real-world view in real time, enriches the user's experience through the resulting composite view. In essence, AR is a utility, something useful or designed for use.[41] Its usefulness is limited only by our imagination. Both AR and VR offer tremendous educational, training, and social opportunities for many, including libraries. It's further distinguished from adjacent technologies by the level of immersion that it promises the user. Virtual reality stands out as a medium of expression by offering believable presence. Both AR and VR use some of the same types of technology. Both are focused on the user's experience; AR enhances, while VR creates. Both technologies enable new and exciting entertainment and educational experiences that either bring to life new worlds or create layers of interaction with the real world. Experts and investors see great potential in using these technologies in industry and everyday products.[42] Tremendous investments in exponential technologies, including hardware and software development, are spurring adoption of both AR and VR by consumers, businesses, and libraries.

NOTES

1. "Ivan Sutherland," *Wikipedia.*
2. Holly Brockwell, "Forgotten Genius: The Man Who Made a Working VR Machine in 1957."
3. "Virtual Reality."
4. NBC, "Experience the Rio Olympics in Virtual Reality."
5. Amy Ann Forni, "Gartner's 2016 Hype Cycle for Emerging Technologies Identifies Three Key Trends That Organizations Must Track to Gain Competitive Advantage."
6. Troy Lambert, "Virtual Reality in the Library: Creating a New Experience."
7. R. T. Azuma, "A Survey of Augmented Reality."
8. Eric Johnson, "What's the Difference Between Virtual Reality and Mixed Reality?"
9. "The Promise of Augmented Reality."
10. D. Zelter, "Autonomy, Interaction and Presence."
11. Christian De Looper, "Watch the Olympics in Stunning Virtual Reality with the Samsung Gear VR."
12. "Presence," Merriam-Webster.com.
13. Adam Dachis, "How Virtual and Mixed Reality Trick Your Brain."
14. Cynthia Fox, "Virtual Reality vs. Real Life: How Brian Neurons Light Up."
15. Jaywalker Interactive, "Blue Marble."
16. Philippe Fuchs, Guillaume Moreau, and Pascal Guitton, *Virtual Reality: Concepts and Technologies*, 248–50.
17. P. J. Costello, "Healthy and Safety Issues Associated with Virtual Reality."
18. Amit Singh, "More Ways to Watch and Play with AR and VR."
19. G. G. Roberston, S. K. Card, and J. D. Mackinlay, "Non-Immersive Virtual Reality."
20. Aaron Souppouris, "Virtual Reality Made Me Believe I Was Someone Else."
21. Torisu Takashi, "Sense of Presence in Social VR Experience."
22. Owlchemy Labs, "Job Simulator."
23. Heather Bellini, "The Real Deal with Virtual and Augmented Reality."
24. Stephen Babcook, "How One Maryland Library System Is Embracing Virtual Reality."

25. Troy Lambert, "Virtual Reality in the Library."

26. Cynthia Hart, "Trends-day Wednesday, Technology on Display at ALA Midwinter."

27. VARlibraries, "About Us."

28. California State Library, "Virtual Reality Experience Project."

29. SMT, "1st and Ten Graphics."

30. Dennis Williams, "Did Sports Pave the Way for Augmented Reality?"

31. Fitz Tepper, "An NBA Team Is Turning Their Scorebook into an AR Baseball Game."

32. Yannis Ioannidia, Olivier Balet, and Dimitrios Pandermalis, "Tell Me a Story: Augmented Reality Technology in Museums."

33. Detroit Institute of Arts, "Detroit Institute of Arts to Premiere Lumin, a Mobile Tour Using Augmented Reality."

34. Jeff Parsons, "Augmented Reality Children's Books Bring Bedtime Stories to Life in 3D."

35. City of Virginia Beach, "Library Partners with Tagwhat Mobile App to Launch New Chapter in Local Storytelling."

36. Phil Goerner, "The Educational Potential of Augmented Reality."

37. Laura McQuarrie. "The Playstation 3 Wonderbook Uses AR to Bring Stories to Life."

38. Bill Briggs and Marcus Shingles, "Exponentials."

39. Kris Graft, "Q&A: Google's Chief Game Designer Explores the Potential of Virtual Reality."

40. Price Waterhouse, *Tech Breakthroughs Megatrend.*

41. "Utility," Merriam-Webster.com.

42. "Virtual Reality vs. Augmented Reality."

BIBLIOGRAPHY

Azuma, R. T. "A Survey of Augmented Reality." *Presence: Teleoperators and Virtual Environments* 6, no. 4 (1997): 355–85.

Babcook, Stephen. "How One Maryland Library System Is Embracing Virtual Reality." *Technically Baltimore*, August 9, 2016. https://technical.ly/baltimore/2016/08/09/futuremakers-hyattsville-public-library-virtual-reality/.

Bellini, Heather. "The Real Deal with Virtual and Augmented Reality." Goldman Sachs video, February 2016. http://www.goldmansachs.com/our-thinking/pages/virtual-and-augmented-reality.html?cid=PS_02_04_07_00_01_16_01.

Briggs, Bill, and Marcus Shingles. "Exponentials." *Deloitte University Press*, January 29, 2015. https://dupress.deloitte.com/dup-us-en/focus/tech-trends/2015/tech-trends-2015-exponential-technologies.html.

Brockwell, Holly. "Forgotten Genius: The Man Who Made a Working VR Machine in 1957." Techradar, April 3, 2016. http://www.techradar.com/news/wearables/forgotten-genius-the-man-who-made-a-working-vr-machine-in-1957-1318253/2.

California State Library. "Virtual Reality Experience Project." Accessed May 8, 2017. http://www.library.ca.gov/services/libraries/vr.html.

City of Virginia Beach. "Library Partners with Tagwhat Mobile App to Launch New Chapter in Local Storytelling." July 14, 2011. https://www.vbgov.com/news/Pages/selected.aspx?release=171.

Costello, P. J. "Healthy and Safety Issues Associated with Virtual Reality: A Review of Current Literature." *Advisory Group on Computer Graphics*, July 23, 1997. http://www.agocg.ac.uk/reports/virtual/37/chapter2.htm.

Dachis, Adam. "How Virtual and Mixed Reality Trick Your Brain." *Next Reality*, September 9, 2016. https://next.reality.news/news/virtual-mixed-reality-trick-your-brain-0171.

De Looper, Christian. "Watch the Olympics in Stunning Virtual Reality with the Samsung Gear VR." *Digital Trends*, August 5, 2016. https://www.digitaltrends.com/virtual-reality/olympics-streaming-virtual-reality/.

Detroit Institute of Arts. "Detroit Institute of Arts to Premiere Lumin, a Mobile Tour Using Augmented Reality." DIA Press Release, January 10, 2017. http://www.dia.org/news/1952/Detroit-Institute-of-Arts-to-premiere-Lumin,-a-mobile-tour-using-augmented-reality,-Jan-25-Developed-by-DIA-in-partnership-with-Google-and-mobile-developer-GuidiGO-.aspx.

Forni, Amy Ann. "Gartner's 2016 Hype Cycle for Emerging Technologies Identifies Three Key Trends That Organizations Must Track to Gain Competitive Advantage." Gartner, August 16, 2016. https://www.gartner.com/newsroom/id/3412017.

Fox, Cynthia. "Virtual Reality vs. Real Life: How Brian Neurons Light Up." *Bio Science and Technology*, January 12, 2015. http://www.biosciencetechnology.com/article/2015/01/virtual-reality-vs-real-life-how-brain-neurons-light.

Fuchs, Philippe, Guillaume Moreau, and Pascal Guitton. *Virtual Reality: Concepts and Technologies*. Leiden, The Netherlands: CRC Press, 2006.

Goerner, Phil. "The Educational Potential of Augmented Reality." *School Library Journal*, August 3, 2016. http://www.slj.com/2016/08/technology/the-educational-potential-of-augmented-reality/#.

Graft, Kris. "Q&A: Google's Chief Game Designer Explores the Potential of Virtual Reality." *Gamasutra*, January 6, 2017. http://www.gamasutra.com/view/news/288771/QA_Googles_chief_game_designer_explores_the_potential_of_virtual_reality.php.

Hart, Cynthia. "Trends-day Wednesday, Technology on Display at ALA Midwinter." *Inside VBPL* (blog), January 25, 2017. http://insidevbpl.blogspot.com/2017/01/trends-day-wednesday-technology-on_25.html.

Ioannidia, Yannis, Olivier Balet, and Dimitrios Pandermalis. "Tell Me a Story: Augmented Reality Technology in Museums." *Guardian*, April 4, 2014. https://www.theguardian.com/culture-professionals-network/culture-professionals-blog/2014/apr/04/story-augmented-reality-technology-museums.

"Ivan Sutherland." *Wikipedia*. Accessed May 8, 2017. https://en.wikipedia.org/wiki/Ivan_Sutherland.

Jaywalker Interactive. "Blue Marble." Accessed May 8, 2007. http://jaywalkersinteractive.com/bluemarble/.

Johnson, Eric. "What's the Difference Between Virtual Reality and Mixed Reality?" *Recode,* July 13, 2016. https://www.recode.net/2015/7/27/11615046/whats-the-difference-between-virtual-augmented-and-mixed-reality.

Kunkel, Nelson, Steve Soechtig, Jared Miniman, and Chris Stauch. "Augmented and Virtual Reality Go to Work." *Deloitte University Press*, February 24, 2016. https://dupress.deloitte.com/dup-us-en/focus/tech-trends/2016/augmented-and-virtual-reality.html.

Lambert, Troy. "Virtual Reality in the Library: Creating a New Experience." *Public Libraries*, February 24, 2016. http://publiclibrariesonline.org/2016/02/virtual-reality-in-the-library-creating-a-new-experience/.

McQuarrie, Laura. "The Playstation 3 Wonderbook Uses AR to Bring Stories to Life." *Trend Hunter,* January 28, 2015. http://www.trendhunter.com/trends/wonderbook.

NBC. "Experience the Rio Olympics in Virtual Reality." August 21, 2016. http://www.nbcolympics.com/news/experience-rio-olympics-virtual-reality.

Owlchemy Labs. "Job Simulator." Accessed May 8, 2017. http://jobsimulatorgame.com/.

Parsons, Jeff. "Augmented Reality Children's Books Bring Bedtime Stories to Life in 3D." *Mirror*, January 14, 2017. http://www.mirror.co.uk/tech/augmented-reality-childrens-book-brings-9684383.

"Presence." Merriam-Webster.com. Accessed May 8, 2017. https://www.merriam-webster.com/dictionary/presence.

Price Waterhouse. *Tech Breakthroughs Megatrend.* January 2016. http://www.pwc.com/gx/en/issues/technology/tech-breakthroughs-megatrend.pdf.

"The Promise of Augmented Reality." *Economist*, February 4, 2017. https://www.economist.com/news/science-and-technology/21716013-replacing-real-world-virtual-one-neat-trick-combining-two.

Roberston, G. G., S. K. Card, and J. D. Mackinlay. "Non-Immersive Virtual Reality." *Computer* 26, no. 2 (1992): 82–83.

Singh, Amit. "More Ways to Watch and Play with AR and VR." *The Keyword* (blog), February 28, 2017. https://blog.google/products/google-vr/more-ways-watch-and-play-ar-and-vr/.

SMT. "1st and Ten Graphics." Accessed May 8, 2017. http://www.sportvision.com/football/1st-ten%C2%AE-graphics.

Souppouris, Aaron. "Virtual Reality Made Me Believe I Was Someone Else." The Verge, March 24, 2014. https://www.theverge.com/2014/3/24/5526694/virtual-reality-made-me-believe-i-was-someone-else.

Takashi, Torisu. "Sense of Presence in Social VR Experience." *Interactive Architecture Lab* (blog), August 17, 2016. http://www.interactivearchitecture.org/sense-of-presence-in-social-vr-experience.html.

Tepper, Fitz. "An NBA Team Is Turning Their Scorebook into an AR Baseball Game." *Tech Crunch*, April 19, 2017. https://techcrunch.com/2017/04/19/an-nba-team-is-turning-their-scoreboard-into-an-ar-basketball-game/.

"Utility." Merriam-Webster.com. Accessed May 8, 2017. https://www.merriam-webster.com/dictionary/utility.

VARlibraries. "About Us." Accessed May 8, 2017. http://www.varlibraries.com/about-us/.

"Virtual Reality." *Cryptologic Quarterly*, 1992. https://www.nsa.gov/news-features/declassified-documents/cryptologic-quarterly/assets/files/Virtual_Reality.pdf.

"Virtual Reality vs. Augmented Reality." *Augment* (blog), October 6, 2015. http://www.augment.com/blog/virtual-reality-vs-augmented-reality/.

Williams, Dennis. "Did Sports Pave the Way for Augmented Reality?" *AR News*, July 7, 2017. http://www.augment.com/blog/sports-pave-way-augmented-reality/.

Zelter, D. "Autonomy, Interaction and Presence." *Presence: Interoperators and Virtual Environments* 1, no. 1 (1992): 127–32.

Part II

CASE STUDIES

5

Augmenting Orientation

Animating an Interactive Welcome Event at an Academic Library with AR and VR

Julie N. Hornick and Steven Wade

The school year begins and students come flooding back to campus. New students get their dorm rooms set up and try to find their way around campus. Returning students meet up with friends they haven't seen in three months. Faculty finalize syllabi and organize research they worked on over the summer. Libraries plan events and orientations to showcase their resources for the campus community and to get the students in the library doors. These events take many forms, from luaus[1] to tailgate parties,[2] and from table games[3] to complex interactive games based on mystery themes[4] or popular literature like *The Hunger Games*.[5] It was within this back-to-school context that the librarians at Florida Southern College began to plan for our annual open house. As it is for many academic libraries, the challenge for us is not only keeping these annual events fresh but also addressing the perennial problem of students who may be inclined to feel scared, lost, or confused about the prospect of using an academic library.

Florida Southern College is a small, balanced arts and sciences institution with a full-time enrollment of approximately 2,500 students. In years past, the Roux Library open house event at Florida Southern College has been held in conjunction with other student orientation activities on campus and designed to get students to come to the library, meet librarians, learn about the resources we have available, and enjoy some pizza (figure 5.1). However, this year, in an effort to condense the orientation agenda for the incoming 2016–2017 freshman class, the library open house was among events cut from the official schedule. This left us on our own in terms of getting students into the library for our event. Wanting to reach as many students as possible, we were faced with how to best bypass the students' natural anxiety about coming to the library in order to introduce them to the

Figure 5.1. Roux Library Treasure Map. *Florida Southern College.*

resources and information they will need throughout their academic career. The Pokémon GO phenomenon of the summer of 2016 provided the inspiration for incorporating augmented reality into our efforts.

This chapter begins with some background on the technological climate of the summer of 2016, and a consideration of library anxiety. We then discuss how we were led to choose the Aurasma augmented reality and Google Cardboard virtual reality apps based on student interest. The chapter will conclude with a description of how we set up the event. With this case study, we hope to provide similar organizations, as well as school or public libraries without extensive in-house IT support, but with enthusiastic library staff, with an easy-to-follow model of the planning process and the steps taken to set up these interactive activities. At the time of the event we did not do a great deal of assessment or qualitative analysis, and further study is needed to conclusively determine the impact of the event.

BACKGROUND

The Pokémon GO app, launched in the summer of 2016, allowed fans of the long-running video game series to bring the game to life in their own neighborhoods and public parks. The app used augmented reality to display the creatures on a player's mobile device, appearing to place them in the real world. After its debut, it quickly became the most popular mobile game in U.S. history.[6] By the middle of July 2016, the application was drawing in over 25 million daily active users, according to SurveyMonkey Intelligence.[7] In almost any public space, one could see people walking with purpose, phones out, searching for that rare pocket monster they needed to add to their Poké-dex. Would you find a Pikachu in your local library? What about a Tauros lurking at the local train station? Our student workers were discussing the game, proving to us that at least a portion of our college population was, if not actively playing, at least familiar with the game. When the time came for us to plan our annual back-to-campus event, finding activities to capitalize on this interest seemed like a novel way to increase the students' enthusiasm for participating in the open house.

A recent course taken by one of the authors on resources and methods for integrating new and emerging technologies in the classroom suggested a tool we could use. Among the many resources examined in the class was the Aurasma augmented reality application, a relatively easy-to-use online program with an accompanying mobile app. Aurasma allows users to identify a "trigger" (an object or place they want to highlight in the real world) and link an "overlay" (an image, video, words, etc., that will appear on screen) to that trigger. The combination of trigger and overlay is called an "aura" (figure 5.2). While it is clearly more basic in principle and practice than the Pokémon GO game, the parallels between Aurasma auras and Pokémon GO are obvious. Including an augmented reality activity using Aurasma in our

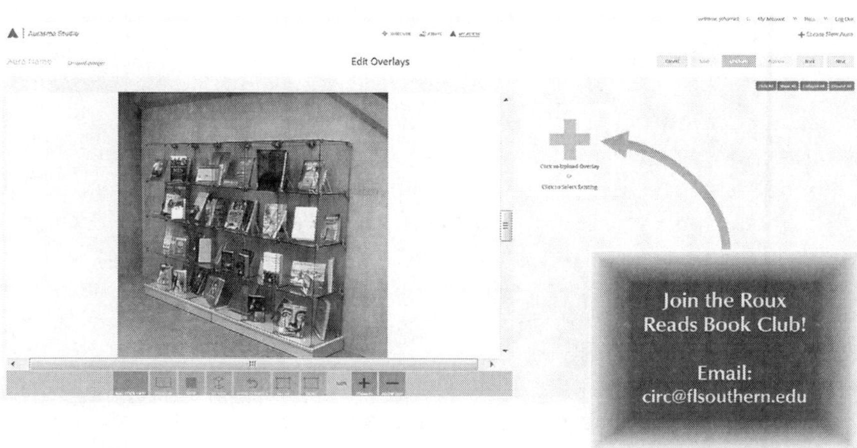

Figure 5.2. Creating an Aura with Aurasma. *Florida Southern College.*

open house event felt like a natural tie-in to an activity that so many students would have been participating in over the summer break; one very likely to increase the engagement of the students in the orientation activity.

The spring and summer of 2016 also saw a surge in interest in virtual reality (VR) devices. The Oculus Rift and HTC Vive headsets were released early in 2016 with great fanfare, and many expected big sales. Early estimates put HTC Vive at around 100,000 units sold by July,[8] although a year in, sales figures still had not been released. *Forbes* cited industry analysts' belief that Vive had sold 500,000 units to Oculus Rift's 250,000 as of April 3, 2017.[9]

These high-tech models are meant to be paired with video game consoles and cost several hundred dollars, pricing them out of range of many of our students. However, we knew that virtual reality can be as simple and inexpensive as Google Cardboard, a do-it-yourself cardboard frame that can be wrapped around a mobile phone. Cardboard was introduced in 2014, and several mobile apps have been released to take advantage of the technology. Content is being developed daily for use with these VR devices, and news organizations in particular have been using VR to connect viewers more intimately with stories using 360-degree video. One such app by the *New York Times*, NYT VR, features educational and informative videos with striking imagery. We believed that demonstrating the app using Google Cardboard would prove to be another effective way to entice students into the library, and would provide us the added benefit of being able to sign them up for access to the *New York Times* through the library's subscription.

AVOIDING LIBRARY ANXIETY

Anxiety is generally acknowledged as one roadblock that keeps students from coming into an academic library, and was something we hoped to mitigate with our event. In her seminal study, Mellon highlighted several characteristics of library anxiety, one of which is that many students do not know how to use a library's resources and are afraid to ask for help.[10] This self-perpetuating cycle can be difficult to break. Van Kampen-Breit and Cooke illustrated this fact in a study that found that a significant percentage of students surveyed were unwilling to ask for help from library staff. Students also perceived librarians to be often too busy to help them with their information needs.[11] There may be many causes of library anxiety, including bewilderment at how the library is organized, unfamiliarity with equipment and resources in the library, and fear of asking questions of librarians whom they perceive as unapproachable.[12]

What can librarians, who know the importance of the library to a student's academic career, do to alleviate that anxiety? One possibility is to schedule introductory events for the students. A number of studies examine the usefulness of this approach. Seeholzer found that social events have the potential to increase the students' perception of the library as a "welcoming" place, and of the library staff as approachable.[13] Logically, according to Kang, the less students have used their academic library, the more likely those students are to feel some anxiety about using that library. The inverse is also true.[14] Van Kampen-Breit and Cooke pointed to the need to "foster stronger relationships with library users" and recommend that libraries look for ways to engage with patrons in "non-threatening" ways to increase their users' comfort with the library staff.[15] Carlile noted that providing students a "positive library experience" in a "non-threatening environment" can also help to allay their anxiety.[16] Her research also indicated that librarians "getting to know students in an informal setting may contribute to their comfort and confidence levels, which, in turn, allows them to feel less anxious about using the library."[17] These findings have been borne out in other studies, as well.[18]

Engaging students in active learning has also been shown to reduce students' anxiety. Halpern reviewed several studies showing that "active learning for information literacy in the classroom environment is more effective than a didactic approach for student engagement . . . and alleviating library anxiety."[19] Additionally, Carlile's research found that instruction that incorporates more affective elements may help to decrease anxiety.[20] Not only is it useful, then, to use engaged learning techniques to lower a student's affective filter, but creating an activity that is fun can also help to accomplish that goal. We decided that gamification of our orientation with AR and VR would add that needed element of fun.

TECHNOLOGY IN LIBRARIES

The use of AR and VR technologies in classrooms and library settings is becoming more common.[21] Many authors take note of their usefulness in developing engaging activities and holding the interest of digital natives.[22] Instructors and librarians are using AR to bring resources to life and to provide valuable or useful extra information about collections, resources, and services.[23] Further, van Arnhem and Spiller noted that using AR allows libraries to "engage with patrons in a way that meets patrons' expectations, a need that is recognized as an integral part of the library experience."[24] Additionally, K–12 school libraries are increasingly using AR to create interest in reading[25] or to invigorate tired orientation lectures.[26]

Academic librarians can thus assume that students will come to campus from high school familiar with these newer technologies, and perhaps even expecting to find AR or VR technologies in place. In his paper discussing the use of AR and VR in libraries, Massis noted that as our patrons become increasingly familiar and comfortable with various digital platforms, it is important for libraries to keep up with the technology, understanding that making these technology-rich experiences available to our students will not only help keep them engaged but also increase their information literacy.[27] Moorefield-Lang observed in her discussion of VR platforms—from those as complex as the Oculus Rift to ones as inexpensive and accessible as Google Cardboard—that VR has the potential to increase student excitement and engagement.[28]

The literature is clear in its analysis that librarians can effectively counter library anxiety in students by providing high-interest, engaging activities in an informal, non-threatening environment. By acting as early adopters of this technology, and by putting AR and VR in the hands of students, libraries will be seen as innovators and will be better positioned to use these technologies as they become more sophisticated.[29] Given the indisputable popularity of Pokémon GO and the increasing excitement about VR, incorporating AR and VR elements into our open house seemed like a promising formula to present an image of the library as both a modern and a welcoming place. Further, using augmented reality to power a self-guided tour of the library gives the students more control over the experience, and gives students the option to complete the activity in a group, individually, or with the help of a librarian, according to their preference.

PLANNING "DISCOVEROUX"

We began planning for the event over the summer by contacting some of our major content providers and asking for giveaways. Prize giveaways have always been a part of Roux Library open house events in the past, and are recognized as an effective motivator in the literature.[30] At our event, students receive pens, highlighters, notepads, and other items by visiting different stations throughout the library. Prizes that feature vendor logos have the added benefit of reminding students about content the library makes available to them. Among the items we received were two Google Cardboard viewers from the *New York Times*, which we decided to promote as a grand prize item for students who completed the treasure hunt. Finally, we planned to offer pizza for students who might not be attracted with anything short of the promise of food.

As the library was no longer a required stop in the campus-wide student orientation, promotion of our event became a new and critical part of our planning phase. We knew that no matter how exciting the program might seem to us, if the students weren't aware of it, they wouldn't come, and putting up a few signs in the library wouldn't be enough. We decided on a catchy name, DiscoveRoux, which the students would recognize from our discovery interface, and which would be illustrative of what the event was designed to accomplish. Our campus Student Solutions office offered the services of their student graphic designers to develop an eye-catching flyer to be posted around campus (figure 5.3), and we designed an in-house poster for table-top displays in the library and our adjacent coffee shop (figure 5.4). In addition, we asked professors to encourage their students to attend and put announcements out through social media and the campus email system.

Figure 5.3. Student Solutions DiscoveRoux Flyer. ***Florida Southern College.***

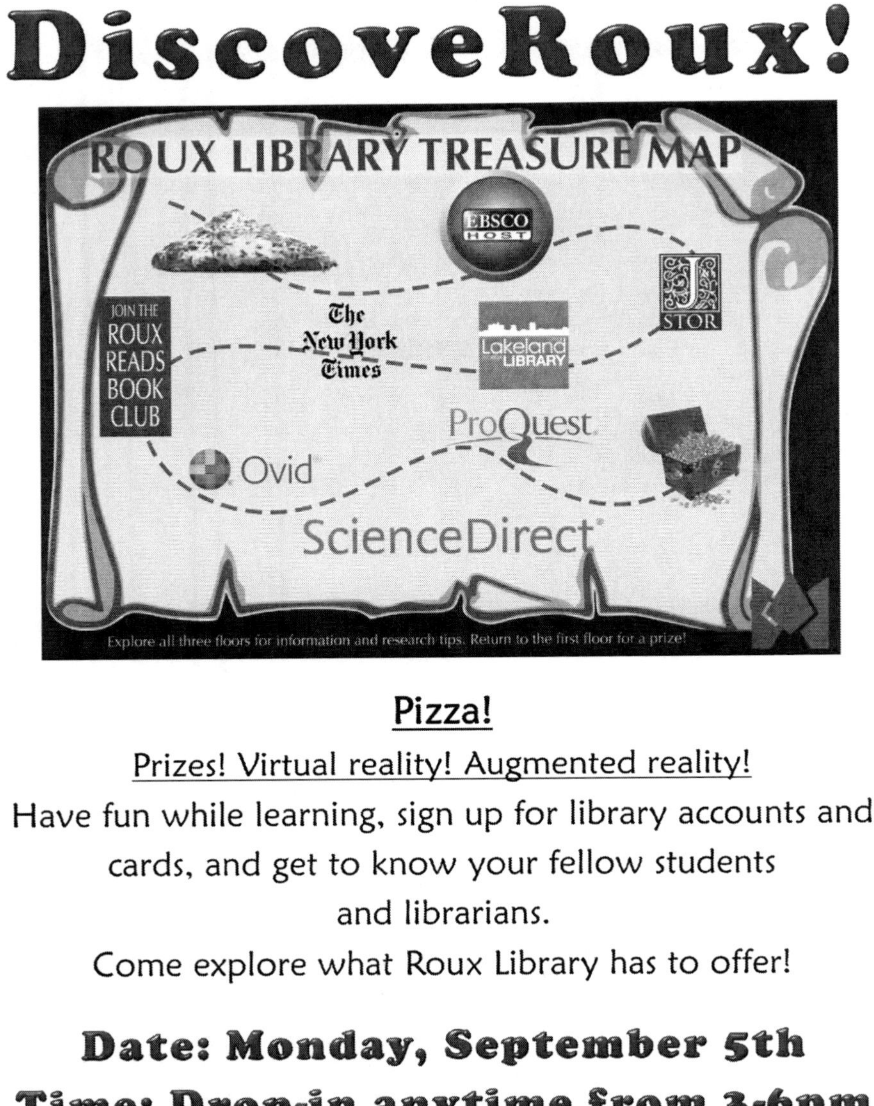

Figure 5.4. In-house DiscoveRoux Flyer. *Florida Southern College.*

Aurasma

In designing our AR activity, we needed something that included a downloadable app that would be free and easy for the students to use. While there were other AR options available (Layar, ZapWorks, and Blippar, to name just a few), many came with a cost, and the authors were familiar with Aurasma. This app is free, making it the natural choice for our purposes. Moreover, using Aurasma Studio to develop AR elements is a relatively straightforward process, as previously described. To plan, we identified areas of the library and specific resources we wanted the students to be aware of (e.g., our DVD collection, our popular books display, the copier/printer area, popular magazines, study carrels, the library classroom), as well as some "points of interest":

- A life-size cutout of a TARDIS
- A larger-than-life brass rubbing of Robert the Bruce
- The record player and record collection
- The fiche reader and microfiche cabinets
- A temporary rare books display

Next, we had to decide what we wanted to do for overlays. Text-based overlays with a description of each site would have been informative, but using text-heavy overlays would have done little to alleviate the discomfort or anxiety students may have had with the library. Instead, we decided to take a more entertaining approach. In the end, we chose amusing GIFs and memes that related in some way to the trigger, and let the students simply discover what the library has to offer them. For example:

- Our brass rubbing of Robert the Bruce was paired with a meme of Mel Gibson as William Wallace (who actually fought by Robert the Bruce's side) yelling, "Freedom!"
- Our game display was overlaid with a nerd culture GIF.
- Our copier/printer area was accompanied by a GIF of the character Samir Nagheenanajar, from the movie *Office Space*, exclaiming in frustration over a malfunctioning copier (figure 5.5).

We still had to find a way to get students to discover the trigger areas, and so we wrote directional clues through which they could learn something about the library, in addition to finding the aura triggers. We made the clues only minimally difficult to figure out in order to keep the frustration to a minimum, while asking the students to think, at least a little bit. For example, the clue for the display of board games read, "Looking for something to do with your friends on a Saturday night? Roux Library has plenty of these to choose from. We promise you'll never get *board*!" To help the students discover our study carrels, they were provided with this clue: "It's finals week. Your roommate is driving you crazy with Zen bells and yoga breathing. You need a space all to yourself to study. Find that place on the second floor."

DiscoveRoux Triggers & Overlays

Trigger	Overlay
DVD collection	horror movie reaction shot
Tardis	flying/spinning tardis
Game display	nerd culture gif
Remnant Trust Display	ancient book being opened/paged through
Popular Books Display	Gaiman quote
Robert the Bruce	Braveheart meme
Copier/Printer area	Office Space printer
Magazines	spinning magazines
Record Player / Records	Lilo
Study Carrels	Lord of the Rings meme
Lakeland Ledger Drawer of the Microforms Files	link to Ledger calendar of events
Fiche Reader	Simpsons fiche GIF
Library Classroom	info lit word cloud

Figure 5.5. Triggers and Overlays. ***Florida Southern College.***

The clues were then included on the activity sheet that all student participants received when they came into the library for the event. Those activities that required the use of the Aurasma app were indicated by the Aurasma logo on the activity sheet (figures 5.6 and 5.7).

After developing the auras, we asked some of our coworkers to test them out to see if everything was going to work smoothly. Getting library staff ready to start the activity pointed out the need to make sure participants had clear instructions so they would know how to access the auras (figure 5.8). Once that issue was resolved, we sent them off to see if they could figure out the clues and get the auras to work. No one had any difficulty with the clues, but most reported that they could not get a number of the auras to work.

From the difficulties they encountered, we realized that we needed to take several pictures of each trigger from several different angles because participants could not be expected to stand exactly where the aura's developer had stood when setting it up. All of the new pictures were then uploaded as triggers, and paired with the original overlays to create the desired auras. We tested them out a second time and found that most of the problems had been resolved. We had to discard a couple of the triggers when it appeared

What's Your Library Treasure Hunt Aura?

	Clues & Activities	Description of the aura/Stamp:
▲	1. "Consumer Reports," "Ebony," "Sports Illustrated," and "Vogue." Read them all at Roux.	
▲	2. If you want to travel through space and time, this is your ship.	
	3. Stop by the Roux Reads Book Club information table. Find out what cool things they have planned for this year. Like what you hear? Become a member!	
▲	4. Your paper is due in 15 minutes and your printer is out of ink. Use ours, instead!	
▲	5. "The Martian," "The Force Awakens," "The Revenant," & "Chi-raq": Roux has them all, and many more.	
▲	6. Looking for something to do with your friends on a Saturday night? Roux Library has plenty of these to choose from. We promise you'll never get *board*!	
▲	7 Have you ever held a book that was hundreds of years old? With this special exhibit, you can.	
	8. Love to read? Want to check out even *MORE* DVDs and audiobooks? Pick up some information and sign up for a public library card at the Lakeland Public Library display.	
	9. Try out the Google Cardboard VR goggles at the New York Times display and get your account to access "all the news that's fit to print."	
▲	10. There aren't many on the first floor, but it's what you expect to find in a library.	

▲*, use your device/tablet to view the aura with the Aurasma app.*

Figure 5.6. DiscoveRoux Activity Sheet, page 1. *Florida Southern College.*

	11. Visit the EBSCO Host/ProQuest display, sign up for your account, and find out how EBSCO and ProQuest can help you in your studies.	
▲	12. This man fought with the forces of William Wallace in 1298.	
▲	13. Want to experience the phonic sound of vinyl? Somewhere on the second floor, you can.	
▲	14. It's finals week. Your roommate is driving you crazy with Zen bells and yoga breathing. You need a space all to yourself to study. Find that place on the second floor.	
▲	15. Are you dying to find out what happened in Lakeland on December 20th, 2013? You're in luck. Find the Lakeland Ledger in the huge filing cabinets on the second floor.	
▲	16. OK, now you've got the little sheet of plastic. How do you read it? The fiche reader!	
	17. Are you a nursing or health sciences student? Ovid is an excellent source of information. (Special goodies available for all nursing/health sciences students while supplies last.)	
	18. JSTOR aims to expand access to scholarly content around the world and to preserve it for future generations. Sign up for an account and start using their resources today. App and loot available, too!	
▲	19. On the third floor, you might come here with a class to learn more about how to research effectively.	
	20. If you're now taking any science courses, or will take any in the future, ScienceDirect is an excellent source of information for your studies. Sign up for an account today and pick up some swag while it lasts!	

▲, *use your device/tablet to view the aura with the Aurasma app.*

Figure 5.7. DiscoveRoux Activity Sheet, page 2. *Florida Southern College.*

Name: ______________________________

Contact Info: ________________________

What's Your Library Treasure Hunt Aura?

Your mission, should you choose to accept it, is to complete as many Treasure Hunt and Aura activities as possible. If you complete at least 15 of the 20 possible tasks, bring your form to the prize table to claim your choice of prizes.

Completed forms will also be entered into a drawing to win a set of New York Times Google Cardboard virtual reality goggles!

Some tasks require you to find the appropriate station, and collect a signature/stamp after you have completed the activity at that station.

Other tasks ask you to use the Aurasma app (available for free in the App Store or Google Play; or, you may use the library's iPad when it is available) find the triggers in the library that correspond to the clues, lock in on the trigger, watch the aura that comes up, and fill in the description of that aura. To get started, be sure to download the app and follow our auras:

1. Go to the magnifying glass search button in app.
2. Type in the account name (jnhornick).
3. Select any one of the aura pictures that come up.
4. Press 'follow'. The auras will then be available to your device.

You're free to complete the auras/stations in any order you like – you don't have to move from 1 to 2 to 3, etc.. (HINT: you won't need to open any doors or drawers to finish the activity.)

When you've filled in at least 15 of the 20 spaces on your game sheet, bring it to the prize table for your choice of available prizes.

Plus, all completed sheets will be entered in a drawing to win the Google Cardboard grand prize. Just put your name on the sheet along with a contact number/email and drop in the grand prize container.

▲, *use your device/tablet to view the aura with the Aurasma app.*

Figure 5.8. Treasure Hunt Aura Instructions. *Florida Southern College.*

that they were too specific or variable; for instance, an aura of the circulation desk did not work because pen holders, staplers, mice, and other objects kept getting moved, making the original snapshot obsolete.

Another factor to consider was the students' access to a mobile device that they would want to use for the activity. In order to work with the auras, students would need to download the free Aurasma app to their devices and then link to our auras. However, we realized that a student might not be able, or willing, to download the app to their device. With this in mind, we decided that we would make the library's iPad available for them to use, which took care of the issue. The activity also included several clues that could be completed without the use of AR for students who preferred not to use either the Aurasma app or the library's iPad.

Virtual Reality

Our VR activity used the Google Cardboard viewers and was less interactive than Aurasma, but was expected to be equally engaging. Although there are several apps that take advantage of a phone's motion sensitivity to add an interactive element to the Google Cardboard experience, our demonstration using VR videos from the *New York Times* did not use this feature. With NYT VR videos, users can turn their heads to view different angles of the scene, but there is no interactive "game" aspect involved (figure 5.9). The Google Cardboard viewer requires very little assembly and is held together

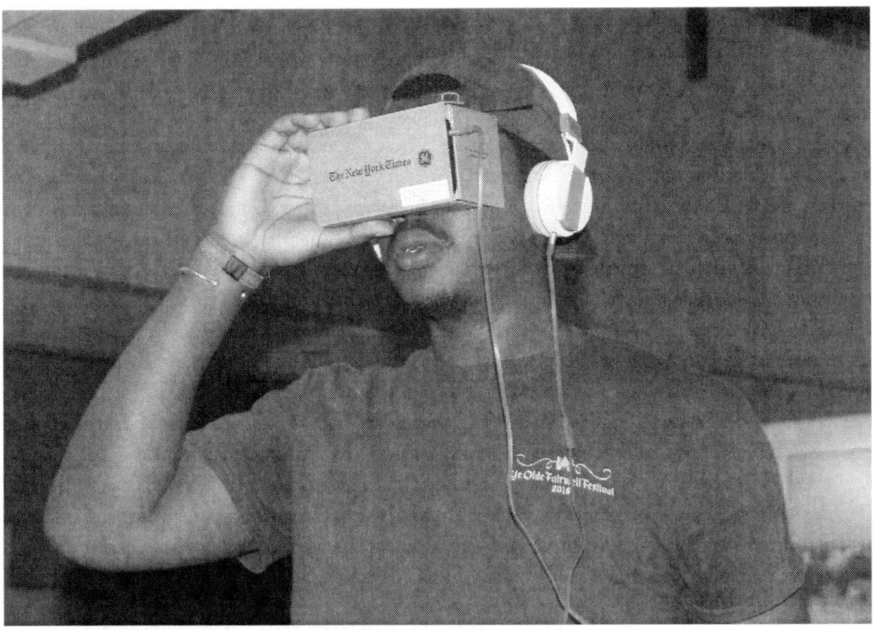

Figure 5.9. Florida Southern College Student Experiencing VR. ***Florida Southern College.***

with Velcro®. For convenience, we used one of the authors' smartphones, pre-loaded with two NYT VR videos and attached to headphones to enhance the user experience.

Although its popularity is steadily increasing, virtual reality is still a new concept for many students, and Google Cardboard is the preferred format for many VR users.[31] To capitalize on this, we set up our VR station on the first floor in full view of anyone walking through the library or using the coffee shop next door. We also had an extra Google Cardboard viewer that we advertised as a grand prize for students who completed the AR activity and visited each database information treasure hunt station. Those students who participated fully in this orientation activity showed a great deal of interest in the possibility of winning the Cardboard viewer. We asked those who wanted to enter the drawing to provide their contact information so they did not need to be present to win. At the end of the evening, we drew for the winner and notified her the next day.

DiscoveRoux

On the evening of the DiscoveRoux open house, the pizza was delivered and the student workers who would be helping participants to sign up for database and public library accounts were set up at their stations around the library. The Google Cardboard VR viewers were ready, and our treasure hunt activity sheets were printed, complete with instructions. As attendees dropped in, we asked them to sign in on the computer, and gave each an activity sheet to use as a guide in completing the treasure hunt.

We found that even with the written instructions for using Aurasma, most participants required some personal assistance in downloading the app and accessing the library auras. However, once those steps had been completed, the students were able to complete the activity with few problems. There were a couple of the triggers that still seemed difficult to zero in on sufficiently to get the overlay to appear: notably, the DVDs, record albums, and microfiche drawers. The difficulty likely occurred because the chosen triggers lacked clear enough detail for the cameras on the devices to register them well. Of all who participated, only three students opted to use the iPad: one because his phone was not able to download the app, and two simply because they preferred not to download it. Those who used the iPad did not have the same issues as people using their own phones, because it was already set up for the activity.

CONCLUSION

Successes

Overall, we felt that the open house event achieved our goal of getting students to feel comfortable in the library. We estimated about one hundred participants, which was consistent with previous years when the event was part of the college's formal orientation. From an informal survey that students could complete if they wished, about two-thirds of those who participated in the AR activity reported that they enjoyed following the clues and discovering the overlays, commenting that they appreciated the "fun pictures and memes" or found them "cute." Further, we observed that most were excited to choose from among the available prizes when they turned in their activity sheets. Most of the attendees entered the Google Cardboard drawing, while some opted out. Although we did not do any formal assessment at the time of the event, a number of students have returned to the library to check out the Google Cardboard viewer, and our end-of-year student survey revealed that, nearly eight months later, students who had attended the event in September still thought the open house was, in the words of one student, "awesome."

Lessons Learned

The event was not without a few glitches and lessons learned for next year. While free pizza was a powerful draw to get the students into the building, many of them left immediately after grabbing their slice without participating in any of the activities. Other students started the Aurasma activity, but became bored and did not bother finishing. From the one-third who indicated on the informal survey that they did not enjoy the activity, comments included that they felt the activity "didn't have a point" or was too easy or too time-consuming. Even with our efforts to overcome library anxiety with fun, low-pressure activities, there is a need to keep the students interested and engaged so that we can accomplish our goal of exposing them to our resources and services.

Some modifications to the Aurasma activity may help prevent frustration or boredom in the future. As suggested by Kang, having a sign or symbol by the target location in the library can streamline the activity by providing a set object for the students to focus on with their devices. This would reduce the frustration of looking for the right angle.[32] As some of the survey respondents felt it was "hard to find things," having fewer clues may also be effective, although striking the right balance will take some trial and error. Presenting the activity as a group competition could be another option to generate more interest. We hope to re-create the AR and VR activities in the coming years, working out the kinks as we go and collecting concrete data on how effective the event is at lowering the participants' affective filter with regard to the library.

Finally, both our AR and VR activities were visually oriented, but not demanding physically; while we did not encounter any students with physical or cognitive disabilities that would have hindered their ability to participate in any of the activities, we are aware of the need to be sensitive to this eventuality. Having student employees available as "buddies" to assist patrons with visual or other impairments would be one way to meet this need in the future.

It is an ongoing challenge to bring new students into the library each year and communicate the value of our resources. Augmented and virtual reality provide fresh opportunities to reach students in relevant and exciting ways, and can be implemented with very little impact on budgets.

NOTES

1. Ellysa Stern Cahoy and Rebecca Merritt Bichel, "A Luau in the Library?"
2. Nancy Noe, "Party with a Purpose: The Library Open House."
3. Willie Miller and Mindy Cooper, "Library WOW! Fun Outreach and Orientation in an Academic Library."
4. Anna-Lise Smith and Lesli Baker, "Getting a Clue: Creating Student Detectives and Dragon Slayers in Your Library."
5. Kylie Bailin, "From 'The Research Games' to Tours: The Evolution of First Year Orientation Activities."
6. Robbie Allan, "Pokémon GO Usage Statistics Say It's the Most Popular Mobile Game in U.S. History."
7. Robbie Allan, "Has Pokémon GO Peaked? The Data Say 'Yes.'"
8. Aaron Pressman, "It Doesn't Look Like Virtual Reality Is a Thing Yet."
9. Charlie Fink, "HTC Vive VR Celebrates Its First Anniversary with Viveport, Freebies and Deals."
10. Constance A. Mellon, "Library Anxiety: A Grounded Theory and Its Development," 163.
11. Doris J. Van Kampen-Breit and Rachel Cooke, "Do They Think We're the Frenemy? Examining Student Anxiety and Service Perception in Today's Academic Libraries," 12.
12. Heather Carlile, "The Implications of Library Anxiety for Academic Reference Services: A Review of the Literature," 133–34.
13. Jamie Seeholzer, "Charting a New Course: A Case Study on the Impact of Outreach Events at Kent State University Libraries," 131.
14. Ji Hei Kang, "Research Design to Evaluate an Academic Library's Orientation Program Applying Mobile Augmented Reality," 218.
15. Van Kampen-Breit and Cooke, "Do They Think," 12, 14.
16. Carlile, "Implications of Library Anxiety," 138.
17. Ibid., 137.
18. Kang, "Research Design to Evaluate," 219.
19. Rebecca Halpern, "Active Learning Works! Until It Doesn't: Measuring the Effectiveness of Activity-based Learning Exercises on Information Anxiety," 243.

20. Carlile, "Implications of Library Anxiety," 136.
21. Carli Spina, "Keeping Up With . . . Augmented Reality."
22. Kang, "Research Design to Evaluate," 219.
23. Jolanda-Pieta van Arnhem and Jerry M. Spiller, "Augmented Reality for Discovery and Instruction"; Spina, "Keeping Up With."
24. van Arnhem and Spiller, "Augmented Reality for Discovery," 216.
25. Carol Thompson, "Aurasma Attack in the Library!" 39.
26. Beth Ebenstein Mulch, "Library Orientation Transformation: From Paper Map to Augmented Reality."
27. Bruce Massis, "Using Virtual and Augmented Reality in the Library," 798.
28. Heather Moorefield-Lang, "Libraries and the Rift: Oculus Rift and 4D Devices in Libraries."
29. Rob Green, "Virtual Reality: Time to Put the Goggles On?"
30. Katelyn Angell and Katherine Boss, "Adapting the Amazing Library Race: Using Problem-based Learning in Library Orientations."
31. Robert Workman, "Understanding the Virtual Reality Demographic."
32. Kang, "Research Design to Evaluate," 227–28.

BIBLIOGRAPHY

Allan, Robbie. "Has Pokémon GO Peaked? The Data Say 'Yes.'" *SurveyMonkey Intelligence Blog*, July 21, 2016. https://medium.com/@sm_app_intel/has-pok%C3%A9mon-go-peaked-the-data-say-yes-130c4a577c9d.

———. "Pokémon GO Usage Statistics Say It's the Most Popular Mobile Game in U.S. History." *SurveyMonkey Intelligence Blog*, July 13, 2016. https://medium.com/@sm_app_intel/pok%C3%A9mon-go-usage-statistics-say-its-the-most-popular-mobile-game-in-u-s-history-ea09ea2bf6df.

Angell, Katelyn, and Katherine Boss. "Adapting the Amazing Library Race: Using Problem-based Learning in Library Orientations." *College and Undergraduate Libraries* 23, no. 1 (2016): 44–55. doi:10.1080/10691316.2014.935547.

Bailin, Kylie. "From 'The Research Games' to Tours: The Evolution of First Year Orientation Activities." *College and Research Libraries News* 76, no. 11 (December 2015): 586–89. http://search.ebscohost.com/login.aspx?direct=true&AuthType=ip,uid&db=eue&AN=111439402.

Cahoy, Ellysa Stern, and Rebecca Merritt Bichel. "A Luau in the Library?" *College and Undergraduate Libraries* 11, no. 1 (May 10, 2004): 49–60. doi:10.1300/J106v11n01_06.

Carlile, Heather. "The Implications of Library Anxiety for Academic Reference Services: A Review of the Literature." *Australian Academic and Research Libraries* 38, no. 2 (2007): 129–47. http://search.ebscohost.com/login.aspx?direct=true&AuthType=ip,uid&db=a9h&AN=26518450.

Fink, Charlie. "HTC Vive VR Celebrates Its First Anniversary with Viveport, Freebies & Deals." *Forbes*, April 3, 2017. https://www.forbes.com/sites/charlie

fink/2017/04/03/htc-vive-vr-celebrates-its-first-anniversary-with-viveport-freebies-deals/#53f6ca431c5a.

Green, Rob. "Virtual Reality: Time to Put the Goggles On?" *CILIP Update* (November 2016): 30–31.

Halpern, Rebecca. "Active Learning Works! Until It Doesn't: Measuring the Effectiveness of Activity-based Learning Exercises on Information Anxiety." *Journal of Library and Information Services in Distance Learning* 10 (2016): 242–53. doi:10.1080/1533290X.2016.1219201.

Kang, Ji Hei. "Research Design to Evaluate an Academic Library's Orientation Program Applying Mobile Augmented Reality." *Journal of the Korean Society for Library and Information Science* 49, no. 2 (2015): 215–33. doi:10.4275/KSLIS.2015.49.2.215.

Massis, Bruce. "Using Virtual and Augmented Reality in the Library." *New Library World* 116, nos. 11/12 (2015): 796–99. doi:10.1108/NLW-08-2015-0054.

Mellon, Constance A. "Library Anxiety: A Grounded Theory and Its Development." *College and Research Libraries* 47, no. 2 (1986): 160–65. http://crl.acrl.org/content/47/2/160.full.pdf.

Miller, Willie, and Mindy Cooper. "Library WOW! Fun Outreach and Orientation in an Academic Library." *Indiana Libraries* 33, no. 2 (2014): 58–60. https://journals.iupui.edu/index.php/IndianaLibraries/article/view/17953.

Moorefield-Lang, Heather. "Libraries and the Rift: Oculus Rift and 4D Devices in Libraries." *KnowledgeQuest* 43, no. 5 (2015): 76–77. http://search.ebscohost.com/login.aspx?direct=true&AuthType=ip,uid&db=a9h&AN=102556301.

Mulch, Beth Ebenstein. "Library Orientation Transformation: From Paper Map to Augmented Reality." *KnowledgeQuest* 42, no. 4 (2014): 50–53. http://search.ebscohost.com/login.aspx?direct=true&AuthType=ip,uid&db=eue&AN=94845354.

Noe, Nancy. "Party with a Purpose: The Library Open House." *College and Research Libraries News* 77, no. 4 (April 2016): 184–87. http://search.ebscohost.com/login.aspx?direct=true&AuthType=ip,uid&db=eue&AN=114279803.

Pressman, Aaron. "It Doesn't Look Like Virtual Reality Is a Thing Yet." *Fortune*, July 5, 2016. http://fortune.com/2016/07/05/virtual-reality-htc-sales/.

Seeholzer, Jamie. "Charting a New Course: A Case Study on the Impact of Outreach Events at Kent State University Libraries." *Public Services Quarterly* 7, nos. 3–4 (2011): 125–35. doi:10.1080/15228959.2011.623595.

Smith, Anna-Lise, and Lesli Baker. "Getting a Clue: Creating Student Detectives and Dragon Slayers in Your Library." *Reference Services Review* 39, no. 4 (2011): 628–42. http://dx.doi.org/10.1108/00907321111186659.

Spina, Carli. "Keeping Up With . . . Augmented Reality." *Keeping Up With . . .* (blog), February 2016. Association of College and Research Libraries. http://www.ala.org/acrl/publications/keeping_up_with/ar.

Thompson, Carol. "Aurasma Attack in the Library!" *School Library Monthly* 31, no. 4 (2015): 39. http://search.ebscohost.com/login.aspx?direct=true&AuthType=ip,uid&db=eue&AN=101766381.

van Arnhem, Jolanda-Pieta, and Jerry M. Spiller. "Augmented Reality for Discovery and Instruction." *Journal of Web Librarianship* 8, no. 2 (2014): 214–30. doi:10.1080/19322909.2014.904208.

Van Kampen-Breit, Doris J., and Rachel Cooke. "Do They Think We're the Frenemy? Examining Student Anxiety and Service Perception in Today's Academic Libraries." *Library Leadership* 30, no. 1 (2015): 1–16. http://search.ebscohost.com/login.aspx?direct=true&AuthType=ip,uid&db=eue&AN=110871164.

Workman, Robert. "Understanding the Virtual Reality Demographic." [a]listdaily, June 23, 2016. http://www.alistdaily.com/digital/understanding-virtual-reality-demographic/.

6

Augmented Archives

Engaging Students in Archives and Special Collections through Augmented Reality Technology

Heather Calloway and Raven Bishop

Imagine walking into a space filled with unknown objects. The walls are covered with photographs. Artifacts are sitting in cases on display. Rare books are under a Lucite cover, and while you yearn to turn the pages of a book to see what follows, it is sadly locked under the case, stuck on pages 233–34. If only these objects could come to life and tell their stories!

This is the central problem that archives and special collections libraries face in their efforts to engage visitors and students with the objects in their collections. In an increasingly technological world, how do we leverage emerging technologies to connect viewers with the historic objects in our collections? This is the problem we are seeking to address through our project, Augmented Archives, at Washington College.

The Washington College Archives and Special Collections houses artifacts of historic significance to the college and surrounding colonial-era community. Washington College dates back to 1782, and was the first college in the new American republic. This is important to mention because of the depth and breadth of the items in its holdings. While the college suffered two devastating fires, in 1827 and 1916, it has been able to collect and preserve historical artifacts dating from the medieval period to the present day. It wasn't until 2012 that the college renovated the library space and created archival storage for special collections. Simultaneously, professional archival staff were hired and tasked to engage students (and others) with the rare materials. These moves enabled research and instruction with the collections for the first time, but—like most special collections libraries—we were seeking ways to involve and immerse undergraduates in the collections' rare and unique objects and artifacts in a way that appeals to students' twenty-first-century technological sensibilities.

In 2015, the Washington College Archives began an ongoing collaboration with the college's academic technology department, which we titled Augmented Archives. This initiative is designed to explore the use of augmented reality (AR) to increase visitor access to and engagement with primary source materials in Washington College's Archives and Special Collections. What makes the Augmented Archives project distinctive is that it is driven by student research and interaction with artifacts in the collection. This initiative presents an opportunity for students to curate AR-enhanced exhibits of historical artifacts and significant objects. Students receive training in both the investigative curation skills and the technological proficiencies needed to plan and execute an AR-enhanced exhibit.

This chapter details a case study of our experience in initiating the use of AR in an academic library as both an outreach and an instructional tool. In this chapter we describe the process of developing the first instructional sequence in this ongoing initiative, and discuss the instructional and technological considerations and challenges we encountered through the implementation process.

PHASE I: RESEARCH AND DEVELOPMENT

This project began with a full semester of research and development in which we explored several applications of AR and prototyped exhibit exemplars so that we could experience the types of challenges our students would encounter as they worked toward creating their own exhibits.

Review of Existing Projects

We began by researching how other institutions—particularly museums and higher education institutions—implemented initiatives that leveraged AR technology to increase visitor and/or student engagement. Examples that most closely matched the goals of our project included the Skin and Bones exhibit at the Smithsonian National Museum of Natural History, which overlays 3D models, video, and additional information over skeletons in the museum's Bone Hall; the British Museum's A Gift for Athena project, which leads young students through the museum's Parthenon exhibit by way of an AR-enhanced scavenger hunt; ARchive LAPL, a collaboration between University of Southern California Annenberg School for Communication and Journalism and the Los Angeles Public Library, in which students from the university created augmented content triggered by permanent physical fixtures and portions of collections, including the children's and rare books collections; and an augmented walking tour titled The Call of Lovecraft, created by Brown University students, that leads walkers through five H. P. Lovecraft–inspired locations in Providence, Rhode Island.[1]

During this phase of the process, we made it a point to test several AR apps so that we could experience a variety of the AR applications available in the consumer market. Applications we explored included Crayola's Color Alive coloring books and the augmented anatomy worksheet Anatomy 4D; InkHunter, an app that allows viewers to view tattoo designs on their skin; PixelPress Floors, which augments students' hand-drawn video game designs into playable video games; Monocle, the AR functionality in the Yelp app that overlays information about local businesses within view of the user's smartphone; Google Translate, which overlays translated text over text in a different language; and Leafsnap, which identifies plants by the shape of their leaves. This wraparound approach to exploring the AR medium exposed us to of the breadth of possibilities that AR presents, and the broad view perspective provided us with ample inspiration while allowing us to craft our own vision for this project rather than duplicating an already existing project.

Selecting an AR Platform

Our review of other institutions' AR projects and our exploration of AR apps acquainted us with a variety of end-user AR authoring platforms through which we were able to determine our AR platform needs: we were seeking an AR platform that would be cost effective, easy to use, and supported across multiple platforms (iOS/Android phones and tablets). After testing multiple platforms, we concluded that Aurasma best met all of the criteria we were seeking in an AR platform. Its drag-and-drop authoring interface is intuitive for students as creators of augmented reality content, and its mobile app interface is intuitive for visitors to interact with. It works across iOS and Android devices (both phones and tablets). Aurasma is free to use and there is the option of having the company "white label" (create an app with an institution's name and needs built in) for a fee. This was an attractive feature, as it would allow us to pilot the use of Aurasma and prototype the initial projects for free with the opportunity to grow into a more robust, instance-specific app in the future.

Each AR platform has its own set of vocabulary to describe components of its functionality. In this chapter we will use the following platform-specific vocabulary when discussing the creation of AR content using Aurasma:

> *Aura*: the visual augmented reality (AR) experience produced when connecting digital assets like videos and web pages to a real-world image or object that Aurasma can recognize. The key components of an Aura are a Trigger Image and an Overlay (the digital element that is launched on [a] mobile device

when the Aurasma viewfinder recognizes a Trigger Image). Auras can include multiple Overlays, and those Overlays can have various commands attached to them. Auras are created in Aurasma Studio and viewed with the Aurasma app.

Trigger Image: the physical real-world images or objects Aurasma recognizes in order to deliver an AR experience to a mobile device. Strong Trigger Images ensure the Aura will activate smoothly and the Overlays will track well. Qualities for strong Trigger Images are:

- Tonal variation and contrast
- Unique shapes and forms
- Lots of detail across the entire image

The physical real-world objects that trigger an Aura must be photographed and imported into Aurasma Studio in the following format:

- JPEG or PNG file
- Less than 500,000 pixels in size (width × height)

Overlay: the digital content that is launched on the screen of a mobile device when the Aurasma recognizes a Trigger Image. Overlays can include videos, images, 3D scenes, web pages, or any combination thereof. Overlays can appear individually or as part of a group (multiple Overlays and sequenced Auras). Actions can be added to each Overlay to direct a user's interaction with the Overlay. Each Aura can have up to 50 Overlays attached to it. The placement, sequencing and interaction with Overlay content is designed in Aurasma Studio.

Aurasma Studio: the online workspace used for creating Auras. Users create an Aurasma account to upload and access Trigger Image and Overlay assets and to design and publish Auras that can be viewed with the Aurasma app.

Aurasma app: the mobile device application used for viewing and interacting with Auras. The Aurasma app is free and can be downloaded onto iPhones and iPads, and Android phones and tablets version 4.0 and above. In the free version of the app, viewers log in to the Aurasma app and "follow" other users' accounts to view those users' Auras. White label versions of the Aurasma app make it possible to view account-specific Auras without the need to "follow."[2]

Prototyping

After selecting Aurasma as our chosen AR platform, we began a prototyping process in which we created three models for how students may approach designing their AR-enhanced exhibits. These models allowed us to combine some elements of projects we reviewed with elements of our own design in ways specific to our collection. The resulting models—the Zimmerman Ludoscope Display, Augmented Walking Tour, and Talking Portraits of Washington College—allowed us to encounter and work through the physical, technological, and instructional challenges and considerations present in each model prior to introducing these processes into an instructional sequence.

The Zimmerman Ludoscope Display was our exploration of AR in a behind-glass exhibit of artifacts. Our collection includes several artifacts related to William H. Zimmerman, a notable Washington College physics professor who served as the college's vice president from 1873 to 1882. The Zimmerman collection includes several of Zimmerman's inventions, prototypes, patents, and personal effects. For an AR-enhanced exhibit of this collection, some of these objects would be exhibited in a display case while others would appear digitally in the Aura. We determined that just Zimmerman's ludoscope (an optical toy invented by Zimmerman) and its accompanying disc accessories would be physically on display. Other parts of the collection would be on exhibit through the Aura. Overlays for the Aura included scans of patents for the invention, photographs of Zimmerman and his experiments with mechanizing the ludoscope, and scans of disc prototypes made by Zimmerman's wife. We created a curatorial video to contextualize the significance of these Overlay images to the invention and to explain Zimmerman's significance to the college. This video was also an Overlay in the Aura for the display (figure 6.1).

Creating the Zimmerman Ludoscope display led us to consider what to use as Trigger Images for behind-glass exhibits. Though Aurasma has the ability to trigger augmented content from a three-dimensional object, we chose to augment caption cards to accompany the objects instead of augmenting the objects themselves. Aurasma is sensitive to changes in light, so if the shadows on an object change, then the device cannot recognize the Trigger Image properly and no Aura will be produced. Two-dimensional images, such as captions, are less susceptible to changes in light that affect Aurasma's ability to recognize the Trigger Image. We also discovered the need to include photographs as part of the caption cards because text-only captions were not visually unique enough to trigger an Aura (figure 6.2).

This prototype brought to our attention the usefulness of video in contextualizing still images in an Aura. The narration in a video provides the viewer with a curator's commentary without requiring the presence of a curator. This enables the viewer to better understand the images contained in the Aura. Instructionally, this meant that students would require training in creating and editing digital video in addition to instruction in the use of photography and scanning applications and equipment. Further, the use of video would necessitate closed captioning. In our prototype, we were able to provide a closed-caption version of the video by uploading it to YouTube and using the captions feature to add captions to the video. We added a closed-caption "button" to the Aura that links the viewer to the captioned video on YouTube. The

LUDOSCOPE

1902; Tin machine with cardboard discs
Dimensions: 10" x 10" x 7"
Prof. William H. Zimmerman (1839-1922)
Maryland, USA

A MERRYWHEEL FOR MOTION PICTURES

Zimmerman's ludoscope was a motion picture optical toy. It was operated by the viewer resting his or her forehead against the viewing hood and spinning a slotted wheel through which a connected printed disc was viewed, creating an animated effect.

The invention was patented in the USA in 1904 and in England in 1905. It was sold with six discs with more available for purchase. The Washington College Archives collection includes the original six discs as well as several hand-drawn prototype discs--many of which were created by Professor Zimmerman's wife, Jennie.

Figure 6.1. Caption card for Zimmerman Ludoscope display prototype. This image contains AR content. To view the Aura, download the Aurasma app. After logging in, follow askWCarchives and scan the image with the in-app viewer. ***Washington College.***

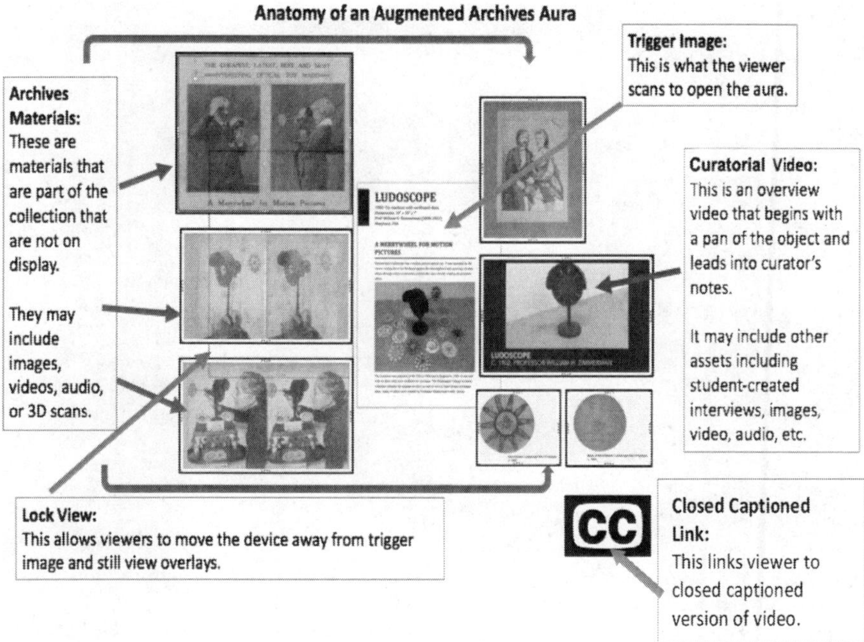

Figure 6.2. Caption card for Zimmerman Ludoscope display prototype as it appears in the Aurasma Studio workplace. *Washington College*.

need for closed captioning added a further instructional consideration for the use of video in student-created Auras in that students would need instruction in captioning videos, either through YouTube or another program.

A second prototype was an Augmented Walking Tour, spearheaded by an archives student assistant who was working with a collection of campus photographs from the 1950s. The vision for this prototype was to create a walking tour that would use campus buildings as Trigger Images, with a photograph of the building from the 1950s as the Overlay (figure 6.3).

The student was successful in creating such an Aura, and the effect was quite impressive as the viewer watched the building "transform" into a view of how it looked in the past. The AR experience, coupled with the experience of the viewer occupying the same space as the building, had the effect of transporting the viewer back in time. Unfortunately, due to the same light sensitivities previously explained, the Aura only worked on sunny days and at a particular time of day. Any change in lighting impeded the ability to trigger the Aura. We attempted to respond to this problem by using the GPS trigger feature in Aurasma as an avenue for a location-based AR experience, but the GPS functionality was not granular enough to pinpoint a building-specific Aura. We were able to aug-

Figure 6.3. In the Augmented Walking Tour prototype, a college dormitory (left), when viewed through the Aurasma app, revealed an Overlay of itself in the 1950s. The Augmented Walking Tour prototype (right) as viewed through Aurasma (the Overlay has been lightened to increase visibility). Since Aurasma is sensitive to changes in light, the Aura was only visible under very specific weather and time conditions. *Washington College*.

ment markers that a viewer could scan to trigger the Aura, but the effect was not as impressive as using the building itself as a Trigger Image.

This prototype brought to our attention the impact of space in a viewer's experience with an AR-enhanced exhibit. However, the execution of such an endeavor proved instructionally complex since students would need to test the Auras on location. At the time, the college Wi-Fi did not support students working in Aurasma Studio on laptops outdoors, so the workflow for creating this type of Aura would involve a great deal of running between indoor and outdoor locations while creating the Auras. Further, it would mean that instructional and technological support would have to happen on location, with instructors needing to circulate to groups at separate locations. Ultimately, we opted not to pursue this type of AR experience as part of our project due to the instructional complexities it presented.

A third prototype was the Talking Portraits of Washington College. This prototype took the form of a scavenger hunt in which viewers searched for augmented portraits around the campus. We used the portraits that hang in buildings throughout campus as Trigger Images. Photographs of these portraits were animated using the simple free web application Blabberize so that the portraits appeared to "come to life" and talk. These videos were also closed captioned using YouTube. We wrote scripts imagining what the individuals pictured in the portraits might say, and asked volunteers to voice-act for each character in the portraits. These animations became the Overlays for the Auras in the scavenger hunt. We also included digital "buttons" in these Auras that, when tapped, link viewers to specific portions of the college website related to the portrait (such as linking viewers from a portrait of a college library patron, Clifton Miller, to a web page documenting the dedication ceremony in which the campus library was renamed in his honor). This prototype represented a different approach to Overlays than the previous two prototypes in that it used links to born-digital archival information contained in the college website instead of digitized facsimiles of physical objects residing in the archives (figure 6.4).

Figure 6.4. A portrait from the Talking Portraits of Washington College scavenger hunt prototype. This image contains AR content. To view the Aura, download the Aurasma app. After logging in, follow askWCarchives and scan the image with the in-app viewer. *Washington College*.

This prototype brought to our attention the need to codify an approach to user interaction with Auras. It would be important for student curators to use a single set of icons linked to specific actions to create a consistent experience for visitors. We also realized the need to develop formatted templates for caption cards so that students could create a cohesive exhibit and spend their time focused on research and interaction with objects in the collection. To address these considerations, we set up several folders in our institution's cloud storage system that contained icon files and formatted caption templates as well as style guides for creating the exhibit. Instructionally, this would mean that we would need to educate students in not only the research portion of curation but also the types of stylistic considerations that arise during the curation process.

Preparing for Instruction

The semester-long research and development phase of this project provided valuable insights and illuminated key considerations for how we might implement student-curated, AR-enhanced exhibits in an instructional sequence. Toward the end of the prototyping portion of our research and development phase, an instructional opportunity well suited to the Augmented Archives initiative emerged. We would work with students enrolled in freshman pre-orientation, a five-day program preceding incoming freshmen's first semester at the college. The resulting project combined aspects of the Zimmerman Ludoscope display and Talking Portraits of Washington College prototypes. During this sequence, students would work to create a behind-glass AR-enhanced exhibit of our rare books collection, which would be on display in the vestibule and lobby of the college library. Each book on exhibit would be accompanied by a student-created caption card. The caption card would serve as the Trigger Image for the Aura; scans of the most significant portions of the book would become Overlays for the Aura, allowing the viewer to digitally "turn the pages" of the closed book on display. Where appropriate, students would include "buttons" in the Aura to link viewers to pertinent web content about the book (figure 6.5).

PHASE II: EDUCATING STUDENT CURATORS

Washington's Secret History: Freshman Pre-orientation Program

The legend of George Washington is more than a myth at Washington College. It has provided a solid history to which students are attracted and

BOOK FOR A LADY

Washington College's rare book library holds two copies of Sir Walter Scott's *Lady of the Lake*. One of the copies was a part of Sophie Kerr's personal library. This book was published by Porter & Coates, a firm based in Philadelphia. It contains engraving illustrations completed by Sir John Gilbert, which are also contained in an earlier edition of the book that the library owns. Interestingly, the editions are published by different publishers yet contain the same illustrations.

Lady of the Lake
1871
Sir Walter Scott: August 15th 1771-September 21st, 1832
Porter & Coates Philadelphia

Figure 6.5. Student-created caption card from the Washington's Secret History pre-orientation program. This image contains AR content. To view Aura, download the Aurasma app. After logging in, follow askWCarchives and scan the image with the in-app viewer. *Faith Stahl, Washington College.*

inspired to follow. When new students are asked why they chose to attend Washington College, many mention the history of George Washington as a foremost attraction. We were approached by the college's pre-orientation program staff to help design a program that would capitalize on the allure of the college's historical significance to help new students connect with the college. The resulting program, Washington's Secret History, became a part of the college's pre-orientation program in fall 2016 as a way to attract a new type of student to pre-orientation—those who have an interest in historical research. In previous years, the program had a heavy emphasis on outdoor and environmental programs that highlight the college's geographic connection to the Chesapeake Bay and its estuaries. In this new pre-orientation program, students would dive into the college's rich colonial history by way of the artifacts and resources contained in the college archives. Working with a professor whose expertise is in rare books and manuscripts, we designed an instructional sequence for this program in which students would get a behind-the-scenes look at curating an AR-enhanced exhibit by working with the volumes in our rare books collection.

Working with Artifacts

As part of the Augmented Archives program, Washington's Secret History afforded students a level of involvement with artifacts that normally does not occur until graduate school. Traditionally, teaching done with underclassmen focuses on document analysis. Students examine one item and attempt to describe it. In fact, many projects for undergraduates are similar to what TeachArchives.org advocates, which is "creating specific and tailored prompts for each document that your students will examine."[3] Our project focused on what we have come to call *investigative curation,* instruction that focuses on students' hands-on interaction with an artifact, leading them to ask authentic questions about the object and seek to answer those questions and share their findings through curating an exhibit that engages all types of patrons coming to the library.

Few of the students had been in an archives before. We had three professionals (an archivist, an English professor, and an instructional technologist) and one undergraduate archives assistant who worked as a team to teach and lead the project. There were 13 undergraduate students in the program, and this was their first experience on the college campus. They were surprised that we allowed them to interact, hold, and examine the objects so closely. We provided each student with an archival kit containing a document storage box, white cotton gloves, a mylar sleeve, and an archival folder. We bought these from an archival supply company and wanted the students to leave with them as a souvenir of their experience. Each student was loaned an iPad and laptop for the duration of the project (figure 6.6).

Students were given access to a professional still-life photography studio that resides in the college's archives. This piece of equipment consists of a lighting kit mounted above a white molded plastic cyclorama backdrop, the curved corners of which provide a soft, seamless background to photograph artifacts against, eliminating the need to retouch photographs for use in digital exhibits. Students were also taught how to construct a similar do-it-yourself photography setup using poster board and a strong light.

We were careful to regard technological equipment as not separate from the canon of archival tools, but incorporated them as a matter of course during archival work. Students were instructed in the use of these items, as well as the care and handling of rare books.

Each student was given time to explore a large number of preselected rare books or browse the stacks of the rare books room. After browsing the materials, the students each selected one or two rare books that they wanted to investigate more closely and present through their AR-enhanced exhibit. Students then set about reading the title pages, notations, and any other "clues" found inside the volumes. They carefully documented these "clues" by pho-

Figure 6.6. Students photographing artifacts in the college Archives using the professional still-life photography studio (right) and a temporary photography setup (left). ***Washington College.***

tographing and scanning them. Aided by a rare books specialist and archivist, students then worked to construct a thoughtful caption card about the book. Working with an instructional technologist, students used this caption card as a Trigger Image for their Aura and added the photographs and scans of their "clues," as well as buttons linking viewers to pertinent Internet resources, in the Overlay of their Aura.

Technological Proficiencies

It is important to note that involving students as creators of AR content involves the acquisition of technological proficiencies beyond the use of the specific AR platform. In our case, students needed to become proficient in not only the use of Aurasma Studio and the Aurasma app but also basic digitization techniques, including scanning and photography, in order to create the augmented caption cards for their exhibit. Because the acquisition of these skills would be in addition to the skills students were gaining in working with artifacts, and because the instructional sequence took place over a short period of time, we designed our approach to rely heavily on the use of iPads to consolidate the number of devices needed to accomplish the tasks for the project and mitigate the technological learning curve our students faced. We made use of an iPad loaner program available through the college that assigned each student an iPad for the week. The iPads allowed students to test their Auras as they created them. For photography and scanning, we trained students to use the free iPad app CamScanner. This app allowed students to take high-quality photographs of their books and perform basic photo-editing tasks like cropping and contrast adjustments. The app also allowed students to scan pages within their books and "straighten" those scans as we had done in our Talking Portraits prototype. CamScanner uploads to its own cloud storage solution, so students were able to pull their scans from their accounts on the CamScanner website onto their laptops and then into the Aurasma Studio workspace when they began creating their augmented caption cards.

Because students in the pre-orientation program were assembled from high schools throughout the country, and this was their first college academic experience, there were disparities in the basic technological proficiencies students possessed. One unexpected challenge we encountered was that while our students easily adapted to working with Aurasma Studio and CamScanner to create their augmented content, they struggled with the more basic technological skill of working with cloud storage. We relied heavily on the use of our college's cloud storage solution to distribute assets such as icons and caption-card templates and to provide students with a space to gather, share, and organize their research assets from their work with the rare books for the exhibit. We had made the assumption that students would come to college prepared to work with files "in the cloud." What we discovered was a significant number of students who had no formal experience working "in the cloud," and those who did had gained this experience from attending high schools that had adopted cloud storage solutions as part of the schools' information technology infrastructure. To address this gap, we added breakout sessions to our instruction so that students who needed to gain these skills had an opportunity to do so, and noted that we would need to make this type of technological onboarding a part of future instructional sequences until working with cloud storage becomes more ubiquitous in K–12 educational systems.

Installing the Exhibit

Once the Auras were complete, students began to install their exhibit at the entrance of the library. They were provided with exhibit supplies—book snakes and book rests, Lucite caption holders, and glass shelving. They worked collaboratively to take ownership over making the exhibit look polished and professional. They moved shelves, rearranged furniture, attached items to the walls, and more. The final product was a welcoming and engaging exhibit filled with rare books, archival supplies, and technology, which instantly drew patrons to look at and immerse themselves in the story of the rare books in a collection seldom visited by patrons of the library.

Patron Interaction

We approached patron interaction from both a physical and technological perspective. Technologically speaking, user interaction was fairly simple to facilitate. Setting the devices—iPods and iPads—to guided access mode restricted use of the devices to the Aurasma app, so the only function the devices served was as AR viewing mechanisms.[4] We were fortunate to be able to utilize iPads from the college's Academic Technology device loaner program for the exhibit. This was important because we found that providing devices as part of the exhibit was key to patron's interaction with augmented content in the exhibit. Though the Aurasma app is free to download, we found that patrons were unwilling to download the app to their personal smartphones. Furthermore, Aurasma uses a social media model of creating an account and "following" creators' accounts to access augmented content created by other users. The process of downloading an app, creating an account, and searching for and following the Washington College Archives account proved to be too many steps for a patron to go through to engage with an already unfamiliar technology. Providing devices that were set on the app and set to just "scan and go" made the augmented content readily available to patrons and facilitated their interaction with it (figure 6.7).

Physical measures to facilitate viewer interaction with the exhibit were more extensive. The devices were attached to the wall under the display case using device security locks. We attached Lucite brochure holders to the walls alongside the display case to hold the iPads and iPods at eye level. We affixed stickers with instructions for viewing the Auras on these holders so viewers would know how to utilize the technology to view the AR content.

Since the free version of Aurasma does not have any reporting mechanism to help assess patron interaction (certain white label versions do), we relied on observations to assess how patrons would interact with the exhibit. Observing patron interaction with the exhibit afforded us with insights on how to improve the exhibit.

One such improvement became evident when we realized that, although viewers understood the concept of Trigger Images, they were not sure which objects in the exhibit served as Trigger Images. We placed stickers that read "Scan Me" on the Lucite card holder for each caption card to identify these as Trigger Images. We also observed that some viewers had trouble reaching their arms up high enough to access Trigger Images on the top shelves of

Figure 6.7. A patron viewing augmented content in the student-curated exhibit. *Washington College.*

the display cases. To remedy this, and to make the exhibit more accessible to viewers who use wheelchairs and those with limited mobility, we printed two booklets containing all of the caption cards for the exhibit. Viewers could view all of the Auras in the exhibit by scanning the booklet. We placed the booklets on lecterns that are part of the college's historical furniture collection, which added to the history-meets-contemporary aesthetic of the exhibit.

Academic and Pedagogical Value

At a liberal arts institution, posing critical research questions is essential. For students to be able to conduct research utilizing primary source materials is even more valuable, particularly for incoming first-year students who might not otherwise have firsthand access to these rare objects. Traditionally, undergraduate students seldom, if ever, get the opportunity to work closely with rare primary source materials; instead, they work with facsimiles of these materials found in books and online. Augmented Archives leverages AR technology to give students their first opportunity for hands-on engagement with rare materials, and gives faculty the ability to craft instructional sequences to fulfill discipline-specific learning objectives using our collections.

Undergraduate students often don't know where to begin when introduced to primary source materials. In fact, "the use of archival material takes them into an environment different than a library and one with which they are not familiar."[5] By utilizing a new technology such as augmented reality, students can be encouraged to use special collections, and we can further enhance this involvement.

Comments from student interviews we conducted at the end of the five-day pre-orientation sequence indicated that students valued working with primary sources throughout the experience. One student noted, "It was definitely a great experience to work with rare books and rare artifacts throughout the week and actually get to touch them instead of stare at them behind glass."[6] Another student commented, "Doing the research for the book, I felt like a detective just trying to figure out this book's secrets."[7] Indeed, all 13 students were able to produce an augmented caption card that illustrated the fruits of their "detective work," accurately describing each book's significance. They were able to select pertinent information from and about each book for the digital Overlays to support the assertions they made about the book's significance—much in the same way they would find themselves citing this information in research-based writing.

Initiatives like Augmented Archives can provide an avenue to acquaint students with rare materials with a distinct and focused objective to educate the public through the crafting of highly engaging AR-enhanced exhibits. A third student noted that she valued "learning what you do as an archivist or a curator and how to do those things. We got some experience with being an archivist and curating our own exhibit."[8] This approach fosters learning environments for each student to engage in authentic research as well as acquire and employ technological proficiencies in a highly interactive, project-based instructional sequence with real-world applications.

From an archives and museum perspective, the use of augmented reality in the curation of exhibits helps to bridge the gap between the physical and digital in ways that other technologies and practices cannot. Though digitization practices have helped archives and museums to preserve and share primary sources with the public through the web, these digital repositories do not offer the same patron experience as the close-up viewing of objects "in real life." At the same time, limited physical exhibit space can relegate interesting and valuable artifacts in a collection to reposing in storage, out of sight to patrons. By using augmented reality in projects like Augmented Archives, institutions can have the best of both worlds by making the physical and digital available in one cohesive patron experience.

The Augmented Archives initiative continues to expand access to primary sources. Having gained valuable instructional and technological insights from the implementation process of Washington's Secret History, we are able to introduce this program to the larger Washington College community.

After viewing the students' exhibit, one biology professor expressed interest in using Aurasma for tree identification around campus. Another professor created an augmented PowerPoint presentation for her children's literature course. One professor assigned students in a museum education internship to use Aurasma to augment an exhibit through a partnership with a local museum after hearing one of the students from the Washington's Secret History pre-orientation program describe how useful augmented reality was in the curation process.

In curating AR-enhanced exhibits through this initiative, students are able to develop skills where they can discover, analyze, and present information in a real and meaningful way to the larger community. Students are able to learn how to effectively use digital tools and emerging technologies in learning sequences that ask them to actively apply these skills. Collections that previously were untouched are now revealing secrets to students and viewers in new and exciting ways. Faculty and staff members are able to tap into the Augmented Archives initiative by collaborating with the library and Academic Technology team to craft engaging instructional sequences that leverage AR technology in investigative curation processes.

NOTES

1. Laura Geggel, "Smithsonian App Brings Fossils to Life"; Ben Davis, "The British Museum: Five Lessons in Augmented Reality"; Ani Boyadjian, "Augmented Library"; "Class Creates Lovecraft Tour."
2. Aurasma, "Aurasma Community Network."
3. Julie Golia and Robin M. Katz, "Our Teaching Philosophy."
4. Apple, "Use Guided Access with iPhone, iPad, and iPod Touch."
5. Marian J. Matyn, "Getting Undergraduates to Seek Primary Sources in Archives," 349.
6. Student interview (Student 1), in discussion on camera with authors at the conclusion of the pre-orientation program, August 24, 2016.
7. Student interview (Student 2), in discussion on camera with authors at the conclusion of the pre-orientation program, August 24, 2016.
8. Student interview (Student 3), in discussion on camera with authors at the conclusion of the pre-orientation program, August 24, 2016.

BIBLIOGRAPHY

Apple. "Use Guided Access with iPhone, iPad, and iPod Touch." Apple Support. Accessed February 13, 2017. https://support.apple.com/en-us/HT202612.

Aurasma. "Aurasma Community Network." Accessed February 13, 2017. https://aurasma.zendesk.com/hc/en-us.

Boyadjian, Ani. "Augmented Library." Thedigitalshift.com, September 17, 2014. http://www.thedigitalshift.com/2014/09/mobile/augmented-library-technology/.

"Class Creates Lovecraft Tour." *News from Brown*, August 21, 2013. https://news.brown.edu/articles/2013/08/class-creates-lovecraft-tour.

Damala, Areti, Eva Hornecker, Merel van der Vaart, Dick van Dijk, and Ian Ruthven. "The Loupe: Tangible Augmented Reality for Learning to Look at Ancient Greek Art." *Mediterranean Archaeology and Archaeometry* 16, no. 5 (2016): 73–85. http://maajournal.com/Issues/2016/Vol16-5/Full8.pdf.

Davis, Ben. "The British Museum: Five Lessons in Augmented Reality." Econsultancy, December 4, 2013. https://econsultancy.com/blog/63929-the-british-museum-five-lessons-in-augmented-reality/.

Geggel, Laura. "Smithsonian App Brings Fossils to Life." Live Science, January 14, 2015. http://www.livescience.com/49454-smithsonian-skin-and-bones-app.html.

"A Gift for Athena-MW2015: Museums and the Web 2015." MW2015: Museumsandtheweb.Com. Accessed February 10, 2017. http://mw2015.museumsandtheweb.com/bow/a-gift-for-athena/

Golia, Julie, and Robin M. Katz. "Our Teaching Philosophy." TeachArchives.org. Accessed April 26, 2017. http://www.teacharchives.org/articles/our-teaching-philosophy/.

Matyn, Marian J. "Getting Undergraduates to Seek Primary Sources in Archives." *The History Teacher* 33, no. 3 (May 2000): 349–55. http://www.jstor.org/stable/495032.

"Skin and Bones: Mobile Augmented Reality App for the National Museum of Natural History's Hall of Bones." Naturalhistory.Si.Edu. Accessed February 10, 2017. http://naturalhistory.si.edu/exhibits/bone-hall/.

Smith, William. *An Account of Washington College, in the State of Maryland: Published by Order of the Visitors and Governors of the Said College, for the Information of Its Friends and Benefactors.* Philadelphia: Joseph Crukshank, 1784.

Washington's Secret History 2016 Pre-orientation Student Interviews, August 24, 2016.

7

"Blipping" through Information Literacy

Using the Blippar App in Instruction

Bethanie O'Dell and Art Gutierrez

With the release of Pokémon GO in 2016, augmented reality (AR) is now a common technology term murmured in every library, school, and college, with uses including instruction, outreach, exhibit promotion, and increased engagement with patrons. The University Libraries and Archives at Emporia State University (ESU) is no exception.

Over the last few years, ESU librarians have been reflecting on the unique challenge of incorporating AR throughout the library as well as embedding an AR unit in an information literacy course. In order to enhance students' research skills and technology usage, the library faculty utilized the augmented reality app and software Blippar to instruct students on digital media and presenting a topic. This chapter will demonstrate how AR was used to meet key learning outcomes for a specific information literacy course, UL100: Research Skills, Information, and Technology, which is taught by library faculty at ESU. Assessment of the pros and cons of using Blippar as an educational tool, how this critical approach fits the digital literacy theme, and how millennial students reacted to using AR technology will also be covered.

Blippar is a visual discovery browser that interacts with real-life objects using a mobile device, and just like Pokémon GO, it uses 4G network, camera access, and touch screens to connect the user to the virtual object.[1] Blippar is a privately owned company launched in 2011 by Ambarish Mitra and Omar Tayeb. The vision of Blippar is to "[transform] the way people connect with the world, with brands, and with each other."[2]

Blippar is free and easy to use. The user will download the app to any iOS or Android mobile device, granting access to the device's camera. By using the camera, the user will aim the device at specific objects to identify "blipps" ("digital content that has been added to an image in the real world") in the area.[3] The app can identify basic objects (keyboard, laptop, dog, etc.) but will also identify customized markers (name-brand objects, photographs, etc.).

Advanced users can access the Blippbuilder by creating a personal, company, or educational account at https://web.blippar.com. This access allows the user to develop their own blipps for specific objectives or images.

INFORMATION LITERACY AND AR

When looking at augmented reality and the larger information literacy landscape, digital literacy is a natural connection. The ALA Digital Literacy Task Force defines digital literacy as "the ability to use information and communication technologies to find, evaluate, create, and communicate information, requiring both cognitive and technical skills."[4] The first part of the definition, "the ability to use information and communication technologies," speaks to the skills and experience of learning how to use new tools. Blippar is just one in a new realm of AR tools. The more students use these tools, the more intuitive they become as they build a knowledge base of how these systems work and increase technical skills.

Students will continue to find and evaluate information in the research process, but the way that they create information is being enhanced. The traditional way we assess the process of research skills and abilities is through a very cognitive use of a static object like a written paper or presentation. AR, through Blippar, opens up a new, unique way for students to showcase the research they have done by creating a blipp. The user's ability to interact with the content in the blipp is what makes this assignment more engaging compared to the PowerPoint alternative.

There are currently two types of AR: location oriented, and vision based.[5] Pokémon GO is a good example of the location-based implementation of AR. Blippar is the latter, with emphasis being placed on creating a target image that is then transferred into a blipp. The focus is on communicating information in a new and engaging way, not only for the creator, but also for the consumer. By presenting information in this format, students are interacting with research topics in an intentionally digital way.

The Information Creation as a Process frame from the *Framework for Information Literacy for Higher Education* states that

> Information in any format is produced to convey a message and is shared via a selected delivery method. The iterative processes of researching, creating, revising, and disseminating information vary, and the resulting product reflects these differences.[6]

The re-organization of information literacy into the new framework puts a focus on the process of information creation. It highlights the fact that the process is not to be viewed as linear, but more of a cycle that repeats steps as needed, as determined by the user, until the process is complete. With most digital tools, the iteration process is enhanced by the ability to view, edit, and create objects from multiple devices, and with Blippar this is easily done. The Blippbuilder is web based and compatible with Macs and PCs. Additionally, through Blippar, students can incorporate information sources, including social media sites such as Facebook, Instagram, Twitter, and LinkedIn, with additional ways coming in the future.

The interface for the Blippbuilder has a similar layout to other web-based interfaces (figure 7.1). As a final project, students create an online portfolio using Wix.com. The site editor for Wix and the Blippbuilder have similar layouts, such as a toolbar from which users can select content and the option to rearrange the content on the page. This what-you-see-is-what-you-get (WYSIWYG) interface is user friendly and encouraging to students who do not have coding skills. Users can easily create content by dragging and dropping features from the provided menu onto the image they intend to blipp.

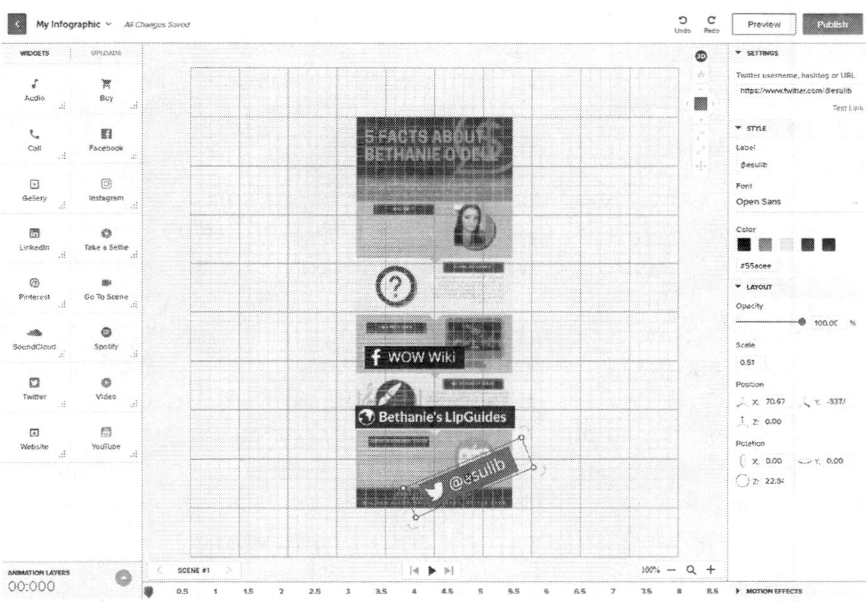

Figure 7.1. A screenshot of the instructor's Blippbuilder layout account. *Emporia State University.*

INTRODUCING BLIPPAR TO THE CLASSROOM

Emporia State University is a Midwestern liberal arts university with just under 6,000 students and full-time enrollment of 4,951.[7] The University Libraries and Archives at ESU offers at least five sections of UL100: Research Skills, Information, and Technology every semester, with four sections face-to-face and one online. UL100 is a two-credit-hour general education course that introduces the skills and concepts for locating, evaluating, and using information from a variety of resources. This course meets the information technology requirement for undergraduates because it teaches students how to identify credible information and use it ethically.

In collaboration with the online section, one of these face-to-face sections incorporated Blippar as a learning tool. The purpose of this collaboration was to identify ways to incorporate active learning through the use of technology while meeting specific general education and course outcomes. The following were the primary outcomes used during this project:

- To acquire proficiency in core skills necessary for academic success, including written and spoken communication, quantitative reasoning, and information technology and literacy (general education outcome)
- To develop the skills necessary to access information effectively and efficiently (UL100 course outcome)
- To identify ethical, legal, and social issues reflecting the changing nature of information in a technological society (UL100 course outcome)
- To analyze and synthesize information for the purpose of creating new knowledge (UL100 course outcome)

According to Tina Stavredes, author of *Effective Online Teaching: Foundations and Strategies for Student Success*, active learning is a method that places the responsibility for learning on the learner by having the student take responsibility for his or her learning through active engagement in course reading, writing, and discussion in order to make meaning from the content.[8] While the student takes responsibility for their engagement, the instructor facilitates by providing engaging content, multimedia, and assignments that allow students to experiment with what they are learning.

Active learning is a challenge for both online and face-to-face communities because it requires learners to take responsibility for their learning, and a 2016 article by Snipes and Slone states the current educational system is not preparing them for this sort of involvement.[9] Instead, the learners wait until they are told the answer.[10] One technique for enhancing student motivation is to use online tools that will help illustrate the information presented in the course, as well as allow students the ability to interact and experiment with the content.

To emphasize active learning in UL100, students were introduced to the concept of information being presented anywhere and everywhere through a demonstration video of how name brands are using Blippar to market.[11] Students were able to see that even objects they encounter every day can often present information. Therefore, finding credible information applies to their daily lives, not just in their academic careers.

Blippar is an excellent tool that demonstrates accessing credible information in the digital world. However, in order to illustrate that anyone can create information, regardless of their credibility, students were required to create their own blipp featuring content from their research topic and to present it to their peers. In order to meet Family Educational Rights and Privacy Act (FERPA) guidelines, students did not include any personal information, and images used to create individual blipps were submitted through Canvas, the university's learning management system. Blippar also includes an education account option, which locks blipps from being viewed publically unless provided a specific code. With this code, students have control over whom they share their blipp with.

WHY BLIPPAR?

Through the exposure to AR by using Blippar in the safe environment of the classroom, instructors create a foundation for students to build on as they move forward with their education and, ultimately, in the workplace. This experience will allow students to experiment with a new technology that will encourage them and increase their willingness to try new tools in the future.

As the use of QR codes is being replaced with AR, there are many different AR apps that can deliver media content (audio, video, hyperlinks, etc.) to smart devices—Layar, Wikitude, and Aurasma, to name a few.[12] Many AR apps require the use of GPS signals (Wikitude),[13] which can limit the service for distance students, and with companies taking advantage of this new trend, many apps also require a paid subscription to use the services. While Wikitude is one of the leading apps in AR, using iOS, Android, and Windows devices to access audio, video, and social media content, Blippar has similar features and is a more cost-efficient alternative.[14] At the time of the first Blippar assignment with UL100, Blippar was in the beta stage with the Blippbuilder. Therefore, there was no cost to use the services and, as of this writing, no cost advertised as the service transitions from beta stage.

The app does not require a location like many AR apps do, but looks at the markers embedded into the blipp from the Blippbuilder. Blippar also creates a code for each blipp that can be shared between users. The code is entered through the app settings and allows the user to instantly view the blipp. This is an ideal option for education accounts that want to create blipps but only want specific users to access the content.[15]

HOW BLIPPAR WAS USED

The basic curriculum for all UL100 sections is for students to select a research topic to focus on throughout the semester. At the end of the semester, students will have an infographic displaying key facts on their topic, an annotated bibliography of credible sources, and an online portfolio that displays their work throughout the semester. For this collaborative project between the face-to-face and the online instructor, an additional assignment required students to create an infographic (or use an image representing their topic) and use it as the marker for a customized blipp.[16] Assignment guidelines instructed students to embed a video of themselves demonstrating a library database and including at least two web links to credible online sources on their topic, and a link to their online portfolio.[17]

A common issue the ESU library faculty have encountered when teaching online and face-to-face classes is students waiting until the last minute to turn in their assignments. This issue resulted in the need to identify tools to help facilitate active learning. Therefore, the instructions for the Blippar assignment stated that students should be aware that a blipp takes approximately 24–48 hours to go live. While there were still a few students who did not acknowledge this feature until the day the assignment was due, most of the students in the class were able to submit a live blipp on time.

Another concern was that students would react negatively toward the Blippar assignment due to lack of prior knowledge about augmented reality or experience with Blippar. As recommended in Stavredes's textbook,[18] an FAQ section was provided for students to access, linking an instructor-made video, tutorials by Blippar, and step-by-step guides for individual features in the Blippbuilder. This helped prevent the massive amount of technical questions students would have while completing the assignment.

STUDENT REFLECTIONS AND ASSESSMENT

In Stavredes's textbook,[19] she states that reflections are a vital part of critical thinking and help enforce active learning. Many instructors assume that reflection should be at the end of an assignment, but Stavredes acknowledges the benefits of adding a pre-reflection assignment before the initial unit. While she recommends doing a discussion board that has students reflect on their expectations based on the course objectives, another method could include doing a pre-survey.

It is hard to predict the sorts of technology questions students will ask, but knowing what kind of technology they are using will help identify what sorts of guides will be essential. For example, the instructor of the online UL100 section created a pre-survey at the beginning of the semester to gather information about the current technology usage among the online students. This assessment also allowed the instructor to predict whether the students were ready to tackle the learning curve of augmented reality. In this survey, the instructor asked:

- what sort of mobile devices the students had
- what desktop/laptop computers they had
- whether they could tell the difference between an .mp3 and an .mp4 file
- whether they could use the camera and app store functions on their mobile device.

Figure 7.2 demonstrates that 95 percent of the online learners surveyed had an iPhone, which was useful for the instructor when creating a video

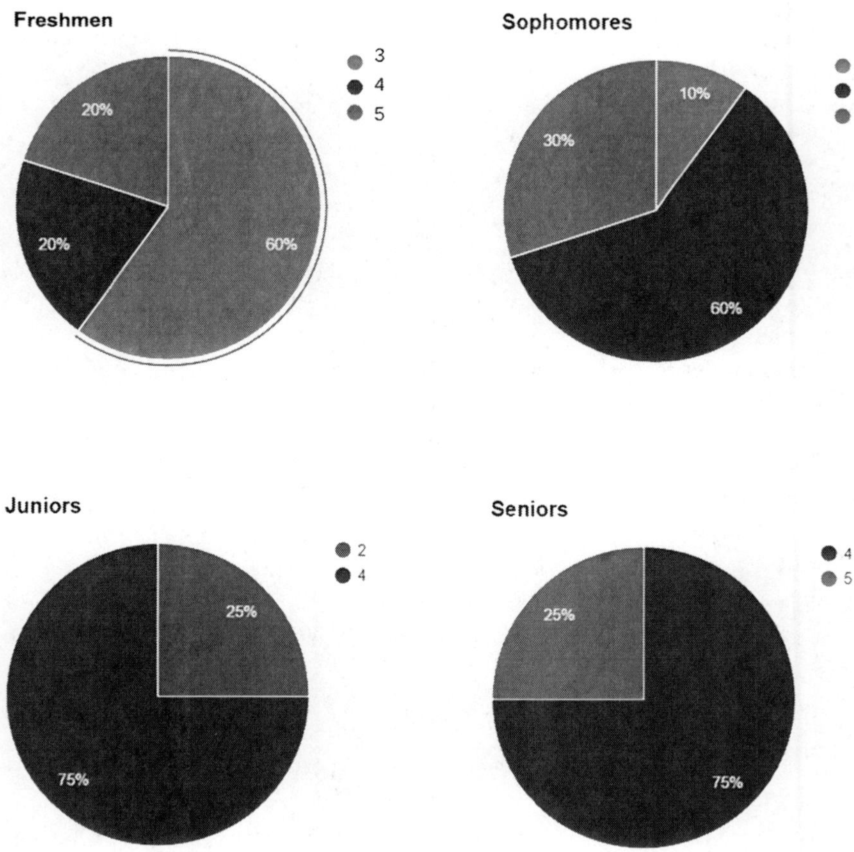

Figure 7.2. The percentage of students enrolled in the online UL100 course that say they have experience with specific types of technology. *Emporia State University.*

demonstration. This survey also showed that all the students could use the camera and app store features on their mobile devices, but only a small portion of students could state the difference between an .mp3 and an .mp4 file. Knowing how to identify the difference between these files is critical for successfully completing the Blippar assignment, which required embedding a video file (.mp4) into the blipp. Therefore, the instructor clarified the differences between these files in an earlier module.

To obtain perspective on where these students were with augmented reality, the UL100 instructors also created a pre-assessment survey for both sections, which asked the students specific questions about their interpretation and expectations of augmented reality. This survey included questions about the students' background (class standing) and other demographic information. It also included the following questions,[20] asking students to rank their opinion on a 1–5 scale:

- Using augmented reality will improve my performance in communicating information and content.
- Using augmented reality will enhance my effectiveness in communicating information and content.
- I find augmented reality to be useful in communicating information and content.

Figure 7.3 shows that the majority felt confident (ranking 4 for the statement) that "using AR will improve my performance in communicating information and content."

After completing their blipp, students were required to submit a 250-word (minimum) reflection on their experience using the app and Blippbuilder. There were not any requirements as far as the content of the summary, just a word limit. Student reflections covered a range of positive experience, concerns about the assignment, and ideas for future use. Some students noted that the tool is great for marketing, but advised that Blippar needs to market this tool better in order for companies, brands, and consumers to see the benefits of using it for marketing. A few students suggested that Blippar would be a great marketing tool for museums and schools that want to feature an exhibit and make it more interactive.

BLIPPAR AND ACCESSIBILITY

One of the primary challenges of using augmented reality are the limitations many AR/VR apps have regarding screen readers. According to a feature

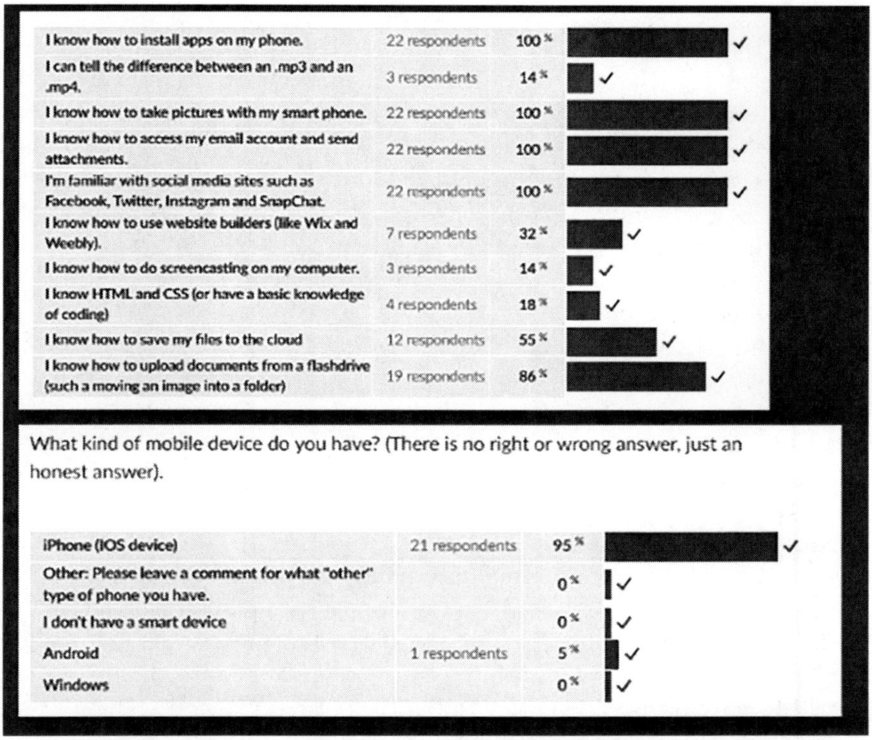

Figure 7.3. Percentage of students based on class standing and how they felt regarding AR improving performance in communicating information and content. ***Emporia State University.***

article on Blippar's website,[21] there have been successful experiments with using Blippar in the classroom. This article focused on how the students, faculty, and parents of A. Harry Moore School of New Jersey City University used Blippar to assist in creating their school newsletter and other assignments. To make the poster more accessible, the braille on the poster was used as the trigger point to activate the blipp, creating access to video, audio, and web content.

At the time, the authors were not aware of the advanced features of assigning triggers for blipps, and had not considered the accessibility option of adding braille. However, these features allow assignments incorporating Blippar to be engaged, interactive, and overall more inclusive by meeting the learning needs of all students. It might take an extra learning curve to understand how these advanced features work, but they are available and it is worth branching out to make sure they are accessible to everyone.

CONCLUSION

Teaching students how to use AR and present knowledge through a new form of technology was the overall goal of this project. While there were a few challenges with Blippar updating its Blippbuilder layout a few times during the semester, resulting in outdated videos and guides, students were still able to successfully present their project using AR. As expected, there were a few students who resisted this assignment and either did not complete it or completed it after the deadline. However, there were also students that continued their AR journey and sought out other projects they could market (such as making an interactive map of the Appalachian Trail) or looked for other blipps as consumers.

Regardless, student enthusiasm for this project was extremely encouraging, and the feedback we received from students aligned with our original course outcomes. Therefore, it is likely that the library faculty at ESU will continue to incorporate augmented reality in their information literacy course. Since the beginning of this project, the use of Blippar has expanded beyond just UL100 and information literacy sessions. The University Libraries and Archives also incorporated Blippar as a marketing strategy for Banned Books week events, presented at a children's tech camp to highlight the May Masse book collection, and played a key role in promoting the World War I and the Memorial Union: Honoring Veterans, Serving Students exhibit in the university's archives.

While there are always setbacks when introducing new technologies, introducing Blippar to the ESU campus has slowly evolved from just a small class assignment to highlighting some of the libraries' primary events.

APPENDIX A: *THE STORY OF FERDINAND*

Below is an example of what UL100 students submitted for their Blippar project. To access the blipp feature embedded in the image below, download Blippar to your mobile device and aim your camera lens at the image. You should see a loading screen before the screen presents the blipp content.

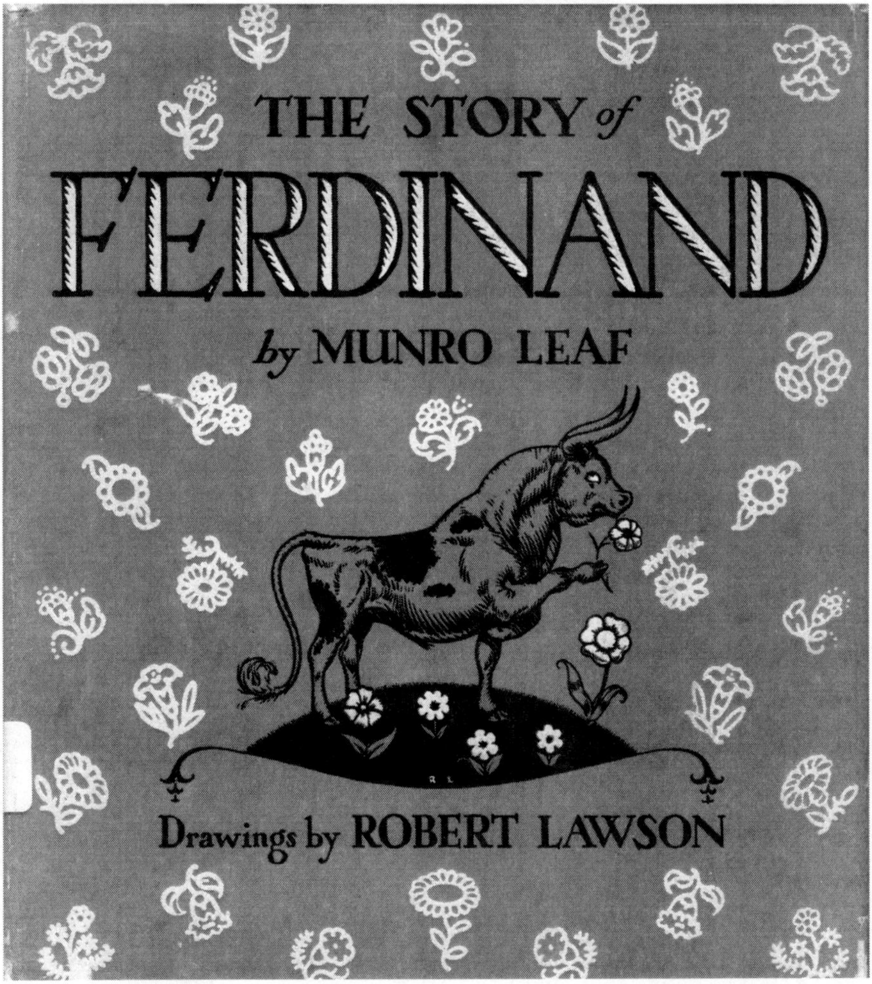

Figure 7.4. *The Story of Ferdinand* by Munro Leaf. *Emporia State University. Blipp Creation* © *Art Gutierrez*

APPENDIX B: ASSIGNMENT 1

This assignment sheet is specific to the online section of UL100 taught by Bethanie O'Dell.

Introduction to Blippar Assignment

Part of being information literate is being informed of trends that are currently being used to display information. I'm sure many of you were aware of the craze last year over Pokémon GO. Well, this assignment is going to look at the idea of augmented reality (which is what is used in Pokémon GO) and will provide you a brief introduction that will let you experiment with augmented reality and show you how information can be displayed in different formats other than the general book, journal, and Internet search.

Assignment Details

First, you will need to download:

- Blippar on your mobile device (which can be downloaded through the app store). Since we all have different devices, I won't create a tutorial. However, if you have issues installing the app let me know.
- Create an account at the actual Blippar site: https://web.blippar.com/blipp-builder#Blippbuilder (links to an external site). When it asks you what type of account, select personal account (which is free).

Second, use the image of yourself that you used in your infographic assignment and upload it to the Blippar site.

Basic Requirements: Include at least three "links" to the blipp: one link should be a video link (like YouTube) or embedded video (uploaded as .mp4) of the Database Demo you created in Module 5; one link should be a website link that links to your online portfolio; and one link needs to be any website link of your choice that relates to your research question (a link to an article, video, etc.).

So three things: the blipp will include your Database Demo, link (URL) to your online portfolio, and something linked that relates to your research question.

Keep in mind that most blipps take 24–48 hours to go live, so manage your time wisely.

Submission: To submit this assignment, upload the picture of you used for the blipp, and include a short reflection (150 words minimum) about your experience with Blippar and your opinion of augmented reality.

Additional Notes: Blippar is a new program, so I can imagine there may be a few hiccups along the way. If you have issues at all with accessing, using, or submitting this assignment, please let me know ASAP so I can help troubleshoot any issues.

APPENDIX C: ASSIGNMENT 2

This assignment sheet is specific to the face-to-face section of UL100 taught by Art Gutierrez.

Create your own Blipp using Blippar!

What is Blippar?

Blippar is an augmented reality tool. Download the app to your mobile device; you can find it on iTunes or the Google Play Store. Currently, the app does not work with Windows Phone devices. The app lets you access the blipps you create or that others create. To create the actual blipp you need to go to https://web.blippar.com/ and sign up for an account. Once you have an account you can access the Blippbuilder on https://web.blippar.com/ to create your blipp.

Links to Blippar Videos: These are helpful videos on what Blippar does and how to use it.

https://www.youtube.com/watch?v=YIPWq_sAC2M (What is Blippar?)

https://www.youtube.com/watch?v=x2td0r8ULaA&t=302s (Tutorial on how to use Blippar)

Rationale

We will be exploring your research materials in a new and different way than you have in the past. We will be using augmented reality to present your research findings and information about your research topic. This exposes you to a new technology, which is a goal of this course, and also allows you to interact with traditional research in a new and fun way!

Getting Started

First you need to create an account. To do this, go to https://web.blippar.com/. Then, using the main navigation bar at the top of the page, select Augmented Reality > Blippbuilder. On the next page choose Sign Up.

You will be taken to a sign-up screen where you will enter your name, username, password, country, and how you will use Blippar. Please choose Personal as your use category.

Next, check the I Agree to Terms box, and uncheck the Notify You of Product Updates box.

Finally, click Create Account. You should receive an email that you will need to open and follow the link to verify you Blippar account.

Basic Requirements

Create a Trigger Image for your blipp. This can be a selfie or another image related to your research.

You will also need to identify four information resources related to your research topic to add to your blipp. These sources can be videos, articles, or another source that you can connect to digitally.

Once you have verified your account, you can follow the steps above to log in to the Blippbuilder and create your blipp.

We will be going over how to navigate and use the Blippbuilder in class the Monday before the assignment is due.

Assignment Submission

To complete the assignment, please upload the Trigger Image you created in the assignment submission area of Canvas.

NOTES

1. Irene McDermott, "Fun with Virtual and Augmented Reality," 27.
2. Blippar, "About Us."
3. Ibid.
4. ALA Digital Literacy Task Force, "Digital Literacy Definition."
5. Matt Dunleavy and Chris Dede, "Augmented Reality Teaching and Learning."
6. Association of College and Research Libraries, *Framework for Information Literacy for Higher Education.*
7. Office of Institutional Research and Assessment, "Data Book: Fall 2016."
8. Tina Stavredes, *Effective Online Teaching: Foundations and Strategies for Student Success*, 107–8.
9. Phyllis Robinson Snipes and Mary Beth Slone, "Successful Flipped Instruction," 18.
10. Ibid.

11. "What Is Blippar?"

12. Jon Fletcher, "Augmented Reality: Is It Really Fit for Your Purposes?"

13. Ibid., 22.

14. Brenda Roberts, "Create Magic in Your Library with Augmented Reality (AR)!"

15. Blippar, "About Us."

16. Appendix A includes an example of a blipp.

17. Appendixes B and C include copies of the assignment provided to UL100 students.

18. Stavredes, *Effective Online Teaching*, 192.

19. Ibid., 113.

20. Ibid.

21. Blippar, "How Blippar Education Supports Special Needs Students to Improve Learning."

BIBLIOGRAPHY

ALA Digital Literacy Task Force. "Digital Literacy Definition." *ALA Connect,* September 14, 2012. http://connect.ala.org/node/181197.

Association of College and Research Libraries. *Framework for Information Literacy for Higher Education.* February 2, 2015. http://www.ala.org/acrl/standards/ilframework.

Blippar. "About Us." Accessed April 3, 2017. https://blippar.com/en/resources/faq/.

———. "How Blippar Education Supports Special Needs Students to Improve Learning." Accessed November 11, 2017. https://blippar.com/en/resources/blog/2015/05/28/how-blippar-education-supports-special-needs-students-to-improve-learning/.

Dunleavy, Matt, and Chris Dede. "Augmented Reality Teaching and Learning." In *Handbook of Research for Educational Communications and Technology*, edited by David Jonassen, Michael Spector, Marcy Driscoll, M. David Merrill, Jeroen van Merrienboer, and Marcy Driscoll, 735–46. New York: Springer, 2008.

Fletcher, Jon. "Augmented Reality: Is It Really Fit for Your Purposes?" *Multimedia Information and Technology* 38, no. 3 (August 2012): 22–23.

Givens, Earl, Art Gutierrez, Bethanie O'Dell, and Ashley Todd-Diaz. "Augmented Reality Pre-Survey." Google Forms, February 3, 2017. http://bit.ly/pre-surveyaugmentedreality.

McDermott, Irene. "Fun with Virtual and Augmented Reality." *Online Searcher* 40, no. 6 (November 2016): 27–28.

Office of Institutional Research and Assessment. "Data Book: Fall 2016." Emporia State University. Accessed July 13, 2017. https://www.emporia.edu/oira/documents/ESU-Datatbook-Fall-2016-2.pdf.

Roberts, Brenda. "Create Magic in Your Library with Augmented Reality (AR)!" *Teaching Librarian* 22, no. 2 (January 2015): 20–22.

Snipes, Phyllis Robinson, and Mary Beth Slone. "Successful Flipped Instruction." *School Library Monthly* 31, no. 6 (April 2016): 18–19.

Stavredes, Tina. *Effective Online Teaching: Foundations and Strategies for Student Success.* San Francisco: Jossey-Bass, 2011.

"What Is Blippar?" YouTube, posted by "Blippar," September 20, 2013. https://www.youtube.com/watch?v=YIPWq_sAC2M.

8

Dance Magic Dance

A Case Study of AR and VR/360 Video and the Performing Arts

Melanie Hibbert, Gabri Christa, Alexis Seeley, and Abby Lee

Barnard College, Columbia University, has a nationally recognized Department of Dance, and library administrators in collaboration with faculty piloted media and digital tools for dance research, performance, and composition. This chapter highlights three projects: the use of an augmented reality (AR) app, VR/360 video, and long-exposure LED photography as it relates to dance education and the performing arts at Barnard College. While these technologies are new and still in the exploratory stages, this descriptive case study supports the idea that AR and VR/360 tools can offer innovative methods for recording, scholarship, and instruction around the performing arts.

These three projects were the result of a collaboration between Barnard dance faculty members and Barnard IMATS (Instructional Media and Technology Services). While each project was different in technology and scope, all three had a similar goal: to capture, represent, and experience dance in new and innovative ways. This includes (a) giving audience members an opportunity to view dance pieces via an AR mobile application that also incorporated archival photographs and site specificity; (b) offering an immersive and viewer-directed method to watch dance via VR/360 video; and (c) recording dance scales through time-lapse technology, representing movement through an original method. All three projects have implications for dance education and scholarship. In addition, all of these projects were made possible through a supportive environment that encourages piloting and experimentation.

In a broad sense, the state of technology and higher education is one of "great disruption"[1]; while there are many anxieties and concerns related to the intersection of technology and education,[2] there are also many possibilities and affordances.[3] In the current moment, AR/VR (augmented reality and virtual reality) occupies significant interest and development. The reach of these emerging technologies includes video games and digital entertainment (the Oculus Rift and HTC Vive); mobile applications (Pokémon GO and Google Daydream); and film (*Dear Angelica*, which premiered at the 2017 Sundance Film Festival's New Frontiers exhibit). The application of these tools in library or educational settings is currently atypical; these technologies occupy a space where little has been researched or implemented, so there are no "best practices" or guidelines for their use. There is the chance that AR/VR will be viewed as a trend or a "flash in the pan" in the future, but there are rich instructional possibilities around immersive realities and visualizations.[4] This case study supports the fact that these tools have educational affordances, especially in relation to movement-based activities such as dance.

BACKGROUND

Virtual reality (VR) is a technology that has been "new" since its inception in the 1980s; one best-selling book from 1993 by Ken Pimentel and Kevin Teixeira titled *Virtual Reality: Through the New Looking Glass* is echoed in similar language over 20 years later, such as a 2015 article in the *New York Times*, "A Virtual Reality Revolution, Coming to a Headset Near You." The application of VR at Barnard College, via 360-degree video, is through the capture and creation of "three-dimensional realities" experienced through a VR headset or cardboard viewer; this form and function reflects the VR definition from over 25 years ago.

Augmented reality (AR), as Ronald Azuma defines it, "allows the user to see the real world, with virtual objects superimposed upon or composited with the real world . . . AR supplements reality, rather than completely replacing it."[5] The widespread adoption of smartphones and mobile devices has allowed AR to become more accessible, and currently hundreds of AR mobile applications are available for Android and iOS, such as Augmented Car Finder (to help users find their car in a parking lot) or Google SkyMap (to identify stars, planets, and constellations based on phone location and camera). AR is increasingly used in several industries, such as the design, architecture, and construction fields, in order to visualize plans before execution.[6]

Subject areas that combine space, movement, and visualizations would seem a "natural" fit for AR/VR technologies, as they apply the affordances of these tools. Because dance and the performing arts involve space, movement, and visuals, there are many possibilities with AR/VR, especially when considering teaching and archiving. (Consider the possibilities of learning dance from another continent, such as 360-degree recordings from Africa or other locations, without needing to physically travel to those locations.) AR/VR is not widespread in dance education, but there have been some projects such as a pilot by Yan and colleagues using the tool OutsideMe (incorporating an Oculus Rift headset). Dancers wore head-mounted displays that created an "external self-image" so they had a 360-degree view of their own performances; dancers were also able to train with a virtual dance partner (either as a lead dancer or extra dancer).[7] Preliminary results demonstrated greater practice efficiency, where eight participants self-reported their dance practice efficacy as higher with OutsideMe as opposed to regular training. In another project incorporating AR/VR and performance, Mazzanti and colleagues introduced the concept of the "augmented stage," outlining metrics to create an interactive experience. The "augmented stage" allows audience members to perceive virtual objects superimposed with the performance stage, via their mobile devices; audience members also have the ability to input and manipulate information, real-time, which in turn contributes to the performers and the stage.[8]

Again, these are new and emerging technologies, and there is a dearth of literature in the research related to AR/VR and education, particularly in relation to higher education, libraries, dance, and the performing arts. This case study aims to contribute to the growing body of knowledge around VR/AR as it relates to these topics.

SETTING

Barnard College is a women's liberal arts school located in New York City. It is proximal to and a partner with Columbia University. Founded in 1889, Barnard remains an institution dedicated to women's education and advancement. There are approximately 2,500 undergraduate students, with 28 academic departments and 20 academic programs. The academic library, or Barnard Library and Academic Information Services (BLAIS), has a focus on certain collections, such as the Zine collection, and includes archives, as well as a personal librarian program where all undergraduate students and faculty are assigned a research and instruction librarian.

At BLAIS, there is a performing arts librarian as well as an Archives and Special Collections, which collects the history of dance at Barnard, as well as special collections relating to dance. Barnard collects dance materials at a research level for Barnard and Columbia; collection materials from the library and archives include books, periodicals, media, and other materials (such as paper programs). Barnard's institutional archival dance collections include documentation and recordings of the Dance Uptown series; special collections include the Gloria Fokine Dance Collection, and the American Ballet Theater and NYC Ballet programs, newsletters, and repertory notes. The Archives and Special Collections collects recordings of Barnard dance performances in digital and analog formats. These materials are accessible to researchers.

Instructional Media and Technology Services (IMATS) is a department within the organizational structure of BLAIS. The core purpose of IMATS is to use technology and media to serve research, instruction, and learning at Barnard. There are two units of IMATS: Audiovisual Technology Services (AVTS) and Instructional Media Services (IMS). AVTS offers audio and visual services, equipment, and operators for classrooms, conferences, lectures, and other campus events. IMS includes an equipment room that manages over 800 checkouts per semester; this is a service available to all Barnard and Columbia faculty, staff, and students (figure 8.1). The equipment room offers a wide range of video cameras (from handi-cameras to advanced 4k camcorders), audio equipment (shotgun microphones, Tascam recorders, XLR cables), lighting, digital cameras, projectors, screens, portable speakers, and other items. It is staffed by approximately 20 Barnard undergraduate student workers. IMS also fulfills video recording services for the college, producing over 100 videos each semester of events, classes, conferences, and so forth; this has led to several flipped classroom projects. Periodically there are more "produced" video projects that are scripted or documentary, at times including green-screen, animation, and other intensive post-production work.

IMATS works extensively with faculty, such as consulting on syllabi and curricula; utilizing Canvas (Barnard's learning management system); teaching workshops in courses on digital tools and software such as podcasting, Adobe Photoshop, or video editing; assisting with research data collection and analysis; and other types of projects. IMATS is uniquely positioned to test out and experiment with new educational technologies. This intersection of media equipment and digital production, instruction and research, and administrative staff and faculty members has led to fruitful cross-disciplinary projects, including the ones outlined below involving IMATS staff and the Barnard Department of Dance. Additional examples of cross-disciplinary collaborations include working with a German course on a unit for which students produced German soap operas (involving scripting, shooting, and editing); producing interactive videos with embedded quiz questions for a flipped classroom project with a chemistry professor; and teaching students how to create interactive maps and "walking tours" related to the Harlem Renaissance for an art history course.

Figure 8.1. One section of the Barnard IMS equipment room, which handles over 800 checkouts per semester. *Barnard College.*

PROJECT 1: BARNARD AUGMENTED (AR)

In 2014, the Barnard College Department of Dance offered a site-specific composition course that invited students to integrate archival research and AR technology in their choreographic processes. Conceived by Professor Paul Scolieri and performance-based artist Adam Weinert, the course asked students to select dance photographs from the college archives and interpret them in two-minute (125 seconds), site-specific compositions.

This project received internal funding from Barnard through a COOL (Committee on Online Instruction) grant. An external developer was hired using these funds, and through the customization of the open source Dance-tech app (hosted by the Aurasma platform), the Barnard Augmented app was created. Barnard Augmented allowed users to scan archival images located at specific locations on the Barnard campus, which made the dances associated with the site appear on the viewer's smartphone (figure 8.2). The project culminated in a multi-day event, "125 Barnard Dances," where students, alumni, and other guests were invited to participate in this AR project with the assistance of tour guides and audio guides. 125 Barnard Dances was part of broader campus

Figure 8.2. The Barnard Augmented mobile app, built on the open source Dance-tech app, licensed from Aurasma. *Barnard College*.

programming related to Barnard College's 125th anniversary, including readings, music performances, lectures, screenings, and other events.

Upon reflection, the Barnard Augmented project received positive qualitative feedback from viewers and students as to its creative approach and innovation. For example, in a video produced about the project, one student comments: "There's an interesting experience that happens being in a physical space and watching something that happened in that same space but at a different time, and in a slightly different context." The artist Adam Weinert offers, "It's a nice opportunity to both look back into Barnard's history but also bring it into the 21st century."[9] While no formalized assessments were conducted in relation to this project, staff members present during the 125 Barnard Dances event recollected how participants were engaged with a novel approach to a campus tour and viewing archival materials.

There were also constraints and limitations. Thorny questions arose while developing content, such as how does one choreograph for an iPhone, or what does it mean to adjust and experiment with scale and have performance shrink to such a small size. There were technical considerations: Will all participants have smartphones? Is the app compatible for both iOS and Android? Is the cellular or Wi-Fi network strong enough to stream the performance without lags, pauses, and crashes? There was also user-experience "friction" involved in the project, which included downloading the app, scanning the archival images (as one would scan a QR code) and, at the time of its implementation, the image-recognition capabilities of the software were imperfect. For example, the mobile phone had to be held very still over the image for the app to work properly; there were also delays between the scan time and the video loading time.

Dance and the performing arts are embedded in the history of Barnard College, and this AR project was interdisciplinary in its combination of dance, technology, and historical archives. Site-specific events—inherent characteristics of both dance and AR—call attention to a location, its histories, and other spaces, both real and imagined. This project invited the viewer to reflect on and interact with the history of Barnard College—the physical campus and institution, as well as students past and present (figure 8.3). There are many implications and possibilities with AR and archival materials, and this project brought images into conversations and wider circulations. It highlights the ways in which AR can link archives and inaccessible cultural heritage to broader audiences and spaces, and how historical archival material can be "brought to life" in new and innovative ways. The future potential for projects involving AR, archival materials, and the performing arts is compelling.

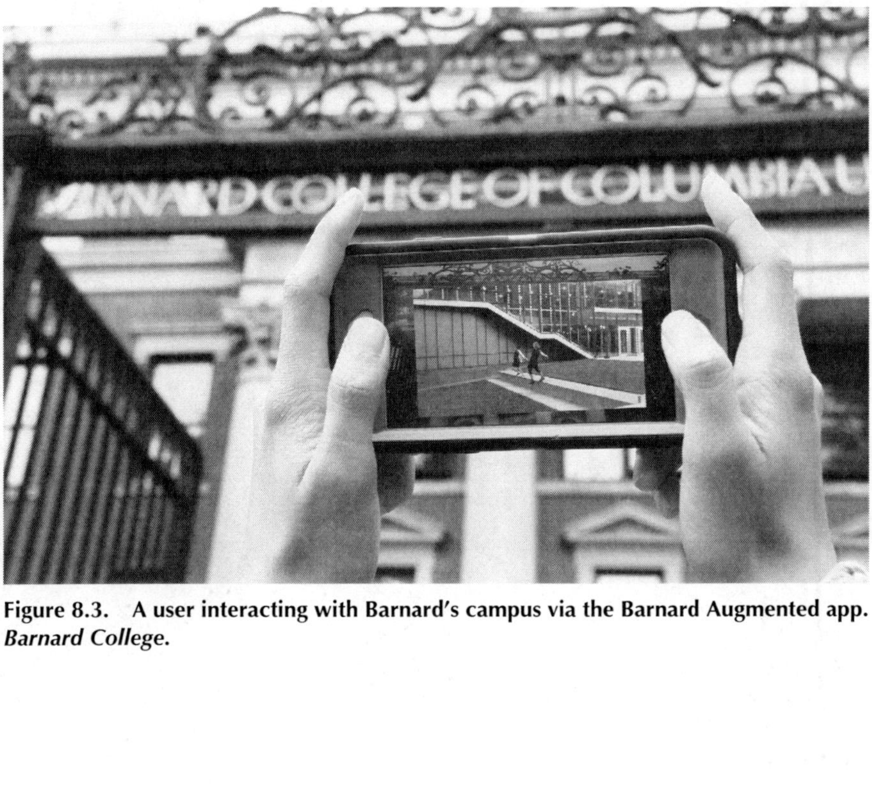

Figure 8.3. A user interacting with Barnard's campus via the Barnard Augmented app. ***Barnard College.***

PROJECT 2: VR/360 VIDEO

In fall 2016, IMATS and the Barnard Department of Dance collaborated on a VR/360 video pilot. We used a Ricoh Theta 360-degree camera, which is pocket-sized, lightweight, and relatively inexpensive (currently priced below $300). Our experience with this camera was that it was relatively easy to use; the recording function just entails an off/on switch (with no settings to customize white balance, frame rate, exposure, and so forth). The post-production process with 360-degree video includes "stitching" the footage from the two lenses together (figure 8.4), then running through a "spatial media metadata injector," and uploading to YouTube, which is free and supports VR/360 video. Viewers then use a VR headset (we had $15 cardboard viewers) (figure 8.5) with their mobile phone, and this creates an immersive experience in which viewers can look up, down, or in any direction and perceive a "3D" environment.

Barnard College offers a wide range of dance faculty, courses, and genres to students. This was an optimal context to try VR/360 video, and we were fortunate to have high levels of cooperation among faculty. We visited several different dance classes and student clubs, and recorded tap, ballet, modern dance, improvisation, classical Indian dance, hip-hop, ballroom, and other genres. We recorded dance warmups, showcased rehearsals, and improvised routines. The number of dancers in these recordings ranged from four to over twenty. We tested different angles with the 360-degree camera, and attempted various tripod positions, from elevated angles to low-to-the-ground perspectives. These videos all have their own qualitative value and textures, but through trial and error we decided our "best practice" for recording

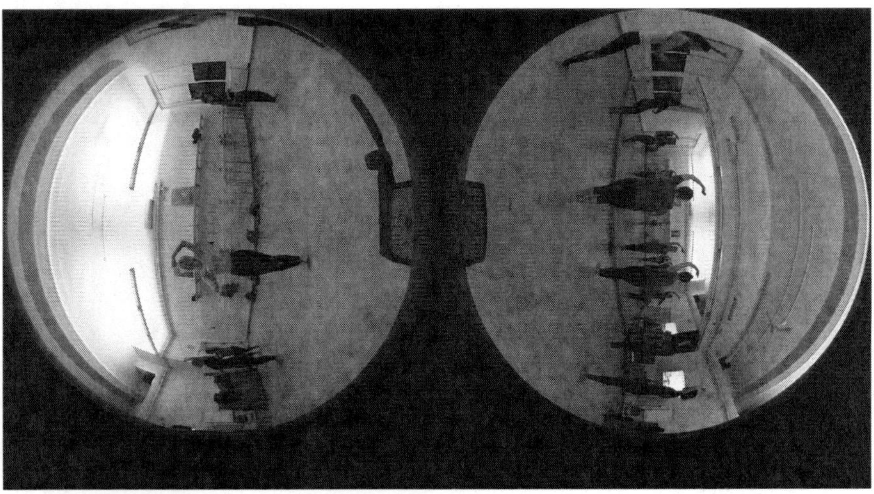

Figure 8.4. Raw footage of a dance rehearsal from a 360-degree camera, before it is stitched together and uploaded online. ***Barnard College.***

360-degree video of dance entails (a) positioning the camera in the center of the room, so that it is in the middle of the performance and at a slightly lower height than eye level, and (b) using a tripod (recording tests where participants danced while holding the camera led to dizzying footage).

We considered the VR/360 videos of dance footage to be exploratory, untied to measured outcomes. However, these recordings were used to review rehearsal performances for shows at New York Live Arts by the choreographers in order to gain additional feedback on which sections needed more practice. Because of the dynamic "3D" experience of 360-degree video, there are significant implications for the recording and notation of choreography. There are also implications for learning dance, and the ability to "see" dance and movement in a new way. With VR/360 video, the viewer is able to focus on specific dancers or on specific choreography—this is in contrast to "flat," two-dimensional video recordings.

At this point in time, there are certainly drawbacks. The technology is still "early" and low-resolution. VR/360 gives some people motion sickness.[10] The most technologically advanced virtual reality systems—even if powerful supplemental instructional tools—will never fully replace real-time, person-to-person instruction in dance. Yet there are many powerful affordances of this tool, which were evident from the earliest test shoots. First of all, there are documentary and archival implications of VR/360, especially considering all of the rich sensory details that are captured, some of which we might not even be cognizant of, and what value they might have for future generations to

Figure 8.5. A cardboard viewer for watching VR/360 video. *Barnard College.*

review. The immersive qualities of VR/360 can also offer transportive experiences; examples might include giving someone disabled or in a wheelchair the firsthand perspective of what it is like to ballroom dance, or expanding the livestreaming "portal" to dance performances such as the New York City Ballet and the American Ballet Theatre to audience members unable to afford a ticket. VR/360 video could also be used to help dancers rehearse choreographed routines, and could cut down on rehearsal times and/or rehearsal spaces. We plan to continue future projects and research regarding the instructional media aspects of VR/360 video and dance, especially as the technology continues to improve in terms of higher-resolution cameras and capture systems that allow for smoother and even more immersive experiences.

PROJECT 3: LED MOVEMENT SCALES

A third project example of using digital tools and media in dance research and performance is an LED Movement Scales project. Under the same thread as the VR and AR pilots, this endeavor used technology to capture and represent dance/movement in an original way. AR allows a viewer to access a dance recording in conjunction with an on-campus site and archival photographs; VR allows a viewer to experience a dance performance in a first-person, 360-degree perspective. While the LED images are more abstract, they visualize dance and movement in a provocative way.

This pilot was a collaboration between IMATS and Barnard dance faculty member Paul Scolieri, inspired by the "Visualizing Space Harmony" project (visualizingspaceharmony.com) led by Marie Percy, movement analyst and assistant professor in residence at the University of Connecticut. The LED Movement Scales was a test of long-exposure photography and light-painting video to capture movement scales based on the work of Rudolf Laban, a pioneer in modern dance. Laban created a movement theory and practice called Space Harmony or Choreutics.[11] Choreutics/space harmony scales follow sequential patterns, and end in the same place where they begin; principles of countermovement, parallelism, symmetry, and repetitions are at the core.

Students in Scolieri's movement analysis course were willing participants for this pilot. We were able to use a completely light-proof space in a production studio, and set up a DSLR (digital single lens reflex) camera with a manual, long-exposure photography setting. We also used the free iPhone app Pablo, which captures light-painting videos. The student dancers affixed LED gloves and bands around their wrists, arms, and legs; the lights varied in color, and some could be customized to flash at slow or fast intervals. One by one, students performed movement scales (ranging from 10 seconds to 45 seconds) (figures 8.6 and 8.7), which were recorded as still images and light-painted videos.

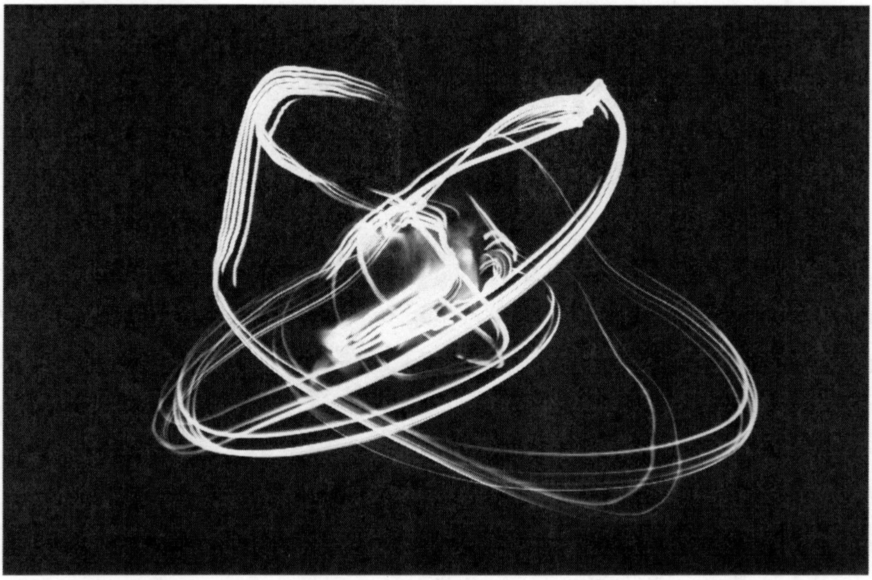

Figure 8.6. Long-exposure photograph of an LED movement scale, approximately 10 seconds. *Barnard College.*

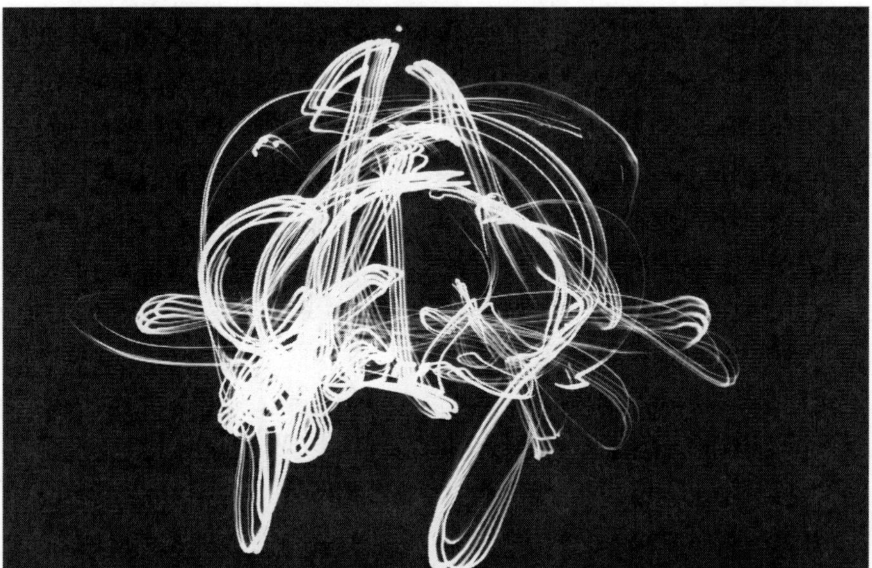

Figure 8.7. Long-exposure photograph of an LED movement scale, approximately 30 seconds. *Barnard College.*

The resulting full-color videos and images elicited positive responses based on anecdotal, firsthand experiences. This project generated interest among colleagues at the Columbia University library; there are current discussions for creating a similar project with sign language and possibly other forms of nonverbal communication. The LED photographs and videos also sparked interest with the Barnard development office and led to a collaboration on an LED light-painting video for a fundraising event.

This was a short-term pilot project, but these abstract "movement paintings" created during this session raised questions and implications. For example, is this technique allowing us to see something we might not see otherwise? If two dancers performed the same movements, but different images emerged, what implications might that have? Do these images reflect forms of dance notation, and could therefore be a record of choreography? Does the ability to visualize movements (such as space harmony scales) help students with the learning, comprehension, and performance of dance? While this pilot raises more questions than offers findings, it was something that led to cross-department partnerships. It was also a project that was an inexpensive undertaking, both in time and materials.

TAKEAWAYS

Here we summarize some of the main outcomes from three projects at Barnard College. These are not meant to be conclusive "results," but rather summations from these projects and suggestions for other institutions interested in implementing these tools or continuing further research into AR/VR applications.

- The three pilot projects were able to occur in an environment supportive of collaboration and experimentation.
- Augmented reality (AR) and dance are inherently site-specific, and there are affordances in the ways AR combined with dance can call attention to a location, its histories, and other spaces, real and imagined.
- VR/360 has implications for learning dance, and the ability to "see" dance and movement in a new way (e.g., the ability to focus on specific dancers or on specific choreography).
- AR and VR/360 currently have user experience friction considerations, such as app loading times and motion sickness.
- The LED Movement Scales project led to additional cross-campus collaborations.
- VR/360 Video and the LED Movement Scales projects were inexpensive in materials, time, and post-production.

AR/VR offers accessibility affordances and constraints. On one hand, there are limitations with AR/VR technologies for those who have visual impairments, and some AR applications may not be fully accessible to those with motor impairments. There are also financial barriers to entry in terms of equipment (such as mobile smartphone devices, headsets, headphones)—but libraries can mitigate this by offering equipment for patron checkout. This is something Barnard IMATS has been piloting, by adding 360-degree cameras and VR headsets to the equipment inventory, available for free checkout to all Barnard and Columbia patrons. As far as the learning curve for production and creation, VR in our context has proved to be quite accessible, with low barriers to entry for producing a VR/360 video. Conversely, AR in our context was fairly complicated to produce and required outside development assistance.

More broadly, VR has implications for accessibility, as it offers immersive experiences of other environments. This is an affordance that sets it apart from other technologies, and can offer engagement in new ways. As a basic example, users can experience a place that they would never have been able to visit, such as experience what it's like to be under a glacier in Antarctica. VR can open up spaces unavailable to those limited by economics or physical disabilities, such as what it's like to be scuba diving or what it's like to view dance performances in European theaters. This is not to offer a false equivalence between experiencing something firsthand and experiencing something via simulation, but this immersive potential is relevant for other fields, including journalism, geography, and the social sciences.

CONCLUSION

A collaboration between Barnard IMATS (Instructional Media and Technology Services) and Barnard dance faculty led to three projects involving the use of new technologies to record and engage with dance and the performing arts. A key factor for these projects was collaboration with the Barnard Library (of which IMATS is a part) and the Department of Dance. These would not have been possible without a supportive administration willing to try new tools and experiment in this realm (especially because some of these technologies are very recent and have no "best practices"). It is also of note that both the LED Movement Scales and VR/360 projects were not very costly.

These three projects included Barnard Augmented, an AR mobile application that was an interdisciplinary project involving historical archival college photographs and site-specific dance performances; VR/360 video, a pilot project where multiple dance courses and genres were recorded, offering an "immersive" record of performance; and time-lapse photographs and light-painting videos of LED movement scales. These projects offer qualitative support that AR/VR has significant affordances in relation to the teaching, learning, and scholarship around dance and the performing arts, and that, as these tools continue to improve and proliferate, more opportunities will surface for future applications. Nothing will replace physical presence, especially in relation to dance, and there is no "one way" to learn the performing arts, but movement-based activities offer interesting possibilities with virtual and augmented reality.

NOTES

1. C. M. Christensen, S. Aaron, and W. Clark. "Improving Higher Education through Disruption."
2. David R. Johnson, "Technological Change and Professional Control in the Professoriate."
3. New Media Consortium, *The Future of Higher Education: How Technology Will Shape Learning.*
4. Jeremy N. Bailenson et al., "The Use of Immersive Virtual Reality in the Learning Sciences: Digital Transformations of Teachers, Students, and Social Context."
5. Ronald T. Azuma, "A Survey of Augmented Reality," 356.
6. Hung-Lin Chi, Shih-Chung Kang, and Xiangyu Wang. "Research Trends and Opportunities of Augmented Reality Applications in Architecture, Engineering, and Construction."
7. Shuo Yan et al., "OutsideMe: Augmenting Dancer's External Self-Image by Using a Mixed Reality System."
8. Dario Mazzanti et al., "Augmented Stage for Participatory Performances."
9. "125 Barnard Dances."
10. Seizo Ohyama et al., "Autonomic Responses During Motion Sickness Induced by Virtual Reality."
11. Rudolf Laban, *The Language of Movement: A Guidebook to Choreutics.*

BIBLIOGRAPHY

"125 Barnard Dances," Barnard College. Accessed May 3, 2017. https://barnard.edu/events/125-barnard-dances. Azuma, Ronald T. "A Survey of Augmented Reality." *Presence: Teleoperators and Virtual Environments* 6, no. 4 (1997): 355–85.

Bailenson, Jeremy N., Nick Yee, Jim Blascovich, Andrew C. Beall, Nicole Lundblad, and Michael Jin. "The Use of Immersive Virtual Reality in the Learning Sciences:

Digital Transformations of Teachers, Students, and Social Context." *Journal of the Learning Sciences* 17, no. 1 (2008): 102–41.

Chi, Hung-Lin, Shih-Chung Kang, and Xiangyu Wang. "Research Trends and Opportunities of Augmented Reality Applications in Architecture, Engineering, and Construction." *Automation in Construction* 33 (2013): 116–22.

Christensen, C. M., S. Aaron, and W. Clark. "Improving Higher Education through Disruption." *The Internet and the University: 2001 Forum* (2002): 19–44. https://www.educause.edu/ir/library/pdf/ffpiu013.pdf.

Johnson, David R. "Technological Change and Professional Control in the Professoriate." *Science, Technology, and Human Values* 38, no. 1 (2013): 126–49.

Laban, Rudolf. *The Language of Movement: A Guidebook to Choreutics*. New York: Plays, Inc., 1966.

Manly, Lorne. "A Virtual Reality Revolution, Coming to a Headset Near You." *New York Times*, November 15, 2015. https://www.nytimes.com/2015/11/22/arts/a-virtual-reality-revolution-coming-to-a-headset-near-you.html.

Mazzanti, Dario, Victor Zappi, Darwin G. Caldwell, and Andrea Brogni. "Augmented Stage for Participatory Performances." *Proceedings of the International Conference on New Interfaces for Musical Expression*, 29–34. NIME, 2014. http://www.nime.org/proceedings/2014/nime2014_413.pdf.

New Media Consortium. *The Future of Higher Education: How Technology Will Shape Learning*. 2008. https://www.nmc.org/pdf/Future-of-Higher-Ed-(NMC).pdf.

Ohyama, Seizo, Suetaka Nishiike, Hiroshi Watanabe, Katsunori Matsuoka, Hironori Akizuki, Noriaki Takeda, and Tamotsu Harada. "Autonomic Responses During Motion Sickness Induced by Virtual Reality." *Auris Nasus Larynx* 34, no. 3 (2007): 303–6.

Pimentel, Ken, and Kevin Teixeira. *Virtual Reality through the New Looking Glass*. Blue Ridge Summit, PA: Windcrest, 1993.

Yan, Shuo, Gangyi Ding, Zheng Guan, Ningxiao Sun, Hongsong Li, and Longfei Zhang. "OutsideMe: Augmenting Dancer's External Self-Image by Using a Mixed Reality System." In *Proceedings of the 33rd Annual ACM Conference Extended Abstracts on Human Factors in Computing Systems*, 965–70. New York: Association for Computer Machinery, 2015.

9

Gotta Catch 'em All

A Case Study about Cal Poly Pomona's Pokémon GO AR Orientation

Kai Alexis Smith and Paul R. Hottinger

We all struggle with engaging students in learning about an academic library and its services. Students are busy. Dana Ingalls states that "students also expect to be able to access most information online and may be unable or unwilling to attend in-person orientation sessions."[1] At Cal Poly Pomona (CPP), we capitalized on the popularity of Pokémon GO by developing a Pokémon GO Augmented Reality (AR) Library Orientation to engage students by using new technology and introducing them to the library space and services. This orientation model was built on an existing paper-based scavenger hunt that is tied to the physical space of the library. The Pokémon GO AR Library Orientation enhanced CPP's library orientation with a new level of interactivity by using existing technologies and connecting the library to popular culture. In this chapter, we will outline why we chose augmented reality and some of the technologies used to create the AR experience, as well as discuss successes and challenges of the orientation. In addition, we will expand on the feedback and assessment from users during our library's Welcome Week and from students in our for-credit course LIB 150: The Information Diet.

CAL POLY POMONA

California State Polytechnic University, Pomona (Cal Poly Pomona), is located in Los Angeles County, 25 miles east of Los Angeles. The campus has approximately 24,000 students, but is predominantly an undergraduate institution (22,000). Cal Poly Pomona consists of eight academic colleges and offers more than 100 degree programs, including undergraduate, graduate, doctoral, credential, and certificate programs.[2] Ranked as one of the best public universities in the western United States, Cal Poly Pomona provides a rich academic experience that encourages hands-on learning in every program, course, and activity on campus.[3] The Cal Poly Pomona University Library (CPP Library) serves approximately 8,000 visitors per day houses more than 2.4 million items, including books, microfilm, maps, periodicals, e-books, online journals, and databases.[4]

LITERATURE REVIEW

Our Pokémon GO AR Library Orientation is in line with the Academic and College Research Libraries (ACRL) Framework for Information Literacy for Higher Education through the frame "Searching As Strategic Exploration."[5] This frame is about the nonlinear and iterative way required to evaluate a range of information sources, and the mental flexibility to pursue alternate avenues as new understanding develops.[6] Students understand the scope of the tasks at hand in the introduction to the Pokémon GO AR Library Orientation. Throughout the orientation, students have to make decisions and problem-solve to match information needs and search strategies to appropriate search tools and locations in the library, as each clue after an activity builds on the other. Students have to complete activities within the orientation at Pokestops that help them explore and search for information. For example, at one Pokestop, the students must search the catalog to find a book that will lead them to their next Pokestop. The clues scaffold learning through activities and help students think about the library space and explore its resources, which puts the library resources in context. The post-tests and in-class feedback reflect the fact that students who completed the AR library orientation learned to identify experts when seeking guidance, were flexible and creative while searching for the next location, developed stronger communication skills while working in teams, and realized that the information sources the library offers vary greatly.

Augmented reality orientation and gaming is not new to libraries, and has been used locally and abroad to enhance learning and change perceptions of the library. In 2011 in Taiwanese elementary schools, Chih-Ming Chen and Yen-Nung Tsai developed the augmented reality library instruction system (ARLIS) to provide students with library instruction education that is often not planned due to limited budgets.[7] By developing ARLIS, students benefited from enhanced learning motivation and performance.[8] In 2014, stateside, Beth Ebenstein Mulch worked with a team at her high school and recorded videos to create an augmented reality library orientation using Aurasma. Mulch incorporated the work of drama students into her orientation.[9] The augmented reality library orientation changed students' perceptions of the library and engaged them. Mulch described the orientation as having "changed students' vision of the school library space from a boring place to a surprisingly fun and cool place to hang out."[10]

Libraries have provided various ways of using augmented reality to support their mission and promote resources and services. A recent project by Yan Lu and Joseph T. Chao from Bowling State University, and Kevin R. Parker from Idaho State University, provided a creative approach to the traditional library scavenger hunt. Using Apple's iOS mobile platform, their prototype "HUNT" AR mobile game was designed to explore learning opportunities through an orientation activity in a university environment.[11] The HUNT mobile game would give users a list of objects that they would have to search for throughout the library. When a user found a listed object, a video or image would display on the screen. Different point values were given to different objects. At the end of the scavenger hunt, a summary and tally of points were displayed to the user. The library determined that their traditional library tour needed to be more interactive and engaging. The library concluded that the HUNT mobile game improved student experiences in a common aspect of their university environment, and increased both their enjoyment and their retention by making learning more memorable.[12]

Going beyond libraries, museums have embraced augmented reality and have woven AR into their orientations and public tours. Marco Mason explained how MIT has incorporated Google Glass and AR software to enhance the user experience when viewing objects on display in the robotics lab. For example, when users wearing Google Glass would look at the Kismet robot, they were presented with options for various facial expressions. These 4- to 5-second videos showed how the robot reacted to the voice of a person "speaking" with it in order to engage people in natural and expressive face-to-face interaction.[13]

WHY AUGMENTED REALITY

Like most libraries, the CPP Library had an activity for students to complete, which oriented them to the library space and resources. This activity was traditionally tied to Welcome Week, the first or second week of the fall quarter. Welcome Week is a week-long event organized by the CPP Library. Students are invited to participate in activities, panels, presentations, and a scavenger hunt to become oriented to the library. The orientation was developed to simply help students become more familiar with the physical library service points. The library orientation involved a passport system in which the students visited "stations" in the library and listened to a summary of services at the locations from library staff or student assistant. At each "station," the student would get a stamp. When all the stamps were collected from every "station" in one passport, the student would turn it in, to be entered into a raffle for prizes.

The passport game had high participation. However, we could only offer it when library staff were available, which limited the opportunities for students to participate. In addition, not all students would actually learn from each stamp on their passport. We found that if large groups of students gathered at a station all at once, the staff would speak to the crowd and stamp all of the passports at the same time. Unfortunately, not all students would stay to listen to the whole description of services offered at each location. To help remedy this and create a more interactive experience, we began investigating how to create an orientation that students would be able to complete on their own, whenever the library was open, involving technology to which most students readily have access, and providing an active learning opportunity. In addition, we wanted to expand the original library orientation's learning objectives to include scaffolded learning through hands-on activities that involved problem-solving. The final learning objectives for the Pokémon GO AR Library Orientation include:

1. The student will learn about the resources the library can offer and become more familiar with the layout of the building.
2. The student will learn to navigate One Search and locate a book using the Library of Congress call number in the library.
3. The student will be able to identify three library services.
4. The student will learn about the technology assistance they can receive.
5. The student will learn about the services of the Learning Resource Center.

TECHNOLOGY SELECTION

We chose to use Aurasma because of the success the librarians had at the University of Houston Downtown (UHD), where they used Aurasma in a Clue-themed scavenger hunt.[14] Aurasma is a free app that can convert everyday objects into videos. It is compatible with both iPhones and Android devices. The app seemed easy to use, and we built off the successes and noted the challenges the UHD librarians faced. Because we are a state institution in California, we have limited access to the technology that the UHD librarians had, such as Adobe Interactive to create videos. We decided to work with what we could access. The technologies we decided to use included Aurasma, Microsoft PowerPoint, Snagit, and YouTube. All of the technology we decided to use was accessible through the university or available for free.

Snagit

Creating the actual videos for the orientation was one of the most complicated and time-consuming aspects of the project. However, before we could actually record our videos, there were some pre-production steps that needed to be accomplished. The first step was to write a script. Preparing a script was crucial because it allowed us to develop an actual narrative for the videos that would cover all of the material we wanted to impart to our audience. Also, it ensured that when we recorded our videos, our narrative would sound more natural. Once the script was completed, we needed visual material to accompany the narrative. Microsoft PowerPoint was used to create a visual timeline for our narrative. This included pictures of the library, the relevant Pokémon for a Pokestop, and text. When we actually recorded the videos, we referred to cues strategically placed in our scripts to notify us when to move to the next slide. We practiced reading the script a few times with the PowerPoint slides before recording the videos. This helped us with production preparation and efficiency.

We needed a program that could capture and record our computer screens, as well as record audio from a microphone at the same time. After researching the available multimedia software on the market, we found many programs to consider. Some were free to use, such as Jing and CamStudio. However, these had some limitations, such as limited recording time. There were also commercial options such as Adobe Captivate and HyperCam, but the price point was not in our library budget. After consulting with our campus IT department, we found that CPP has a license with the software platform called Snagit, by TechSmith. Snagit is a complete software tool that allows for screen capturing and video recording from a desktop computer. Snagit also allows the user to record audio through a USB microphone. It is compatible with both Macs and PCs, and saves videos in standard MP4 format.

Snagit was very simple to use. When we launched Snagit, we were prompted to create a box around the area of our screen that we wanted to record. Drawing a box around our PowerPoint presentation prompted the recording option. After pressing record, we were given a 5-second countdown. After the countdown, recording began. Following the cues within our script, we were able to efficiently create our videos, with minimal retakes.

YouTube

CPP requires that any videos created for students must include closed captioning in order to be deemed accessible and compliant with the American Disabilities Act (ADA). We used YouTube to accomplish this. The first step was to upload our videos. We uploaded them to our Cal Poly Pomona

University Library channel. Once a video was uploaded, we selected the video within our channel and then clicked the closed-captioning logo underneath the video. This opens the video manager menu, which allowed us to add new closed-captioning text. There are a number of options that YouTube provides for adding closed captioning, which include "upload a file," "transcribe and auto-sync," "create new closed captions," and "buy closed captioned translation." We initially tried the "transcribe and auto-sync," but found that YouTube had a hard time translating our voices to text. Some of the words were not transcribed correctly, so the text did not completely match what we were saying in the video. To remedy this, we selected the "upload a file" option instead. This allowed us to upload our actual script, which YouTube would then sync with our video.

To make the transcript, we took our original script, which was saved as a Microsoft Word document, and converted it to a text (.txt) document. This was done by copying and pasting the text into Notepad and saving the file with a .txt extension. Once the .txt file was created, we uploaded the transcript, and YouTube automatically synced the video. It was important to watch the video in its entirety after this process. We found that some of the text had spacing issues. The solution to this problem was to go into the "edit closed captioning" option and alter the spacing within the text itself.

Once the closed captioning was inserted correctly, we needed to download the video. To download the video from YouTube, we used the Windows VLC media player. This created a separate MP4 video file with the video, along with the closed captioning, which we then uploaded to Aurasma.

Aurasma

Aurasma provides easy-to-implement instructions so that anyone can create augmented reality. First, an account must be created. We decided to create an account for the library called "CPP Library Go." Then, we initially took pictures of Pokémon that we printed out to be the Trigger Images for our Auras. Auras are original, user-created, online files accessible within the Aurasma app, which instructs the program to launch a specified video when a user overlays their mobile device on a specific image, also called a Trigger Image. The Trigger Images would act as Pokestops in the library. Once a student points his or her phone over the Trigger Image, the Aura appears on the screen and plays a recorded video. After realizing the strict image requirements for Auras, we worked with the library's in-house graphic designer to create more dynamic images for the orientation. This included creating Trigger Images of Pokémon with contrasting backgrounds in Adobe Photoshop. To help with this, our graphic designer decided on a lightning bolt in back of the Pokémon. After taking a picture of the new designed images, we created Auras by selecting an area, and dragging and resizing the box to create a mask. The mask is the point in the image where Aurasma will respond to and trigger the video. Next, the video is uploaded. We created names for the Overlays and Auras that corresponded with one another and the videos so that there was no confusion about which Overlay went with which Aura. There is an option to create a hashtag for Auras, but we decided not to use this feature since the students would not require alternative ways to discover the Auras in Aurasma. Our students were led to the next Aura by clues at the end of each video. Once these steps were completed, we tested our Auras.

After reading on message boards about some technical difficulties with numerous people using the app and Auras at the same time, we decided to let the students use the login we created to navigate the library with the app. This helped with use, but it opened us up to students possibly editing the Auras. This happened once by mistake; a student changed a video, but it was corrected quickly.

CASE STUDY

We tested the game in two environments: during Welcome Week, and in a controlled classroom environment, a for-credit course titled LIB 150. In order to play the Pokémon GO AR Library Orientation, we printed the Pokémon images we designed with our in-house graphic designer and posted them in key locations throughout the library to represent Pokestops. We secured permission from library administration before adding the printouts to the walls, as there are strict rules on the library appearance. We used painter's tape to temporarily secure the Pokémon images to the walls. For Welcome Week, we decided to leave all of them on the walls all week. However, when students began playing the game, we discovered that the Pokestops were being removed and/or stolen in the evenings/nights. The two Pokestops that were missing were rather popular Pokémon characters: Jigglypuff, and Jesse and James. We replaced the two Pokestops and had student workers check on them when they did their rounds of the floors. After the first incident, only one was consistently removed every night during Welcome Week. This was Jesse and James, which was located in the 24-hour computer lab. The computer lab is not an area that the student workers are required to observe, and we do not have the budget to hire a student worker to guard the Pokestop all day. We did check on the Pokestop each morning, and if the Jesse and James picture was stolen, we would print out another and replace it. This was tiresome, but necessary for the students to complete their quest. After Welcome Week ended, we removed all the Pokestops from the walls throughout the library.

When we conducted the game within a controlled classroom, we decided to put the Pokestops up only during the class time for two hours. In the winter and spring quarters of 2017, three classes completed the orientation. However, in one of the classes, the same incident occurred: the Jesse and James Pokestop in the 24-hour computer lab was once again removed/stolen. This prevented the students from completing the orientation. We developed a few plans to remedy this issue. This included placing the Jesse and James Pokestop out in a hard poster holder and attaching it to the glass window and, for classroom AR library orientations, a student worker was tasked with sitting in the room to observe whether it was removed and, if so, how.

Another issue we discovered was that some of the students were not able to download the Aurasma program on their phone. We discovered that some phones had issues connecting to the library Wi-Fi. Students did try downloading Aurasma over their 4G data service, but they were having trouble getting a sufficiently strong signal in our computer lab as well. Another problem reported was buffering issues when playing the videos in the library. If the Wi-Fi connection became too slow, the video would buffer. Some students had more buffering issues than others, but they informed us that it didn't last very long and was not a serious issue that would hinder them from completing the orientation. Perhaps retooling the Pokestops to be closer to Wi-Fi hotspots would help reduce the buffering or dropped connections.

Noise and interruptions to library services and students studying were a concern when developing the orientation. To help remedy this, most Pokestops were developed on floors not designated as "quiet floors." These floors include those where our service desks are located and those containing open areas with many tables for group work and discussion. During our trial of the orientation, we found that any noise from students conducting the orientation would not interrupt our regular library services or students collaborating on these floors. Only one Pokestop was on a designated "quiet floor." However, we made sure that the Pokestop was far enough from any study carrels to minimize any noise that might interrupt individual students studying.

LibGuide

To assist students with navigating the app and learning how to play the game, we created a LibGuide. A LibGuide is an online content management system used by libraries to organize subject-specific resources and to create and manage websites.[15] The purpose of the LibGuide for the Pokémon GO AR Library Orientation was to provide step-by-step images and instructions on how to download, log in, and use the app, and the instructions for playing the game, as well as a place where students could complete the activity form and the pre- and post-tests (figure 9.1). Since not all students on campus have access to cell phones or have data plans, we created a paper version of the game that students

Figure 9.1. Screenshot of the LibGuide to support the Pokémon GO Library AR Orientation. *Cal Poly Pomona.*

can use to complete the orientation. There are also paper versions of the pre- and post-tests and the activity form. Since it can be completed in the library, once the students reached the end of the orientation they were required to find an available computer and fill out the forms in the LibGuide.

In-class Pilot

Our librarians teach a for-credit course titled LIB 150: The Information Diet. In this course, open to undergraduates, students learn about literacy skills for academic success and how to use and produce information effectively and ethically. To help acquaint the students with the library and orient them to our services, we had the LIB 150 students complete the Pokémon GO AR Library Orientation. Assigning the orientation to the LIB 150 students and dividing them into small groups allowed them to work together and get to know one another on the first day of school.

Each student in the LIB 150 course began by accessing the Pokémon GO AR Library Orientation LibGuide and completing steps 1 through 3, which included registration, pre-test, and setup of Aurasma on their smartphone. Before students left the classroom on their "journey," we had them form groups of five. We did not want all of the students watching and listening to the videos at the same time in the library. We were conscious of not disturbing students near Pokestops, especially since some were on quiet floors. The groups were staggered as they started their journeys so that each group would not be at the same Pokestop at the same time. When the groups returned from their journey, each student in the group was required to fill out the activity form on the LibGuide and complete the post-test. The entire process from start to finish took approximately 45 minutes for the students to complete.

ASSESSMENT

In order to measure learning, we developed a pre- and post-test to assess the students' prior knowledge about the library, and how it improved after the Pokémon GO AR Library Orientation. An activity form was also developed for completion while the student was engaged in learning during activities. This form gauged understanding of the videos, library space, and the instructions (figures 9.2 and 9.3).

Pokemon Go Library Orientation Activity Form

Fill out this activity form during or after you navigate the library orientation. You must complete this before the post test. This form must be completed in order to be eligible for the raffle.

* Required

1. **First AND last name (REQUIRED)** *

2. **CPP email address** *

3. **Where can you find course reserve books?** *
   Mark only one oval.
   - 4th floor Research Help Desk
   - First floor at the entrance
   - Second floor Circulation Desk
   - Second floor Faculty Reading Room

Figure 9.2. The Pokémon GO Library AR Orientation activity form. ***Cal Poly Pomona.***

4. **What iconic building can you see from the grand reading room?** *
Mark only one oval.

- Bronco Student Center
- Kellogg West
- CLA building
- Kellogg Mansion

5. **How many group study rooms are there in the library?** *
Mark only one oval.

- 10
- 105
- 56
- 44

6. **Where in the library can you go for assistance with research (floor and name of the place)?** *
Mark only one oval.

- 3rd floor Faculty Reading Room
- 1st floor Learning Resource Center
- 7th floor Circulation
- Second floor Research Help Desk

7. **What is in the display cases outside of special collections near the Huntley Gallery?** *
Mark only one oval.

- Star Wars display
- Pokemon Display
- The art of Soraya M. Coley
- Primary Sources from Special Collection and University Archives

Figure 9.3. The Pokémon GO Library AR Orientation activity form (2). ***Cal Poly Pomona.***

The data include students who participated in the scavenger hunt during Welcome Week and in the LIB 150 classes during the winter and spring 2017 quarters. A total of 69 students completed the registration form and 59 completed the post-test; that is an 85.5 percent completion rate. Since the LIB 150 students were required to complete the AR library orientation from start to finish as their first assignment, we attributed the 14.5 percent dropout rate to Welcome Week participants who did not complete the AR library orientation.

Before the students left class for the day, we interviewed them. We asked what they thought of the orientation and if they had any suggestions for improvement. Some of the responses we received included "I learned a lot more about the library"; "I liked the activity, it was easy to use"; "Some Pokestops were hard to find. The different elevators in the building made for some confusion"; and "I didn't know we could check out headphones, that's pretty dope!" All of the students were able to complete the orientation during our allotted class time with minimal issues.

CONCLUSION

Traditional paper-based, scavenger hunt–style library orientations have been very convenient to use for library staff. These are easy to develop and do not take a lot of time out of the work day. However, these orientations are not reaching the entire target audience of the library. Students use the library at different times. To truly reach the actual library clientele, an orientation must be available at all hours the library is open. Using augmented reality software such as Aurasma presents an opportunity to provide an interactive orientation to all of our students during all the hours the library is open. Students may not actually use a library service unless they have a reason to seek it out. The AR aspect of Aurasma allows students to learn about a library service, all while interacting with the physical domain of the service. Our past paper orientations brought students to the physical locations of the library services, but did not give them the opportunity to use the service. The interactive use of Aurasma in our AR orientation allows students to not only go to the library service but also experience it. Augmented reality gives us the chance to showcase each area and put in context how that library service will help students with their research needs. In addition, repackaging the library orientation with pop culture is a great way to help students identify and engage with library services. Elizabeth Burns and Sophie Brookover support this notion, explaining that "people are passionate about the aspects of pop culture that interest them most, and these topics can be a powerful lure into the library, not only for your supportive veteran users, but also for those elusive and tantalizing non-library-users."[16] While what is popular in culture can change, it is worth staying on top of trends and capitalizing on them to make library information more palatable for new students. Yes, this may take more time, but the engagement and getting students to connect with the library pay off in dividends.

Use of Aurasma for the Pokémon GO AR Library Orientation was effective for meeting our goals. While we found it rather easy to use, there were some technical difficulties, such as when creating our Auras. However, once we bridged that small learning curve, we found it to be a very easy process to move through. The success we had from this orientation will help us develop more opportunities for outreach. There is already a plan to create a generic AR library orientation that will be available on a regular basis. The Pokémon

GO AR Library Orientation met our learning objectives and allowed us to teach our students the critical services that we offer in our library. More important, our students had a positive experience with the library.

NOTES

1. Dana Ingalls, "Virtual Tours, Videos, and Zombies: The Changing Face of Academic Library Orientation," 83.
2. Cal Poly Pomona, "Academic Programs."
3. Cal Poly Pomona, "Cal Poly Pomona Overview."
4. Cal Poly Pomona, "About the Library"; Cal Poly Pomona, "Dean's Message."
5. ACRL Board, "Framework for Information Literacy for Higher Education."
6. Ibid.
7. Chih-Ming Chen and Yen-Nung Tsai, "Interactive Augmented Reality System for Enhancing Library Instruction in Elementary Schools."
8. Ibid.
9. Beth Ebenstein Mulch, "Library Orientation Transformation."
10. Ibid.
11. Yan Lu, Joseph T. Chao, and Kevin R. Parker, "HUNT: Scavenger Hunt with Augmented Reality."
12. Ibid.
13. Marco Mason, "The MIT Museum Glassware Prototype: Visitor Experience Exploration for Designing Smart Glasses."
14. Bethany Herman, Jovanni Lota, and Megan Hopwood. "Reduce, Reuse, Upcycle: Turning Interactive Instruction into Game-Based Camogogy."
15. Springshare, "LibGuides: Content Management and Curation Platform for Libraries."
16. Elizabeth Burns and Sophie Brookover, *Pop Goes the Library: Using Pop Culture to Connect with Your Whole Community*, 7.

BIBLIOGRAPHY

ACRL Board. "Framework for Information Literacy for Higher Education." Association of College and Research Libraries (ACRL), February 9, 2015. http://www.ala.org/acrl/standards/ilframework.

Burns, Elizabeth, and Sophie Brookover. *Pop Goes the Library: Using Pop Culture to Connect with Your Whole Community.* Medford, NJ: Information Today, Inc., 2008.

Cal Poly Pomona. "About the Library." Accessed May 9, 2017. http://www.cpp.edu/~library/about/about-the-library/index.shtml.

———. "Academic Programs." Accessed May 9, 2017. http://www.cpp.edu/~aboutcpp/calpolypomona-overview/academic-programs.shtml.

———. "Cal Poly Pomona Overview." Accessed May 9, 2017. http://www.cpp.edu/~aboutcpp/calpolypomona-overview/index.shtml.

———. "Dean's Message." Accessed May 9, 2017. http://www.cpp.edu/~library/about/about-the-library/dean-message.shtml.

Chen, Chih-Ming, and Tsai, Yen-Nung. "Interactive Augmented Reality System for Enhancing Library Instruction in Elementary Schools." *Computers and Education* 59, no. 2, (2012): 638–52.

Herman, Bethany, Jovanni Lota, and Megan Hopwood. "Reduce, Reuse, Upcycle: Turning Interactive Instruction into Game-Based Camogogy." Paper presented at the LOEX 2016 (Library Orientation Exchange), Pittsburgh, Pennsylvania, May 5, 2016.

Ingalls, Dana. "Virtual Tours, Videos, and Zombies: The Changing Face of Academic Library Orientation." *Canadian Journal of Information and Library Science* 39, no. 1 (2015): 79–90.

Lu, Yan, Joseph T. Chao, and Kevin R. Parker, "HUNT: Scavenger Hunt with Augmented Reality." *Interdisciplinary Journal of Information* 10 (2015): 21–35.

Mason, Marco. "The MIT Museum Glassware Prototype: Visitor Experience Exploration for Designing Smart Glasses." *Journal on Computing and Cultural Heritage* 9, no. 3 (2016): 1–28.

Mulch, Beth Ebenstein. "Library Orientation Transformation." *Knowledge Quest* 42, no. 4 (March/April 2014): 5–53.

Springshare. "LibGuides: Content Management and Curation Platform for Libraries." Accessed May 9, 2017. https://www.springshare.com/libguides/.

10

That E-book Smell

Curating for the Senses with AR/VR

Michael Ovens and Katie Mills

There is value in the physicality of a library's stacks, books, and journals, which has been lost in the ongoing transition from physical to digital corpora. The sensory experiences associated with a library's physical collections—the texture of a worn page, the location on a particular shelf, the smell of an old book—are both a source of pleasure and a support for learning through memory formation. Augmented and virtual reality (AR/VR), which has the potential to simulate a wide range of sensory experiences beyond the two-dimensional sights and sounds of conventional digital media, has the potential to re-engage future users with the physicalities of traditional collections while maintaining the enhanced accessibility of digital media.

This chapter will explore the ways in which multisensory AR/VR is already beginning to influence developments in digital publishing platforms, and how these new models of presenting and consuming information could impact libraries and library users into the future. In particular, it will focus on the potential for augmented and virtual reality to re-engage users in physical content, and the various roles that libraries might play in the facilitation and mediation of multisensory experience. Potential pitfalls—copyright, equitable access, and technical aptitude—will be discussed, as will new opportunities for collaboration and partnership.

MULTISENSORY MEDIA IN AR/VR

The ongoing transition from physical to digital corpora in libraries across the world has brought with it great benefits in terms of access and data-driven engagement, but it has come at a cost. One of the most visible drawbacks of this transition to digital media has been the "flattening" of different physical media into the singular digital text. Whereas print chapters create a sense of continuity through the spatial flow of its pages across various gatherings, and daily papers conjure a sense of importance through their enormous physical size, studies show that readers have difficulty identifying (or caring) about the difference between e-books, e-journals, and other electronic resources.[1] This may not matter for "born digital" materials, but when it comes to digitized print media, this is a cause for concern since reading (and, by extension, the production of media *for* reading) is a bodily act whose limitations and capacities shape the manufactured text.[2]

The desensitizing of digital media has created an additional problem by erasing the sensory clues used to create cognitive maps of written media. The sensory-motor properties of physical reading—grasp, orientation, olfaction—have been theorized and demonstrated to aid in the retention and comprehension of written information.[3] E-books and other forms of digital text, lacking these sensory-motor cues, appear to inhibit the formation of cognitive maps, which represent the spatial arrangement between objects in an environment.[4] It is little wonder, then, that users of e-books often read less than a chapter at a time and tend to print out those parts for which comprehension or retention is considered particularly important.[5]

Virtual reality has the capacity to roll back these digital shortcomings by simulating the multisensory practice of reading print media in a digital environment. A glimpse at what this might look like can be found in the user interface of the Internet Archive, a wholly digital nonprofit library headquartered in San Francisco, California. The Internet Archive's books, most of which consist of scanned images made searchable through optical character recognition (OCR), are displayed to the reader, two at a time, within a simulated folio whose pages turn back and forth and whose built-up fore edges are visible on either side of the current opening. Technologically speaking, it would be relatively simple to take these two-dimensional scans into AR/VR and give them three-dimensional presence through the simulation, rather than merely the representation, of a book's thickness and the rustling of its pages as they turn. With a little more work, it should be possible to simulate a book's weight, texture, and even its smell.[6] These developments would help to reproduce some of the sensory "hooks" on which hang the comprehensive, retentive, and contextual capacities of traditional print-based reading, while preserving the ease of access and machine engagement made possible by digital publication.

AUGMENTED AND VIRTUAL LIBRARIES

Alternatively, libraries and other institutions might choose to make the most of their existing physical collections by overlaying real-world objects with digital data. As with the wholly digital Internet Archive's use of virtual folios, there exist already examples of real-world libraries using augmented reality to overlay physical collections with digital data. Two of the most common uses of augmented reality are to aid in the location and identification of physical collections, as with the United Kingdom's 2014 Mythical Maze app for children, and to enhance two-dimensional pages with three-dimensional audiovisuals, as with the mixed-media "Wonderbook: Book of Spells" designed for use with the Playstation 3. This use of "sensory-native" media—representing space, for example, in three dimensions rather than a two-dimensional image or a linguistic description—has been shown to provide external support for cognitive processing and to increase the subjective enjoyment of readers. This has the potential to broaden the appeal and engagement of reading for individuals with learning or processing difficulties, such as children with attention deficit hyperactivity disorder (ADHD).[7]

As one of the primary providers of access to e-books and other digital resources, libraries have a key role to play in the development of digitized multisensory reading. Libraries are, for many, deeply aesthetic spaces. Few have described the sensory experiences associated with these spaces more elegantly than essayist and bibliophile Alberto Manguel, who described how important it is for him to "see and touch the pages, to hear the crinkle and the rustle of the paper and the fearful crack of the spine, to smell the wood of the shelves, the musky perfume of the leather bindings, [and] the acrid scent of my yellowing pocket books" before retiring to sleep.[8] The audiovisual sensations of the library, in particular, have been reproduced in exquisite detail in the Quebec exhibition "La bibliothèque, la nuit," a virtual reality collaboration between Manguel and the actor-director Robert Lepage. Using a head-mounted display (HMD) in a seated configuration, participants visit a series of ten libraries, including the U.S. Library of Congress, the lost Library of Alexandria, and the National Academic Library of Sarajevo, Bosnia. Although many of the libraries featured in the exhibition are still in active service, their digital representations are for the most part "dead"—that is to say, their books can be seen on the shelves but cannot be borrowed, existing only "for the acoustics and the ambience."[9]

One potential future for the library as a digital space would see the development of "living" digital libraries through implementation of "themes" or "skins," in which the shelves and books of a digitized fabricated library are connected to the catalog and holdings of a user's local institution. Such skins could come pre-sorted, with each shelf designated a particular role or set of holdings, or they could be customizable based on a user's preferences, putting either romance or Roman history within arm's reach from the moment a user logs in. Users would navigate such a library either in the traditional manner, "walking" from place to place and browsing collections at will, or they could conduct a catalog search and be transported directly to an item's location. Having located an e-resource's location (there's no reason why, in such a model, "born digital" media could not be placed on digital shelves), users could read the resource within the virtual library or they could "check it out" by downloading the files as a traditional e-book or PDF to be read on a flat screen or as a printout.

Within this future, it may be desirable to restrict (or encourage) access to an institution's repositories through its "native" skin, in which the digitized books are shelved in locations corresponding to their real-world counterparts. London's Warburg Institute Library, for example, is divided spatially into the categories of Image, Word, Orientation, and Action, an arrangement designed to reflect founder Aby Warburg's understanding of the narratives of human development as expressed through art, which are lost when accessed through modern random-access retrieval systems.[10] Archival collections, too, could benefit from access through a native skin corresponding to their circumstances of origin. The British Library's Cotton Manuscripts are famously categorized according to their proximity to busts of the Twelve Caesars and two Imperial Ladies; sorting digitized versions of these manuscripts into a digitized reconstruction of the Cotton Library could prove a useful educational tool for students learning about practices of archival discovery and curation.

Moving beyond these spatial sensations, the use of native skins may help in understanding the acoustic, haptic, and olfactory sensations of historical libraries. Although twentieth-century libraries had a reputation for silence, historically (as today) it was often the case that libraries were hubbubs of gentle activity and stimulation.[11] The development of multisensory library spaces in which readers could immerse themselves in the habits and surroundings of past societies would open up new avenues for research and public engagement in the experiential worlds of the past.

HARDWARE, ACCESS, AND EXPERTISE

In recent years, libraries have begun to adopt AR and VR to augment library orientation materials and engage users in library resources, among other activities.[12] However, before simulated books and libraries that provide true multisensory experiences become widespread and the benefits can be realized, there are a number of technical and support challenges that must be overcome.

One of the primary barriers to the development of multisensory experiences is access to high-end virtual reality devices. Devices like the HTC Vive and the Oculus Rift, which are costly in their own right, require a powerful computer in order to operate; according to one estimate, less than 1 percent of the world's personal computers currently have the capacity to support such a virtual reality device.[13] This barrier is likely to decrease as stand-alone and low-spec headsets, like the Windows Mixed Reality Headset, are made available for the masses.[14] Libraries, as key players in fostering digital inclusivity within their communities, are well positioned to extend their existing offerings (3D printers, digital single-lens reflex cameras, laptops, etc.) by providing high-end AR/VR devices for loan or on-site use. Such devices will, however, require justification to administrators who may see the technology as a novelty or passing fad.

One of AR/VR's key selling points is its capacity to facilitate access for individuals with disabilities. It is a core policy of many libraries that services are equally accessible and available to all users, and that crucial services and infrastructure such as screen-reading programs, talking books, and braille texts be provided for individuals with disabilities. In the United States, for example, the American Library Association's Purchasing of Accessible Electronic Resources Resolution strongly recommends that libraries ensure that vendors and service providers comply with WCAG 2.0 or other widely accepted standards of accessibility when purchasing, procuring, and contracting electronic resources.[15] Existing head- and eye-tracked virtual reality devices can offer new freedom to individuals with limited mobility by allowing them to navigate space and information without the use of their hands or feet, while augmented reality devices can bring screen-reading technologies to large-print paper texts. Such devices remain, however, deeply visual in their approach, limiting the engagement of visually impaired individuals. Moving to a multisensory framework, whereby not only sight but also touch can be simulated at a consumer or enterprise level, would help to maintain equitable access to these technologies.

Access to equipment alone, however, is only part of the problem; as Bricken notes, "VR is a new information medium, and like any media, can be used to disseminate propaganda, advertisement, and misinformation."[16] As with print and other digital media, users need to learn how to apply new or existing critical-thinking skills to this new medium. Libraries have traditionally been key players in the development and provision of information literacy education and, in recent years, this has expanded to include digital literacy.

A further expansion of these programs and activities could see libraries providing virtual literacy skills training to their communities. This could include topics such as how to navigate, interact with, and interpret experiences in VR and AR, and the need to think critically about the virtual environments, objects, and texts the user encounters.

Although the use of a VR/AR HMD is relatively straightforward for the general user, a far larger learning curve exists in AR/VR app development. Some public libraries already offer workshops in new technologies and digital skills such as robotics and coding, and both public and academic libraries are beginning to provide spaces and facilities for their communities to come together and teach/share skills through makerspaces and digital labs.[17] These spaces and programs are the perfect setting to introduce people to 3D engines and the basics of app development. This could be achieved through collaboration between libraries and AR/VR developers, who might be able to use the space and equipment and test new apps on library users in return for sharing their skills and time.

PRESERVATION, COPYRIGHT, AND INTELLECTUAL PROPERTY

The use of virtual reproductions of physical items in simulated books and libraries raises a number of questions around intellectual property and copyright. Most countries have copyright laws that grant a copyright owner the exclusive right to not only the dissemination of the original work but also the development of derivative works.[18] This has already created several problems in the neighboring field of game development, where existing copyright laws have been extended and applied to virtual works.[19] The "living" virtual libraries described earlier, in which readers can browse e-books in digital reproductions of physical libraries, may create similar issues to those faced by the publisher Ubisoft in developing Assassin's Creed: Unity, where the freedom of panorama limitations around architecture and sculptures in the French Code of Intellectual Property meant that the developers were unable to replicate the pipe organ at Notre Dame.[20] Some of these limitations might be avoided by using only public domain material, as done with the Chimera Reader's use of Project Gutenberg texts in a wholly virtual library environment, but a more sustainable solution incorporating copyrighted texts ought to be sought in conjunction with publishers and copyright holders.

Augmented reality interfaces, in which digital data is laid over existing texts, may pose fewer copyright challenges than wholly virtual reproductions and might therefore serve as a useful test case in navigating the copyright of virtual libraries. Unlike virtual reproductions, in which a derivative work is created, AR can use a physical object without reproducing in anything beyond the most technical sense, the image on the screen being transient and activated by interaction with a location or object. Caution has to be taken, however, when saving and retrieving elements associated with a copyrighted work; while the U.S. Copyright Act specifies that works must be "fixed in a tangible medium of expression" in order for copyright holders to be able to exercise their rights, AR works may infringe copyright if copyrighted elements from the original work are saved and capable of being retrieved/accessed at a later date.[21]

Once an AR/VR experience is developed, of course, it needs to be preserved if it is to be experienced in the future. Multisensory experiences, though overcoming many of the cognitive and retentive shortcomings of other digital media, pose unique challenges in this regard. The nature of augmented reality in particular means that it relies on users either being based at physical locations or having access to objects that have been overlaid with content. When it comes to location-based augmented reality, the experience cannot be created without the current maps or if the landscape changes. Compare this to holy texts produced over 1,000 years ago that are now held in libraries and museums across the world—a permanence that has led it to be said that "the printed book has a lifetime much greater than the best digital storage option, even though books are a technology many centuries old."[22] The long-term retention and reproducibility of these works needs to be considered.

Libraries may also need to invest in methods of recording the often-ephemeral performances and content produced within virtual worlds, such as the paintings created in Google's Tilt Brush or the sculptures created in Oculus's Medium. The answer to this might be in mixed-reality videos that stitch the virtual environment and the actual user and their movements together into one view. Preservation departments in libraries will need to collaborate with AR/VR developers on the development of mixed-reality capture, which could also be used to promote their software and apps.

Considering the preservation challenges around AR and VR works, it is perhaps ironic that libraries and other institutions may turn to these technologies for opportunities to preserve and provide access to at-risk print materials in their collections. Virtual texts that simulate the original work's weight, texture, and smell could provide a substitute in situations where the original book or manuscript is too valuable or fragile to handle or exhibit. For example, users might be able to turn a virtual page and feel the fragile parchment between their fingers without the worry of damaging the page with the oils from their skin. In this win-win solution, library users would be able to experience some of the sensory hooks of the original works rather than simply relying on a digitized scan online, and libraries would be able to bring their valuable treasures to a much wider audience while preserving the original.

CONCLUSION

Virtual reality, as experienced at the time of this writing, is a niche field that operates almost exclusively within the realm of auditory and visual sensation. It is, however, unlikely to remain this way for long. Collaborative projects, such as the re-creation of the Yellow House art collective in virtual reality at the University of Wollongong, and the Digital Playground at the State Library of South Australia during the 2016 Adelaide Fringe Festival, are just two examples of what is possible when libraries partner with researchers, community groups, and AR/VR companies and developers.[23] By providing equitable access, resources, and partnerships to publishers, content owners, educators, and developers, libraries will be able to ensure that they survive, and even flourish, in the brave new world ahead.

NOTES

1. Michael Levine-Clark, "Electronic Book Usage: A Survey at the University of Denver"; Wendy Allen Shelburne, "E-book Usage in an Academic Library: User Attitudes and Behaviors."
2. Thomas McLaughlin, *Reading and the Body*, 163–94.
3. Thierry Morineau et al., "The Emergence of the Contextual Role of the E-book in Cognitive Processes through an Ecological and Functional Analysis."
4. Liang-Yi Li, Gwo-Dong Chen, and Sheng-Jie Yang, "Construction of Cognitive Maps to Improve E-book Reading and Navigation."
5. Lesley Nelson and Frances O'Neil, "Electronic Monographs in the Academic Library: An Implementation Story."
6. Cecilia Bembibre and Matija Strlič, "Smell of Heritage: A Framework for the Identification, Analysis and Archival of Historic Odours."
7. Stefan Münzera, Tina Seufert, and Roland Brünkena, "Learning from Multimedia Presentations: Facilitation Function of Animations and Spatial Abilities"; Tim N. Höffler, "Spatial Ability: Its Influence on Learning with Visualizations—A Meta-Analytic Review."
8. Alberto Manguel, *The Library at Night*, 15–17.
9. Lepage originally used the term "dead" to describe the real-world Copenhagen Library, but it is equally applicable to the digitized libraries of the exhibition. Jeanette Kelly, "Robert Lepage Virtual-Reality Show Fetes 10th Birthday of the Grande Bibliothèque."

10. Katia Mazzucco, "Fritz Saxl: Transformation and Reconfiguration of Pagan Gods in Medieval Art."

11. William A. Johnson, *Readers and Reading Culture in the High Roman Empire: A Study of Elite Communities*, 4-9.

12. Daniel Ireton, Joelle Pitts, and Ben Ward, "Library Discovery through Augmented Reality: A Game Plan for Academics"; Beth Ebenstein Mulch, "Library Orientation Transformation."

13. Brian Blau et al., *Top 10 Strategic Technology Trends for 2017: Virtual Reality and Augmented Reality.*

14. Microsoft, "Windows Mixed Reality Headsets."

15. American Library Association, "Purchasing of Accessible Electronic Resources Resolution."

16. Meredith Bricken, "Virtual Reality Learning Environments: Potentials and Challenges,"183.

17. Matt Enis, "How to Speak Code"; Fangmin Wang et al., "The State of Library Makerspaces."

18. Daniel Gervais, "The Derivative Right, or Why Copyright Law Protects Foxes Better than Hedgehogs."

19. Ross A. Dannenberg et al., *Computer Games and Virtual Worlds: A New Frontier in Intellectual Property Law.*

20. Anne Lewis, "Assassin's Creed Unity—Notre Dame Wasn't Built in a Day."

21. Copyright Act of 1976, 17 U.S.C. § 102.

22. Barry Lunt et al., "Permanent Digital Data Storage: A Materials Approach."

23. Michael Organ et al., "3D Immersive Collection and Teaching Environments: The Yellow House Project at UOW"; Joshua Gliddon, "The Cube Appears as Fringe Festival and Google Dice with Virtual Reality."

BIBLIOGRAPHY

American Library Association. "Purchasing of Accessible Electronic Resources Resolution." Accessed May 10, 2017. http://www.ala.org/offices/sites/ala.org.offices/files/content/wo/reference/colresolutions/PDFs/electronicresources.pdf.

Bembibre, Cecilia, and Matija Strlič. "Smell of Heritage: A Framework for the Identification, Analysis and Archival of Historic Odours." *Heritage Science* 5, no. 1 (2017): n.p. doi:10.1186/s40494-016-0114-1.

Blau, Brian, Brian Burke, Samantha Searle, and David W. Cearley. *Top 10 Strategic Technology Trends for 2017: Virtual Reality and Augmented Reality.* Stamford, CT: Gartner Group, 2017. https://www.gartner.com/document/3645324.

Bricken, Meredith. "Virtual Reality Learning Environments: Potentials and Challenges." *Computer Graphics* 25, no. 3 (1991): 183. doi:10.1145/126640.126657.

Chheda, Timir. "Intellectual Property Implications in a Virtual Reality Environment." *John Marshall Review of Intellectual Property Law* 4, no. 3 (2005): 483–508.

Dannenberg, Ross A., Steve Mortinger, Roxanne Christ, Chrissie Scelsi, and Farnaz Alemi. *Computer Games and Virtual Worlds: A New Frontier in Intellectual Property Law.* Chicago, IL: American Bar Association, 2010.

Enis, Matt. "How to Speak Code." *Library Journal* 141, no. 3 (2016): 37–39.

Gervais, Daniel. "The Derivative Right, or Why Copyright Law Protects Foxes Better than Hedgehogs." *Vanderbilt Journal of Entertainment and Technology Law* 15, no. 4 (2013): 785–855. http://dx.doi.org/10.2139/ssrn.2233941.

Gliddon, Joshua. "The Cube Appears as Fringe Festival and Google Dice with Virtual Reality." *Traveller*. Accessed May 11, 2017. http://southaustralia.traveller.com.au/article/the-cube-appears-as-fringe-festival-and-google-dice-with-virtual-reality/.

Höffler, Tim N. "Spatial Ability: Its Influence on Learning with Visualizations—A Meta-Analytic Review." *Educational Psychology Review* 22, no. 3 (2010): 245–69.

Ireton, Daniel, Joelle Pitts, and Ben Ward. "Library Discovery through Augmented Reality: A Game Plan for Academics." *International Journal of Technology, Knowledge and Society* 9, no. 4 (2014): 119–28.

Johnson, William A. *Readers and Reading Culture in the High Roman Empire: A Study of Elite Communities.* Oxford: Oxford University Press, 2010.

Kelly, Jeanette. "Robert Lepage Virtual-Reality Show Fetes 10th Birthday of the Grande Bibliothèque." *CBC News*, October 27, 2015.

Levine-Clark, Michael. "Electronic Book Usage: A Survey at the University of Denver." *Libraries and the Academy* 6, no. 3 (2006): 285–99. doi:10.1353/pla.2006.0041.

Lewis, Anne. "Assassin's Creed Unity—Notre Dame Wasn't Built in a Day." *UbiBlog*. Accessed April 30, 2017. http://blog.ubi.com/assassins-creed-unity-notre-dame/.

Li, Liang-Yi, Gwo-Dong Chen, and Sheng-Jie Yang. "Construction of Cognitive Maps to Improve E-book Reading and Navigation." *Computers and Education* 60, no. 1 (2013): 32–39. doi:10.1016/j.compedu.2012.07.010.

Lunt, Barry, Matthew R. Linford, Robert Davis, Hao Wang, Douglas Hansen, and John Dredge. "Permanent Digital Data Storage: A Materials Approach." Paper presented at the 10th International Conference on Preservation of Digital Objects, Lisbon, Portugal, September 2013. http://purl.pt/24107/1/iPres2013_PDF/Permanent%20Digital%20Data%20Storage%20A%20Materials%20Approach.pdf.

Manguel, Alberto. *The Library at Night.* New Haven, CT: Yale University Press, 2008.

Mazzucco, Katia. "Fritz Saxl: Transformation and Reconfiguration of Pagan Gods in Medieval Art." In *The Routledge Companion to Medieval Iconography,* edited by Colum Hourihane, 89–104. London: Routledge, 2017.

McLaughlin, Thomas. *Reading and the Body.* New York: Palgrave Macmillan, 2015.

Microsoft. "Windows Mixed Reality Headsets." Accessed May 1, 2017. https://www.microsoft.com/en-us/store/collections/vrandmixedrealityheadsets.

Morineau, Thierry, Caroline Blanche, Laurence Tobin, and Nicolas Guéguen. "The Emergence of the Contextual Role of the E-book in Cognitive Processes through an Ecological and Functional Analysis." *International Journal of Human-Computer Studies* 62, no. 3 (2005): 329–48. doi:10.1016/j.ijhcs.2004.10.002.

Mulch, Beth Ebenstein. "Library Orientation Transformation." *Knowledge Quest* 42, no. 4 (2014): 50–53.

Münzera, Stefan, Tina Seufert, and Roland Brünkena, "Learning from Multimedia Presentations: Facilitation Function of Animations and Spatial Abilities." *Learning and Individual Differences* 19, vol. 4 (2009): 481–85.

Nelson, Lesley, and Frances O'Neil. "Electronic Monographs in the Academic Library: An Implementation Story." *LASIE: Library Automated Systems Information Exchange* 32, nos. 2/3 (Aug./Dec. 2001): 13–20.

Organ, Michael, Christopher Moore, Rebecca Daly, and Neil Cairns. "3D Immersive Collection and Teaching Environments: The Yellow House Project at UOW." Paper presented at VALA2016: Libraries, Technology and the Future, Melbourne, Australia, February 2016. http://vala.org.au/vala2016-proceedings/978-vala2016-session-16-organ.

Shelburne, Wendy Allen. "E-book Usage in an Academic Library: User Attitudes and Behaviors." *Library Collections, Acquisitions, and Technical Services* 33, nos. 2–3 (2009): 59–72. doi:10.1016/j.lcats.2009.04.002.

Wang, Fangmin, Weina Wang, Sally Wilson, and Namir Ahmed. "The State of Library Makerspaces." *International Journal of Librarianship* 1, no. 1 (2016): 2–16.

11

Wayfinding Narratives

Brian Sutherland

Wayfinding is an essential function of libraries. Libraries are, after all, collections of objects and information services in a physical building, arranged and indexed physically in wings and stacks and on floors, demarcated by signs and symbols, and curated by informed guides. If information access has a physical manifestation, it is in library places! Woven into the search for information is a patron's story, a quest for discovery, finding one's way in an area of interest. Educators call this confluence a "teachable moment"[1] in the sense that people are naturally and logically motivated to learn about a thing they are searching for. A prominent Internet search company ad quipped: "You know who wants a guitar? People searching for a guitar."[2] So it goes that augmented reality (AR), by overlaying *contextual* information on visual fields, is helpful—it is in possession, in part, of a patron's narrative by virtue of processing live sensory information from the same point of view. From that view, an AR application may intelligently filter the mass of information relative to spaces, signs, or physical resources (books, maps, art, multimedia resources) available—helping patrons "find their way."

In applying augmented reality to libraries, our aim has been to help patrons who are enabled by smart devices use these capabilities to be more effective in their information seeking. Nor does it hurt to amaze, amuse, and delight by adding to the unique media experiences libraries normally provide with vast collections of cultural artifacts, across many forms of human expression. Smart device capabilities include, as well, sensory capabilities well beyond patrons' abilities: GPS, motion adjustment, proximity sensing, hyperlinking, and telephony (speed dial), plus a constant connection to dynamic Internet data services, where anything from the exact time of day to the type of object within view might be queried. Augmented reality is a kind of contextually filtered living text, co-constituted as patrons and their devices interact with reality.

In this chapter we will explore three types of AR wayfinding projects. The first application involves geospatial narratives, where the objective was primarily to help patrons find library locations and information. The second involves augmenting individual library spaces, where the objective was to hyperlink signage to websites and contact information. The third involves introducing layers of augmented media onto traditional texts: augmenting book illustrations for interactivity and active learning.

GEOSPATIAL NARRATIVES: AR MAPS OF LIBRARY LOCATIONS

One of the first applications of augmented reality was geospatial; consequently, our first experiments involved location and profiling of a system of libraries in relation to an individual's current position—applying geographical context as a filter to generate a user-centric representation of a patron in relation to the library system. Toronto currently has 100 public libraries and an open data program that makes the global positioning system (GPS) location of each branch easy to find. While people typically go to their neighborhood branch, in the age of mass transit, why always visit the same library when there are so many to explore? This is particularly true in the case of orienting students to libraries—the aim is not just to know *the* library, but to discover what libraries have *in common* by means of cataloging (such as Dewey or LC classification), and *how they are different* by means of special aggregations, collections, and services (for example, the Merrill Collection of science fiction, speculation, and fantasy; Parkdale musical instrument loan program; or the Toronto Reference Library Makerspace).

Figure 11.1 is an illustration of the city public library AR application, constructed in an app called Layar. It has three views: augment, map, and directions. The first photo depicts a shopping mall with a circle augment that illustrates the direction and distance of a library. Nearby libraries show as large circles, with a logical reduction of size with distance, as with normal perspective viewing (figure 11.2). Tapping one of the circles brings up the current details of the branch, including hours and a general inquiry number on speed dial. Speed dial is very handy if you need to call about a popular resource, like borrowing a cello from the Parkdale branch. The convenience of ubiquitous smartphones with regard to AR is, in a sense, an extension of the convenience we discovered in ubiquitous cell phones.

Figure 11.1. AR view of a shopping center. Arrow illustrates small AR circle showing the Toronto Reference Library is 2.2 kilometers to the north. In the upper-right corner, a circle shows the local libraries within range of the patron. *University of Toronto.*

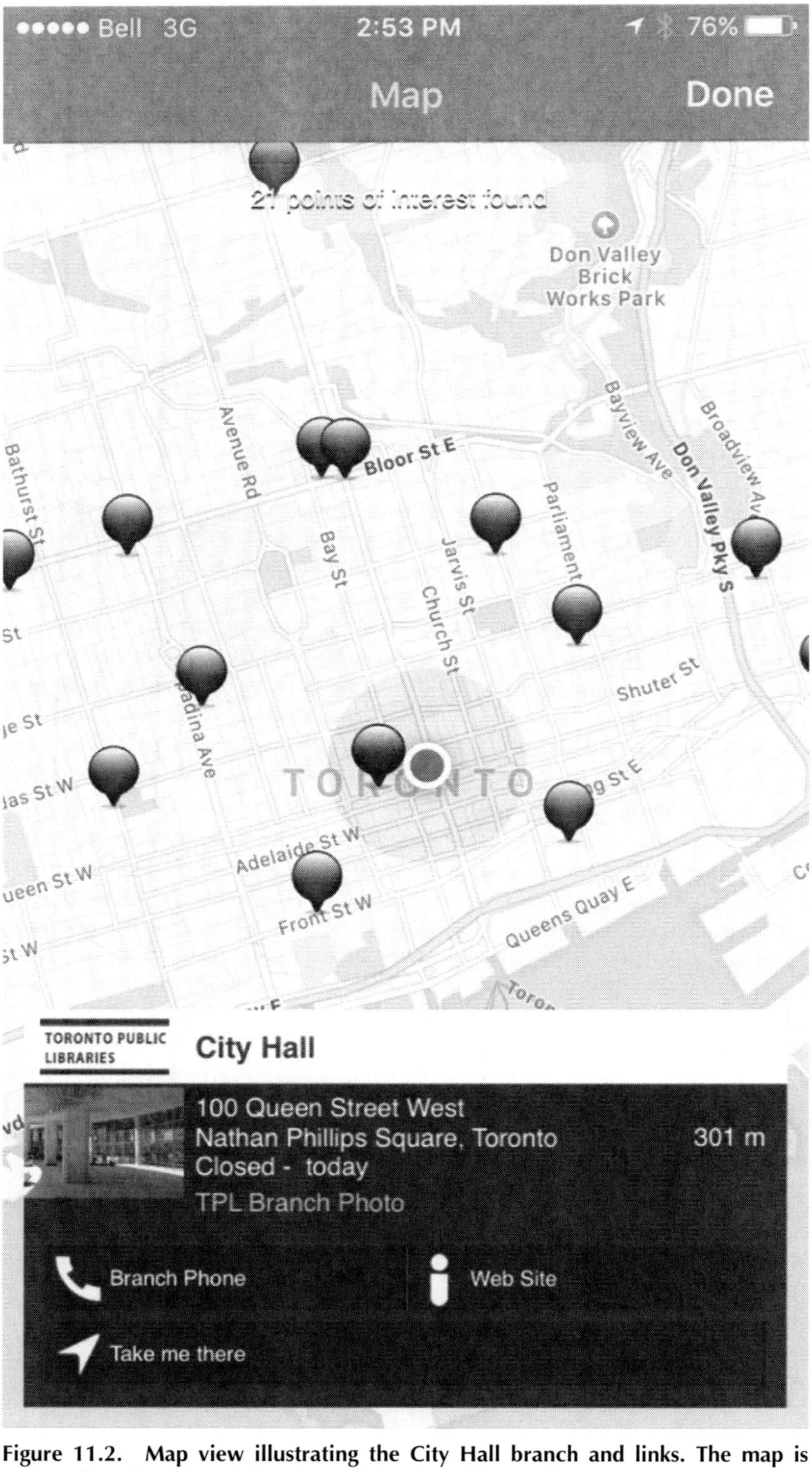

Figure 11.2. Map view illustrating the City Hall branch and links. The map is centered on the patron's location. *University of Toronto*.

Development and Community Stakeholders

To build an augmented reality GPS application for a library system, it is necessary to discuss the project and obtain the consent (and support) of the library system's leadership. Most libraries are interested in experimenting with new forms of service representation alongside existing ones, and everyone recognizes that no one communication strategy suits all patrons. Augmented reality typically benefits patrons who are advanced users of smartphones over traditional users. However, all access strategies must evolve over time as new tools take hold: we must meet patrons in new places, where they are, while maintaining library traditions that are valuable and proven (like designating spaces for silent study, for example).

Part of the process of buy-in is to assemble a team to curate the content, complete graphic design and programming, and conduct quality assurance testing. Depending on the team's skills, this may be a single person or dozens, constituted from within the library system, or in partnership with developer communities. Asking for help from many participants does require more coordination but contributes to the team or community building aspect of the project.

It is useful at an early stage to find out which devices stakeholders own, as there is typically no repository of test devices. Test early and test often as you go, on the actual production machine, if possible. Typically, testing is divided into alpha (development team), beta (internal community of users), and gamma (patrons invited to try the library's test program). There may also be some overlap with social media staff of the library system because testers, in reporting their experiences, often become promoters and early adopters.

Data Gathering

Once you have the consent of management and have organized people to work on the project, obtain a mailing list of the branches or visit the library system website to obtain the postal address, general inquiry phone number, photo, and a short description for each branch. Look up these addresses in a mapping application such as Google Maps, as it can provide the GPS absolute coordinates of each branch location. These mapping applications are surprisingly accurate, provided you zoom in to check the pin and use *all* the decimal places in the latitude and longitude coordinates provided. However, one should be skeptical about any new technology. One way to test GPS is to find a large outdoor parking lot (marked in a grid), then note the coordinates of your smartphone at a specific part of the lot that is easy to locate on a satellite photo, such as a pedestrian island or a memorable juncture of the parking pattern. Then look up the coordinates of the feature on a satellite photo in the mapping application and compare it to your reading. Generally, I've found it is possible to resolve within 10 meters of accuracy in an open space, but we cannot say for certain that the reference maps are equally precise all over the world. That being said, from building many applications like this and testing them—they are often remarkably precise! I once built an AR wayfinding application for a library system 2,500 miles away. When I did finally visit the city, the augments rendered exactly in front of the buildings.

If you're less inclined toward mapping applications for plotting GPS coordinates, it is also useful to turn on GPS tagging in your smartphone's photo app, then stand within a few feet of where you want the augments to appear and snap a photo. You'll therefore have a record of both the place and the GPS location recorded in the metadata of the photo, which you can compare to a reference map. This method is particularly useful if you're dealing with a lot of data where GPS locations might get mixed up in points of interest (commonly known as POIs), or you'd like to crowdsource data collection over the project (everybody send me a GPS-tagged picture of your branch). Note, however, that most social media platforms strip embedded GPS tagging away, so the photos must be shared directly.[3]

In addition to gathering static data about library locations and characteristics, it is also useful to consider a dynamic data strategy where the data provided by the AR wayfinding application is consistent and changes at the same time as other sources. If the library hours change for a single day, for example, this needs to be reflected in the AR data patrons are using. While an administrator can manually change the AR application to reflect changes in the normal schedule, automation and integration are more conducive to the long-term sustainability of the system. By way of this automation, a data question-and-answer system called an application programming interface (API) typically allows smartphones, wall screens, or other communications systems to ask specific questions of databases and receive structured, programmatic responses. North Carolina State University, for example, attributes the rapid development of its mobile application to "existing APIs for services such as the catalog, library hours and computer availability."[4]

Feature-rich IT systems designed for one-way, reference-oriented communication, such as website content management platforms, often neglect APIs that allow developers to build alternative, automated information services. Where there is no API to facilitate the automation of dynamic updates, web-page *scraping* can work very well since the library system's page formatting may remain unchanged for a long period. Web-page scraping means building an automated program designed to read the library's public web page HTML to extract and render current data (such as today's branch hours) in the format your application requires. In my opinion, this is a good investment in dynamic capability. Such a system may work for years, and it has a low organizational impact: the central IT people won't need to build a special bridge to your AR wayfinding project. In the case of the University of Toronto's library, and with the permission of the department, I wrote a script in PHP and installed it to run regularly from a server. It reads the public page http://resource.library.utoronto.ca/hours/ and makes daily updates to the AR database of library locations and hours. A similar script crawls the City of Toronto library system hours.

Building the Application

The world's first AR smartphone application, Layar, was used to build our geo-augmented reality map of the city library system. Essentially, the patron selects the Layar app, the libraries layer specifies a search radius, then the Layar app queries the data service we established, with the location of the patron's smartphone. Our service returns data as to surrounding libraries, a branch photo, and current hours, which Layar renders onto the map view and the AR overlay of the camera. The Layar developer website provided the code and examples for constructing the data service. One of the options for each point of interest is a link to the live map directions API (originally Google Maps, but later switched to Apple Maps), so contextual transit information can be provided from the patron's current location to the branch.

What are the advantages of AR? A responsive design website might make the library's regular pages more accessible to a variety of devices, but in web browsing there is no framework yet for using advanced sensor data from a device, and it's with this rich contextual information that the AR application improves services. AR also provides new ways of visualizing the system: there's nothing quite like rotating around in a circle to see where you are spatially in relation to the branches of the city's libraries, similar to taking a panorama photo, but where the details are *revealed* by AR. Oftentimes you're close to a very interesting collection that needs exploring.

Limitations and Opportunities of GPS-based AR Narratives

While GPS and compass data can work very well to orient urban patrons to their library systems of many branches, specialized collections, and unique services, there are some limitations. If you're walking in an area with a lot of buildings, the accuracy of the GPS may be affected to the degree that your position has significant error. If you're close to a library branch and your smartphone reads your position as on the other side of the building, the directions provided might actually lead you away from the building. Indoors, it frequently doesn't work at all. That being said, in more recent applications, network-based location finding can somewhat accurately locate devices without GPS (see, for example, http://html5demos.com/geo).

Other limitations arise from the nature of smartphone affordances and the type of media AR presentations typically favored. Smartphones and other flat displays lack tactile feedback and often require fine motor coordination. They are therefore difficult for patrons who have visual or fine-motor impairments. Notwithstanding the limitations of devices, AR narratives also tend toward visual interactive narratives rather than audio interactive narratives. That being said, some applications, such as walking tours, can use GPS location to manifest audio direction and narratives automatically.

Indeed, the ability to superimpose digital objects on real outdoor places using mobile computing can reunite digital collections with their original contexts in ways that can invigorate archives, creating "museums without walls."[5] One such narrative is the McLuhan Walk (figure 11.3), a co-production with the Canadian Broadcasting Corporation in Layar. Essentially the smartphone acts as a guided tour, augmenting the physical places McLuhan frequented at the University of Toronto campus with historical images, metadata, and documentary audio commentary of his life and work. This application has automatic GPS triggers for the audio content in addition to ones the user can control, making it accessible to the visually impaired as well as patrons who would simply prefer a more museum-audioguide-style experience. More work definitely needs to be done toward making AR interfaces support universal design.

OBJECT RECOGNITION–BASED AR NARRATIVES: A UNIVERSITY LIBRARY SYSTEM

Barcodes are well known in libraries for managing circulating resources. A laser scanner reads a visually coded object in the collection to retrieve metadata, then the borrower metadata is updated. Object recognition–based AR is similar, but instead of a laser scanner detecting light and dark bars, a smartphone or tablet camera feeds the entire image into a web service that analyzes, matches, and overlays metadata augments. Since the process is visual, it overcomes the precision problem in location-finding narratives. However, there are a lot of objects in a typical scene, and it isn't sufficient to just identify the object—we also need to map its changing position rapidly and adjust the augments sufficiently that they align as explicative callouts.

One way of manifesting object recognition is to incorporate a square barcode or QR code that patrons deliberately scan. Another is to upload representative

Figure 11.3. McLuhan Walk: AR audio-narrated walking tour, a co-production with CBC Spark. ***University of Toronto.***

images that an app can recognize when these are scanned. This latter method was the basis for overlaying digital augments of particular information value, or link value to web-browsing smartphones in the next example.

Obtaining Institutional Support for an Image Recognition System

Image recognition typically involves more processing and data manipulation than GPS/compass-based contextual analysis, so it may be a more expensive system to run. However, the University of Toronto library system was the beneficiary of an AR hackathon contest prize during the image recognition AR experimental phase, so we've been operating the image recognition AR system for many years at no cost. At the time of this writing, Layar Vision costs $34 per image per year (unlimited scans). Alternatively, free computing code libraries such as OpenCV-Python are making object recognition and tracking simpler to implement. If you have an advanced technical team, it may be possible to build your own smartphone image recognition and tracking system upon which to overlay AR, rather than overlaying your contextual information using a commercial application like Layar.

Production Values

It is important to obtain good images of objects people will commonly see—objects that have a high contrast figure, a neutral field around them so as to allow scanning and object recognition from varying distances, and enough edges to produce a unique signature when they are scanned. It is also useful to pick objects that appear in a lot of places (ubiquitous objects), so that the augments are useful across a wide range of contexts. In the case of the university libraries, we taught the Layar app to recognize the university crest and each library branch sign because the crest appears everywhere and branch signs appear many times, typically at every entrance to each branch (figures 11.4 and 11.5). While the prototype images you provide the application need to be quite clear, in terms of actual recognition under variable conditions, the Layar vision system proved remarkably resilient: signage with cast shadows, occluded by heavy snowfall, and even damaged by minor vandalism during orientation were recognized and loaded up the augments we had designed.

In terms of augmentation content, we focused on linking the library's website, general information number, and current events (social media feed). In library spaces in which classes are held, we linked the time-tabling information as an augment, so on a given day students could scan the building sign to look up which room held which class.

Figure 11.4. Scanning the Gerstein Science Information Centre signage makes AR links appear. The shadow cast across the sign seems to have no effect. ***University of Toronto.***

Figure 11.5. The University of Toronto crest, wherever it appears, can be scanned for AR hyperlinks. ***University of Toronto.***

Outcomes

Compared with QR codes that invite patrons to scan them because they are standardized with an express and readily identifiable purpose, it was sometimes difficult for patrons to know that physical building signs could be scanned to reveal augments. In magazine publishing, Layar often adds its logo to the corner of advertising images that are augmented, to illustrate the presence of dynamic interactive AR content. We were not, however, about to turn our institutional signs into ads for the Layar company. Rather, we promoted this capability across a number of campus student events over social media channels.

Another barrier, perhaps, is the fact that many people are uncomfortable with cell phones running cameras in public spaces. In the same way that people often appeared to be talking to themselves in the early days of cell phones, people accessing visual augments often appear to be taking (unwanted) pictures in social spaces. Designating specific spaces is one way to address this problem. Incorporating augments into more subtle forms of visual display, such as augmented reality glasses, may be a future application solution. But AR glasses pose wayfinding difficulties of the walking-and-gum-chewing variety. I have several times tried to read email while walking downstairs using Epson Moverio glasses, without success: one has to stop.

Active Learning AR in Publications

Many have speculated on how interactivity with mobile devices might inform and augment the experience of books.[6] One pioneer in this area is Dr. Helen Papagiannis, author of *Who's Afraid of Bugs?*, the world's first AR pop-up book for iPad2 and iPhone 4. Her work is a children's book that explores and educates on the phobia of insects and butterflies. Reproducing an illustration is beyond the scope of this chapter, but here is a video link: https://vimeo.com/25608606. In the sense that this makes a text interactive and reactive, it has perhaps more value as a didactic narrative, relating through the conventional narrative while also showing the way. Papagiannis has since written a book about many kinds of new sensing available to human experience, *Augmented Human*.

One of our biomedical communications students, Andrea Zariwny, undertook an augmented reality book illustration as part of her master's research project. Her project, Invisible Ear, is similarly a work of education, but it depicts a more complex 3D medical illustration. The AR application renders a real-time, 3D animation model of the mechanism of the inner ear, triggered by a conventional 2D illustration, as would commonly be found in a medical atlas of anatomy (figure 11.6). What is particularly interesting is that

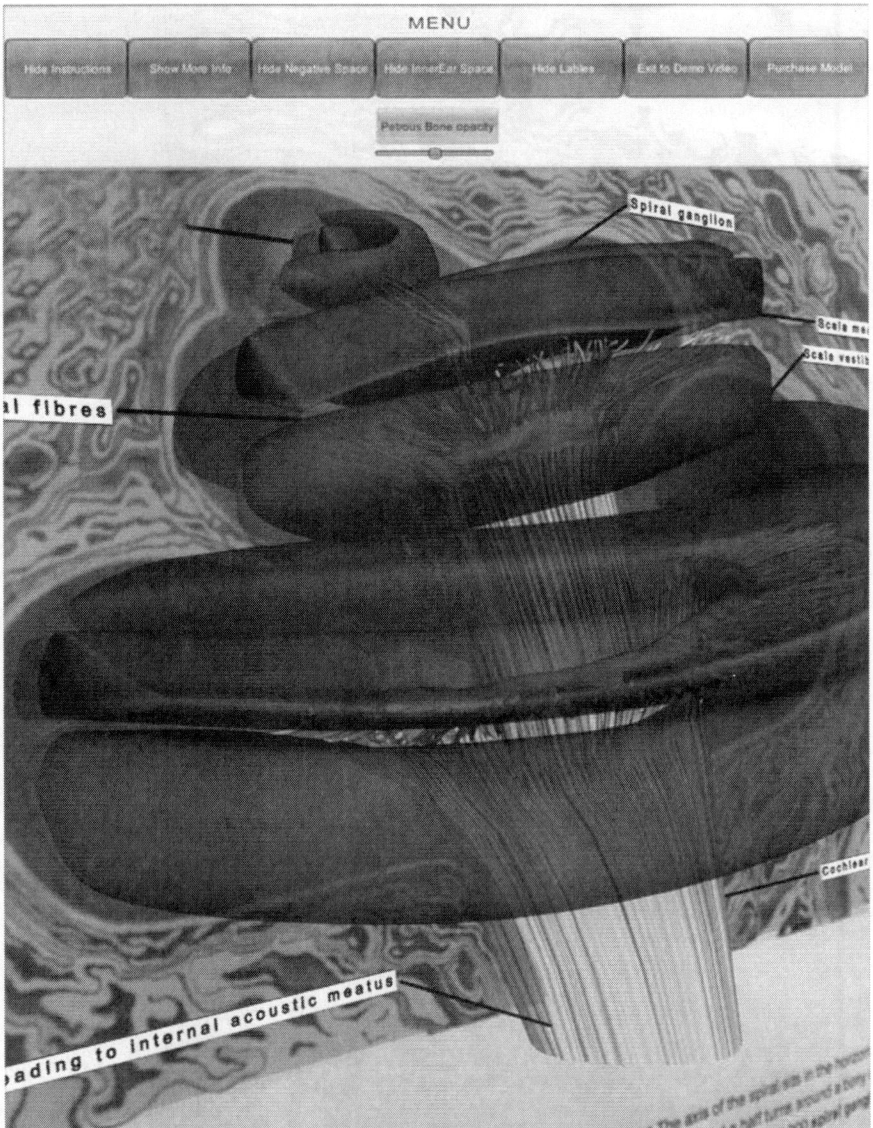

Figure 11.6. Screenshot of the augmented 3D model emerging from the 2D anatomy illustration. ***Andrea Zariwny, University of Toronto.***

the model is moving, and different 3D parts can be hidden or shown for examination. The app and illustration are here: https://itunes.apple.com/ca/app/invisibleear/id764798546?mt=8.

Generally speaking, AR has been slow to find its way in conventional books, perhaps because AR emphasizes visuals, devices, and interactivity, while books emphasize text, paper, and imagination. As digital interaction becomes more integrated into eyewear, the transition between physical and digital will become more seamless. AR layers will become popular in text publications as an alternative mode of experience that educators and students will demand as the emphasis on active, situated engagement addresses a variety of learning styles.

CONCLUSION

While there has been some effort to standardize AR methods in the way the World Wide Web has standardized conventional document and media exchange, there is a ways to go before AR systems are sufficiently interoperable such that AR presents a seamless, ubiquitous experience rather than being particular to places, objects, narratives, and technosocial frameworks.[7] This standardization problem makes elaborate AR work difficult to justify unless it encompasses a significant scope of common objects and environments—high-value ones, as in cultural institutions. Yet augmented reality *is* a powerful method for rendering rich, sophisticated views of contextual information from the point of view of users, and for putting *things* and *digital information about things* in logical adjacency (Mayer's physical contiguity principle, if you prefer).[8] As computing power for visualization grows, simple icons will give way to more sophisticated AR creations. 3D working models of things will not only layer active experiences in mobile settings but also semantically enrich conventional cultural works, connecting them deeply and irrevocably into the digital. Other context-sensing techniques such as Bluetooth proximity sensors, triangulation, and physical Internet devices have further potential to supplement AR-sensing information, increasing the usefulness and accuracy of layering digital information on spaces, for the benefit of future information wayseekers.

NOTES

1. Robert James Havinghurst, *Human Development and Education*, 7.
2. Chris Getman, "Google Ad about Ad Words: 'You Know Who Wants a Guitar? People Searching For a Guitar.'"

3. Photo Metadata Working Group, "Social Media Sites Photo Metadata Test Results."

4. Steve Morris, "NCSU Libraries Mobile."

5. Hannah Lewi and Wally Smith, "Hand-held Histories: Using Digital Archival Documents on Architectural Tours," 1.

6. Any S. Y. Lai, Chris Y. K. Wong, and Oscar C. H. Lo, "Applying Augmented Reality Technology to Book Publication Business."

7. Christine Perey, "Standards Activities Underway."

8. Richard E. Mayer, Julie Heiser, and Steve Lonn, "Cognitive Constraints on Multimedia Learning: When Presenting More Material Results in Less Understanding," 1.

BIBLIOGRAPHY

Getman, Chris. "Google Ad about Ad Words: 'You Know Who Wants a Guitar? People Searching For a Guitar.'" August 30, 2013. https://web.archive.org/web/20180326224351/https:/twitter.com/chrisgetman/status/373385915780976640.

Havinghurst, Robert James. *Human Development and Education*. New York: Longmans, Green, 1952.

Lai, Any S. Y., Chris Y. K. Wong, and Oscar C. H. Lo. "Applying Augmented Reality Technology to Book Publication Business." *2015 IEEE 12th International Conference on e-Business Engineering*. Beijing, 2015: 281–86.

Lewi, Hannah, and Wally Smith. "Hand-held Histories: Using Digital Archival Documents on Architectural Tours." *Architectural Research Quarterly* 15, no. 1 (2011): 69–77.

Mayer, Richard E., Julie Heiser, and Steve Lonn. "Cognitive Constraints on Multimedia Learning: When Presenting More Material Results in Less Understanding." *Journal of Educational Psychology* 93, no 1 (2001): 187–98.

Morris, Steve. "NCSU Libraries Mobile." NCSU Libraries, August 27, 2014. http://www.lib.ncsu.edu/reports/ncsu-libraries-mobile.

Papagiannis, Helen. *Augmented Human: How Technology Is Shaping the New Reality*. New York: O'Reilly Media, 2017.

Perey, Christine. "Standards Activities Underway." *AR Community for Open and Interoperable Augmented Reality Experiences*. Accessed May 2, 2017. http://www.perey.com/ARStandards/standards-activities-underway.

Photo Metadata Working Group of the IPTC. "Social Media Sites Photo Metadata Test Results." *Embedded Metadata Manifesto*, 2015. http://www.embeddedmetadata.org/social-media-test-results.php.

12

VR, AR, and Video 360

A Case Study Toward New Realities in Education

Plamen Miltenoff

The year 2016 marked a breakthrough year for virtualities, including virtual reality (VR), augmented reality (AR), and Video 360. Predictions picture a market ready for VR and AR adoption and the entertainment industry embracing these new technologies.[1] In 2015, the K12 New Horizon Report Edition (http://k12.wiki.nmc.org/Augmented+Reality) made similar predictions. Application of these technologies in education will take longer, considering the need to accordingly rework curricula, course design, and lesson plans. More important, such changes in the curriculum process must be preceded by an educators' mindset evolution. Such an evolution would transform the teaching process to include the rich selection of virtual environments amid other technological and methodological developments, such as the Internet of Things, gaming and gamification, and personalized learning.

This chapter presents a case study from an academic library that applies Video 360 as part of the first step in library orientation, followed by a gamified second step of library instruction. The development of the project, as well as the assessment of students taking both steps (step 1, orientation through VR, and step 2, gamified instruction [http://web.stcloudstate.edu/pmiltenoff/bi/]), reveal the need for scalability during the application of virtual environments in educational settings. Building virtual environments in education and creating corresponding teaching and learning materials can be an expensive and time-consuming process. Therefore, the capacity to change in size and scale needs to be considered.

Gradual expansion of the application of forms of virtuality is mandated by not only dwindling finances in education but mostly the needs of the stakeholders—students, faculty, administration, and parents—to warm up to the idea of learning beyond the traditional classroom and its traditional pedagogy and technology.[2] Further, as part of the educators' force, librarians must understand the inevitability and necessity of working across silos and institutions, and commence collaboration and cooperation on a large scale during the development of complex, costly, and time-consuming projects, such as virtual environments for education and their didactical context.

According to a 2016 survey polling nearly 350 schools from higher education and K–12, only 23 percent of the respondents had tested virtual reality.[3] The number reveals a technology in its infancy both technologically and pedagogically. The obstacles to a broader and quicker adoption entail hesitation over technological issues such as IT infrastructure endurance, to didactical hurdles such as absence of appropriate content.[4]

Keeping in mind the numbers and obstacles mentioned above, it is logical to anticipate slower development, if not complete absence of this trend, in some parts of the world. However, Nigerian scholars prove that virtual reality and augmented reality technology is not a fad and/or prerogative of the developed world only, but a trend to be considered worldwide.[5] The approach of the Nigerian scholars may raise brows in the "Big Brotherly" way they intend to use AR in education, yet it is clear sign that AR and VR are becoming familiar terms in education around the world, even if the methodology and pedagogy will need time to negotiate appropriate application.[6]

DEFINITION

Among myriad other definitions, Noor describes virtual reality (VR) as "a computer generated environment that can simulate physical presence in places in the real world or imagined worlds. The user wears a headset and, through specialized software and sensors, is immersed in 360-degree views of simulated worlds."[7] Noor also presents the following definition: "Augmented Reality (AR) supplements the physical environment with computer-generated sensory input such as sound, video, graphics, or other useful information—essentially overlaying the digital information on top of the physical world."[8] Some consider the popular smartphone game Pokémon GO a form of consumer AR. More resources on VR and AR can be found in the hyperlink list at the end of this chapter.

In this article, we will be using BYOD (bring your own device) in conjunction with VR and AR. Similar to the corporate world, educators adopted BYOD as an opportunity for instructors to use personal mobile devices (e.g., smartphones and tablets) for teaching and learning purposes. More resources on BYOD can be found in the hyperlink list at the end of this chapter.

LIMITATIONS

This study was conceived as a preliminary assessment to establish the need for deeper and wider surveying of students' propensity for the use of VR, Video 360 in particular. Therefore, the time and energy spent on the VR prototype for this case study was deliberately limited in both visual and patron-oriented content. Considering recent surveys on the penetration of VR in education, this study opted to use a low-budget, low-quality approach to test the ground for a serious follow-up VR project that can build on the lessons learned from this prototype.[9]

BIBLIOGRAPHIC OVERVIEW

Hahn refers to the New Media Consortium, the Pew Internet and American Life Project, and the Educause Center for Applied Research as three influential nonprofit organizations concerned with educational technology, VR and AR included.[10] Hahn also evokes projects such as the City of Philadelphia's Department of Records and Miami University's (Ohio) shelf-based library work as exemplary for their application of VR for educational purposes.[11] Massis, like Hahn, provides specific examples for VR and AR apps for mobile devices, as well as an argument for "VR/AR as a learning solution for 'digital natives.'"[12]

Newly emerging studies reflect the educational advantages of VR use, including student engagement.[13] VR and AR are used for new research.[14] VR for education can offer practical purposes such as field trips, anatomy and dissection, as well as coding and 3D design.[15] Virtual and augmented realities open new opportunities for students with special needs and approaches to new areas, such as human empathy.[16] The technologies are expected to have a positive impact on distance and international education.[17] Further, academic librarians can adopt and develop the concept for field trips and transform it into a virtual orientation in an academic library since it fits their environment.[18]

VIRTUAL REALITY IN THE LIBRARY

In addition to Hahn, other librarians have contemplated the future of AR and VR in the library.[19] Meredith sees a close connection between AR and VR in the library in tandem with the proliferation of mobile devices in general, and the BYOD movement in particular.[20] Meredith envisions a wide range of AR applications, including evaluation of user satisfaction by capturing and analyzing facial expression. Similarly, both Gleason and Moorefield-Lang see the immediate VR application in libraries as part of the less-expensive BYOD model.[21]

Similar research is conducted in a dissertation by Ulukuz and in Zaki's research.[22] The authors are comparing users' reactions in museums and libraries through the use of AR and VR. Numerous other studies explore the museum use of interactive approaches, starting with interactive audio in the past to more recent VR and AR projects involving brands such as the Oculus Rift, HTC Vive, and others.[23] Museum innovations are important since their practice and experience can be replicated in similar library environments, such as library orientation. Other studies on VR and AR range from technicalities, such as mobile versus head-worn devices, to the psychological and ethical implications of using VR and AR.[24]

It is important to distinguish the "low-end" model of employing VR for educational purposes, through goggles such as Google Cardboard combined with BYOD, versus the more potent but also more expensive alternatives of VR with the Oculus Rift, HTC Vive, Samsung Gear VR, and AR with Microsoft HoloLens. Such distinctions will be important from financial and pedagogical considerations since, in addition to the cost of the gear, educators also will have to consider the expense of content creation. Such "high-end" solutions are already being considered by some librarians but remain, for the time being, beyond the scope of this research.[25]

The creation of methodologies for education using VR and AR is also in development. Zap and Code propose the application of the evidence-centered design framework to study the impacts of VR and AR on learning.[26] Evidence-centered design (ECD) aims for educational assessment based on evidentiary arguments. As per Mislevy, Almond, and Lukas, ECD is based "on the principles of evidentiary reasoning and the exigencies of assessment production and delivery."[27] Sanabria proposed a Gradual Immersion Method to use AR and VR for enhanced collaboration and creativity.[28]

In 2010, the educational world turned away from the virtual world of Second Life.[29] In 2016, the then-popular Second Life attempted a revival by transitioning/connecting their platform to the experience with VR.[30] When searching for literature on the use of virtual reality in academic libraries, the classification of Second Life as a "virtual world" produced a large number of results referring to Second Life, thus leaving the impression of a gap in sources on VR and AR and their educational application. It will be interesting to follow the resolution to discriminate between overlapping platforms and concepts such as virtual worlds (Second Life) and virtual reality, and help patrons with the accuracy of their bibliography search.

Further, as recently noted, librarians contribute to the confusion around terminology as used in discussion lists by abbreviating virtual reference to "VR" whenever topics related to virtual reference are discussed.[31] Apparently, definitions, theories, and even abbreviations are due for revision, negotiation, and standardization.

Virtual reality, Video 360 in particular, was considered in this case a supplement of, if not a replacement for, the existing lecture-type or guide-type library orientations. Based on current constructivist learning theories, a self-paced individual option for students to acquire information and build knowledge, either on their own or through interaction with peers, will result in better learning.[32] While the allure of a new technology was not discounted, the emphasis in the current experiment of working with Video 360 in library settings is less determined by such ostentatious factors, but rather by the constructivist understanding of providing students with opportunities to foster individual and personalized learning based on interactivity and visualization.

METHOD

The idea for a virtual tour was implemented in the summer of 2016 as a collaboration between a faculty member from the InforMedia Services Group (IMS) and the director of the Virtualization Lab at the university. More information on the IMS and the Virtualization Lab can be found in the hyperlink list at the end of this chapter.

The team employed a Samsung Gear 360 camera to collect footage for the visual orientation. The footage was processed in Gear Action Director, a Samsung developer program. The latest Adobe CC suite has tools to perform similar operations (e.g., stitching) that the Gear Action Director can do. Initially, the team hosted the video with the self-directed orientation on Viar360.com. This third-party service allows the user to insert hot spots in the movie with hyperlinks and additional information, as well as to bring different Video 360 scenes together into one solid movie. Later on, the team discontinued this paid service and wrote its own interface to add interactivity to the Video 360 footage. Without the extra addition of hyperlinks and connecting Video 360 scenes, movies can be uploaded on YouTube. Both visual segments were prepared with the intention of being viewed with goggles—in this case, Google Cardboard goggles.

More information on the technical process of acquiring footage, processing (stitching) the footage, and server hosting can be found in the hyperlink list at the end of this chapter. The ideas for low-cost virtual tours using goggles have already been considered by other libraries.[33]

The prototype for testing the predisposition of students toward the use of VR in an academic library included the creation of two VR settings—one, a movie, and the other, a still-image set. Both visuals were embedded in a SurveyMonkey web page, https://www.surveymonkey.com/r/VRLibrary, where students can conveniently access the video materials through a single departure point and, after the library orientation, continue and take a short survey.

The first Video 360 movie is a 5-minute video introduction (https://youtu.be/LiwAVKQck5Q). In the first video, the students are passive observers in a virtual environment. The team is "leading" the patrons through the library, explaining services, while patrons "look around."

The second Video 360 VR setting (http://bit.ly/SCSUlib360orientation), unlike the first movie, is a set of still VR images. Students can "look around" at their own pace; they are not "led," but rather explore the building and its services and resources on their own. This exploration tour can be achieved by using either their own smartphones and goggles in the VR mode or the Panorama Mode on their electronic devices (smartphones, tablets, laptops, computer lab desktops, etc.) (figure 12.1).

The intention of the first video is to assist students with both becoming acquainted with VR and becoming acquainted spatially with the library and its services. The intention of the second video is to let students learn about the library on their own, and thus solidify the information acquired from the first video.

The VR library orientation (http://bit.ly/VRlib) described in this chapter is followed by gamified library instruction (http://bit.ly/learnlib), a scavenger hunt by the patrons using their mobile devices to learn about basic research

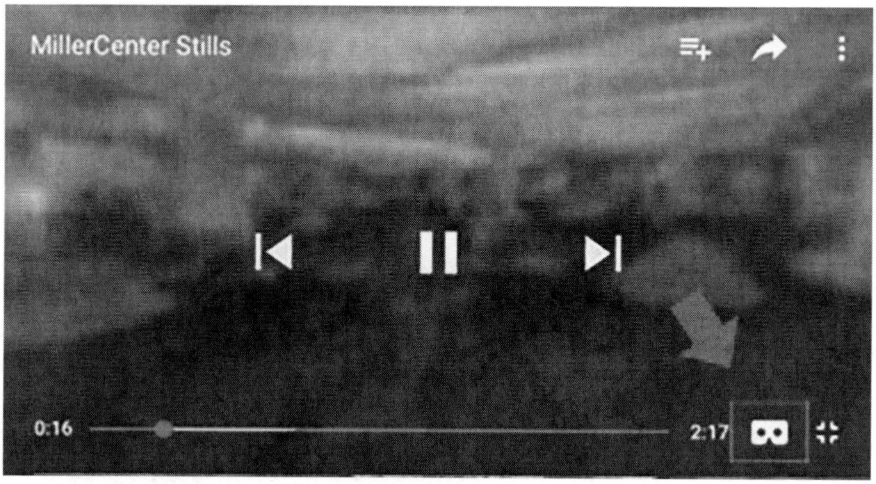

Figure 12.1. The VR mode option on a video. ***St. Cloud State University.***

and library services. The gamified library instruction is beyond the scope of this chapter, which focuses on the use of VR for library orientation.

After finishing their library orientation by watching the first video and next engaging actively with the library orientation in the second VR setting, students proceed to the short survey.

The survey has a threefold goal: to establish whether Video 360, as part of the general VR and AR idea, is a feasible platform for student learning; to find out if learning really happens using VR; and to see if there is any correlation between the first two goals and student demographics. The survey consists of 15 questions. The questions in the survey progress from a general inquiry about library use to questions regarding the specific impact of video 360 on information acquisition and retention.

A total of 221 students from St. Cloud State University (http://www.stcloudstate.edu/) took the survey. Four participants did not respond to seven questions and are excluded from the final results, thus bringing the participants down to 217. The surveyed students were predominantly female (66 percent) and 18 years of age. Half of them (50 percent) were first-year students from places with relatively small populations (10,000–50,000).

FINDINGS

Three questions in the survey (questions 4, 5, 6) aim to measure learning outcomes by asking about the location of services in the library. The rest of the questions are split into two sets: a demographic set and a set of questions seeking to establish patrons' satisfaction with the use of VR in the library.

Based on the responses, most students visit the library at least once a month. This result is not surprising, considering that millennials are an online generation. In addition, the academic library as an institution is gradually moving services and information online (e.g., http://blog.stcloudstate.edu/ims/2015/05/04/lms-and-embedded-librarianship/). Only 6 percent of respondents visited the library at least once per day, whereas 20 percent visited the library less than once a month. With 37 percent selecting "easy" and 41 percent choosing "somewhat easy," patrons find the library an easy place in which to orient themselves.

Open-ended questions regarding aids for finding resources in the library can be clustered in the following responses/recommendations consistent with the traditional role of the library:

- Confirm the benefit of existing services
- Demand for the presence of a real person at the reference/circulation desks of the library

- Demand for tangible/physical orientation aids such as maps, directions, signs, and guides
- Demand for library tour by a real person and a demand for lending of electronic devices from the library

Among the recommendations in the realm of "electronic" services were requests for interactive maps and a library app. The request for a "nap area" was not a new one, but apparently it persisted after the newly designated area for prayers and mediation did not address it.

Based on the three questions evaluating students' ability to orient themselves in the library after experiencing the 360 video, 91 percent correctly identified the location of the scanners, 62 percent correctly identified the location of the archives, and 71 percent correctly identified the music collection. Further research can juxtapose incoming results from the self-guided 360 video library orientation to the results from a person-led library orientation and work on an effective combination of both approaches.

Students' open-ended responses regarding the improvement of the Video 360 content can be clustered as follows: students want the self-guided Video 360 library orientation to include the location of bathrooms, location of the computer lab and single desktop workstations across the library, as well as their availability. Another suggestion was for more detailed information about library services and ways to utilize the library, including lesser-known parts of the library. Additional information was sought regarding library working hours. Meeting such demands has been addressed with technology such as QR codes, and Video 360 certainly can offer virtual displays with hyperlinks to the information, thus merging the virtual experience with the online information and exposing students and faculty to this new type of information integration.

Further suggestions, via open-ended responses, sought specific information about books and procedures to find specific books, the number of books that could be checked out at one time, and the location of color printers and supplies. In addition to interactive maps and a library app, students requested a more detailed Video 360 movie of the library.

In response to the question of whether students like receiving information through VR, 52 percent agreed, 36 percent disagreed, and 10 percent agreed only if the content and format were remodeled. Therefore, the majority of the surveyed students indicated an interest in library orientation in particular, and in learning through Video 360 in general.

The results of this inquiry were cross-tabulated by "year in school." Of the 52 percent (155 respondents) welcoming information through VR, the highest percentage of students interested in receiving information through VR were

Table 1. Do you like to receive information through Virtual Reality (VR)? Gender Crosstabulation		
Do you like to receive information through VR	Female	Male
Yes	79	36
No	51	27
Sure, but different content and/or format	16	7
Total	154	61
Pearson Chi-Square		.884

Figure 12.2. Survey results. *St. Cloud State University.*

first-year students (56 respondents). Gradually, the interest declined: sophomores (28), juniors (17), seniors (8), and graduate students (5).

Through informal inquiry during the library Video 360 orientation sessions, the impression gained was that male students are better acquainted with VR and/or Video 360. Such an erroneous assumption was partially due to a conversation starter regarding gaming and games that preceded the survey. However, according to the survey results, namely a Pearson Chi-Square of .87, there is no significant difference between genders regarding their use of Video 360 (figure 12.2).

Research considers both Generation Z and Generation Y as visual learners.[34] The assumption was that first-year students, being representative of Generation Z, would be more open to new technologies than their older predecessors.[35] However, a Pearson Chi-Square of .88 reveals no significant difference in the use of Video 360 between students in their first and second years and students in their third and fourth years of studies. Considering the short age range between first-year students and seniors, future research may consider fine-tuning the responses for this item by differentiating the Video 360 question, in which the "Yes/No" values were replaced by a five-level Likert scale, thus enabling the quantification, and therefore more precise differentiation of opinions among different-year students regarding their use of virtual reality (figure 12.3).

Although discussion about the digital divide seems to have subsided in recent years, research continues to point out the digital disparity between urban and rural areas.[36] Considering the literature, and based on this author's previous research with students on the same campus, we were

Table 2. Do you like to receive information through Virtual Reality (VR)? Year-n-School Crosstabulation		
Do you like to receive information through VR	Freshman/Sophomore	Junior/Senior
Yes	84	31
No	54	32
Sure, but different content and/or format	16	7
Total	154	61
Pearson Chi-Square		.884

Figure 12.3. Survey results. *St. Cloud State University.*

Table 3. Do you like to receive information through Virtual Reality (VR)? Community Size Crosstabulation		
Do you like to receive information through VR	Community under 50,000	Community over 50,000
Yes	80	34
No	54	23
Sure, but different content and/or format	16	7
Total	150	64
Pearson Chi-Square		.998

Figure 12.4. Survey results. *St. Cloud State University.*

prompted to collect data regarding the place of origin of the students. The intention of such data collection was to understand if an urban-rural divide is a factor in the acceptance of new technologies, VR and AR included. A Pearson Chi-Square of .99 revealed no significant difference in the use of video 360 between students whose main residence has fewer than 50,000 people, and students whose main residence has over 50,000 people. This is another area for further research to bring clarity (figure 12.4).

DISCUSSION

This chapter presents a case study from an academic library that applied Video 360 as part of the first step in library orientation. This preliminary study aimed to establish whether there is interest among students in supplementing and/or replacing the existing lecture-type and/or guide-type library orientation with self-sufficient and interactive methods that can provide students with opportunities to learn on their own. Considering the demographics of the respondents, we expected low student interest in the Video 360 technology, as well as a gender disparity and a rural-urban discrepancy. Our previous research on technology-related use by campus students (e.g., use of podcasts and social media) revealed significant discrepancies from the literature on these issues nationwide. We considered the possibility that such discrepancies were based on the demographic of our students, who are predominantly from smaller communities.[37] In a similar fashion, we expected the similarities and relationship between VR and gaming devices might produce stronger interest among males, considering the stereotype of a predominantly male presence in gaming.[38]

Results overturned all three expectations, as students demonstrated strong interest in this new technology, even as they also clearly revealed expectations for better technical and aesthetic quality and more thorough content. According to the results, gender and community size are not factors in student interest in this technology. Further research can focus on the content components and their successful representation in the Video 360 environment, as well as on the "deeper" content, namely the connection between Video 360 and the successful hyperlinking of resources to the main Video 360 movie. Further research is needed regarding basic technological issues, such as the capability of all mobile devices to play Video 360, the well-known and still existing problem of users becoming dizzy or experiencing motion sickness when interacting with this type of media, among other issues.

CONCLUSION

Approaching this promising technology in a scalable manner follows the same patterns of inquiry as with other educational technologies—start small, and gradually expand the scope and depth of the endeavor. Dire financing is just one reason to seek gradual expansion of VR and AR. Factors such as the inclination of a project's organizers and audience to accept a fairly radical change in their relationship to technology, as well as acceptance of new methodologies for learning and teaching, are just a few elements that must be addressed. VR and AR as teaching methods can present radical changes in both the discourse of the librarians and faculty as well as the perception of the patrons.

When conducting the Video 360 orientation to the library, several students admitted to dizziness when using Google Cardboard goggles. These little incidents were reminiscent of the Oculus Rift issues with motion sickness.[39] While IT professionals and scientists are trying to resolve a very real physiological issue and other technological issues such as infrastructure endurance, one needs to be aware of the most important challenge: the pedagogical/methodological application of VR and AR.[40] Based on our previous experience with the use of new technologies in academia, it is safe to expect that VR and AR application as a novelty to attract patrons' attention will wear off quickly, as it did with numerous other new technologies. Following the "novelty" impact, only methodologically well-constructed and pedagogically well-applied VR and AR curricula will continue to retain patrons' attention. Creating such methodologically and pedagogically sound AR and VR content can be achieved by gradually constructing it in a scalable manner.

In that sense, AR and VR cannot be observed separately, but as pieces of the bigger pedagogical puzzle where gaming and gamification are gradually constructed as part of teaching with constructivism—VR and AR are not attention-grabbing stunts to hold patrons' responsiveness during a lecture, but rather an empowering ambience to create student-centered "zones of approximate development" where patrons have control over information acquisition and build their own knowledge in a peer-supported environment.[41]

NOTES

1. David Nagel, "How Teachers Leverage Mobile Technology"; Jacob Siegal, "Netflix and HBO Launch Virtual Reality Apps on Google Play."

2. Meg Lloyd, "An Open Repository of Learning Space Design"; Nagel, "How Teachers Leverage Mobile Technology"; Sri Ravipati, "5 VR Trends to Watch in Education."

3. Meris Stansbury, "5 Ways Virtual Reality Is Being Used in Education Right Now."

4. Sri Ravipati, "Report: IT Professionals Worldwide Say It's Still Early for AR Adoption"; Stansbury, "5 Ways Virtual Reality Is Being Used."

5. Azubuike Ezenwoke et al., "Wearable Technology: Opportunities and Challenges for Teaching and Learning in Higher Education in Developing Countries."

6. Nick Zap and Jillianne Code. "Virtual and Augmented Reality as Cognitive Tools for Learning."

7. Ahmed Noor, "The Hololens Revolution,"30.

8. Ibid.

9. Stansbury, "5 Ways Virtual Reality Is Being Used."

10. J. Hahn, "Mobile Augmented Reality Applications for Library Services."

11. Ibid.

12. Bruce Massis, "Using Virtual and Augmented Reality in the Library."

13. Laura Devaney, "Teachers Say Virtual Reality Would Boost Engagement"; Phil Goerner, "Augmented Reality: What's Next?"; "Virtual Reality Helping California Students Overcome Learning Barriers"; Stansbury, "5 Ways Virtual Reality Is Being Used."

14. Stansbury, "5 Ways Virtual Reality Is Being Used"; Dian Schaffhauser, "Stanford VR Project Shows Students Oceans of the Future."

15. Stansbury, "5 Ways Virtual Reality Is Being Used"; Frank Smith, "Could HoloLens' Augmented Reality Change How We Study the Human Body?"

16. Arunima Majumdar, "Utilizing Augmented Reality for Special Needs Learning"; Ian Bogost, "Virtual Games Try to Generate Real Empathy for Faraway Conflict."

17. Jerome Yavarkovsky, "Editorial Board Thoughts: The Promise of Immersive Libraries."

18. Hahn, "Mobile Augmented Reality Applications."

19. Hahn, "Mobile Augmented Reality Applications"; Mahmoud Zaki, "Image Recognition and Augmented Reality Technologies in Libraries, Museums and Bookstores."

20. Tamara R. Meredith, "Using Augmented Reality Tools to Enhance Children's Library Services."

21. Ann Whitney Gleason, *Mobile Technologies for Every Library*; Heather Moorefield-Lang, "Libraries and the Rift."

22. Huseyin Ulukuz, *Use of Augmented Reality in Museums: The Relationship Between Children's Engagement and Immersive Visitor Experience*; Zaki, "Image Recognition and Augmented Reality."

23. Kenneth Newby et al., "Interactive Audio Content: An Approach to Audio Content for a Dynamic Museum Experience through Augmented Audio Reality and

Adaptive Information Retrieval"; Ray Lewis, "Virtual Reality: Soon to Become Mainstream in Libraries?"

24. Tony Liao, "Mobile versus Headworn Augmented Reality: How Visions of the Future Shape, Contest, and Stabilize an Emerging Technology"; Ryan Straight, "An Exploratory Study of Augmented Reality and Mobile Games Examining Ingress Player Motivation and Potential Educational Value."

25. Lyn Robinson, "Multisensory, Pervasive, Immersive: Towards a New Generation of Documents."

26. Zap and Code, "Virtual and Augmented Reality as Cognitive Tools."

27. R. J. Mislevy, Russell G. Almond, and Janice F. Lukas. "A Brief Introduction to Evidence-Centered Design"; Russell Almond, Linda Steinberg, and Robert Mislevy, "Enhancing the Design and Delivery of Assessment Systems: A Four-Process Architecture."

28. Jorge C. Sanabria, "The Gradual Immersion Method (GIM): Pedagogical Transformation into Mixed Reality."

29. Jeffrey R. Young, "After Frustrations in Second Life, Colleges Look to New Virtual Worlds."

30. Rachel Metz, "Remember Second Life? Its Creators Are Back with a Virtual Reality Platform."

31. B. Greene, "Re: VR in Community Colleges."

32. Harry Daniels, *An Introduction to Vygotsky*.

33. "Five Ways to Use Google Cardboard in the Library."

34. D. J. Hedderly and Heidi Scott, "Measuring the Effectiveness of Video Training through Technology-Based Education."

35. Caroline Geck, "The Generation Z Connection: Teaching Information Literacy to the Newest Net Generation"; Milan Kubiatko et al., "The Using of and Attitudes Toward Internet and Information and Communication Technologies in Different Age Groups."

36. Michael J. Stern, Alison E. Adams, and Shaun Elsasser, "Digital Inequality and Place: The Effects of Technological Diffusion on Internet Proficiency and Usage Across Rural, Suburban, and Urban Counties"; Jacob L. Vigdor and Helen F. Ladd, "Scaling the Digital Divide: Home Computer Technology and Student Achievement"; Juan-Carlos Torres-Díaz et al., "Internet Use and Academic Success in University Students."

37. P. Miltenoff et al., "The Educational Use of Social Media Cross-Nationally: A Preliminary Descriptive Study."

38. Benjamin Paaßen, Thekla Morgenroth, and Michelle Stratemeyer, "What Is a True Gamer? The Male Gamer Stereotype and the Marginalization of Women in Video Game Culture."

39. Matt Rossoff, "Oculus Founder Explains Why Some People Get Sick When Using His Product."

40. Noah Nelson, "Virtual Reality's Next Hurdle: Overcoming 'Sim Sickness'"; Ravipati, "Report: IT Professionals Worldwide Say."

41. Daniels, *An Introduction to Vygotsky*.

BIBLIOGRAPHY

Almond, Russell, Linda Steinberg, and Robert Mislevy. "Enhancing the Design and Delivery of Assessment Systems: A Four-Process Architecture." *Journal of Technology, Learning, and Assessment* 1, no. 5 (2002).

Bogost, Ian. "Virtual Games Try to Generate Real Empathy for Faraway Conflict." NPR.org, January 25, 2015. http://www.npr.org/sections/alltechconsidered/2015/01/25/379417927/virtual-games-try-to-generate-real-empathy-for-faraway-conflict.

Daniels, Harry, ed. *An Introduction to Vygotsky*. New York: Psychology Press, 2005.

Delahoussaye, James. "Virtual Games Try to Generate Real Empathy For Faraway Conflict." NPR.org, January 25, 2015. http://www.npr.org/sections/alltechconsidered/2015/01/25/379417927/virtual-games-try-to-generate-real-empathy-for-faraway-conflict.

Devaney, Laura. "Teachers Say Virtual Reality Would Boost Engagement." *eSchool News,* July 26, 2016. http://www.eschoolnews.com/2016/07/26/teachers-say-virtual-reality-would-boost-engagement/.

Durbin, Joe. "VR Sales Analysis: Rift and Vive to Sell Under 500,000 in 2016, PS VR to Top 2 Million." UploadVR, November 14, 2016. http://uploadvr.com/superdata-headset-sales-analysis/.

Ezenwoke, Azubuike, Omotla Ezenwoke, Adewole Adewumi, and Nicholas Omoregbe. "Wearable Technology: Opportunities and Challenges for Teaching and Learning in Higher Education in Developing Countries." *10th International Technology, Education, and Development Conference (INTED2016)*. 2016. http://eprints.covenantuniversity.edu.ng/6513/1/1390.pdf.

"Five Ways to Use Google Cardboard in the Library." *Library Administrator's Digest* 51, no. 5 (2016): 6–7.

Geck, Caroline. "The Generation Z Connection: Teaching Information Literacy to the Newest Net Generation." *Teacher Librarian* 33, no. 3 (2006): 19–23.

Gleason, Ann Whitney. *Mobile Technologies for Every Library*. Lanham, MD: Rowman & Littlefield, 2015.

Goerner, Phil. "Augmented Reality: What's Next?" *School Library Journal* 62, no. 9 (2016): 19–20.

Greene, B. "Re: VR in Community Colleges." LITA listserv, January 30, 2017. lita-l-request@lists.ala.org.

Hahn, J. "Mobile Augmented Reality Applications for Library Services." *New Library World* 113, nos. 9/10 (2012): 429–38.

Hedderly, D. J., and Heidi Scott. "Measuring the Effectiveness of Video Training through Technology-Based Education." *SAM Advanced Management Journal* 80, no. 1 (2015): 41–50.

Kubiatko, Milan, Zuzana Halakova, Tibor Nagy, and Sona Nagyova. "The Using of and Attitudes Toward Internet and Information and Communication Technologies in Different Age Groups." *Journal of Current Issues in Media and Telecommunications* 7, no. 3 (2015): 269–81.

Lewis, Ray. "Virtual Reality: Soon to Become Mainstream in Libraries?" *Information Today* 32, no. 4 (2015): 1–29.

Liao, Tony. "Mobile versus Headworn Augmented Reality: How Visions of the Future Shape, Contest, and Stabilize an Emerging Technology." *New Media and Society* (2016): 1–19.

Lloyd, Meg. "An Open Repository of Learning Space Design." *Campus Technology*, October 12, 2016. https://campustechnology.com/articles/2016/10/12/an-open-repository-of-learning-space-design.aspx.

Majumdar, Arunima. "Utilizing Augmented Reality for Special Needs Learning." *eLearning Industry*, August 8, 2016. https://elearningindustry.com/augmented-reality-for-special-needs-learning.

Massis, Bruce. "Using Virtual and Augmented Reality in the Library." *New Library World* 116, nos. 11/12 (2015): 796–99.

Meredith, Tamara R. "Using Augmented Reality Tools to Enhance Children's Library Services." *Technology, Knowledge and Learning* 20 (2015): 71–77.

Metz, Rachel. "Remember Second Life? Its Creators Are Back with a Virtual Reality Platform." *MIT Technology Review*, January 27, 2017. https://www.technologyreview.com/s/603422/second-life-is-back-for-a-third-life-this-time-in-virtual-reality/.

Miltenoff, P., Hoover, J., Tzokov, G., and Schnellert, G. "The Educational Use of Social Media Cross-Nationally: A Preliminary Descriptive Study." *Academia,* 2012. https://www.academia.edu/4919965/The_Educational_Use_of_Social_Media_Cross-Nationally_A_Preliminary_Descriptive_Study.

Mislevy, R. J., Russell G. Almond, and Janice F. Lukas. "A Brief Introduction to Evidence-Centered Design." *ETS Research Report Series,* 2003, i–29. doi: 10.1002/j.2333-8504.2003.tb01908.x.

Mislevy, R. J., Linda S. Steinberg, Russell G. Almond. "Design and Analysis in Task-Based Language Assessment." *CSE Technical Report* (2002). https://eric.ed.gov/?id=ED471471.

Moorefield-Lang, Heather. "Libraries and the Rift." *Knowledge Quest* 43, no. 5 (2015): 76–77.

Nagel, David. "How Teachers Leverage Mobile Technology." *THE Journal*, October 11, 2016. https://thejournal.com/articles/2016/10/11/how-teachers-leverage-mobile-technology.aspx.

Newby, Kenneth, Ron Wakkary, Marek Hatala, Dale Evernden, and Milena Droumeva. "Interactive Audio Content: An Approach to Audio Content for a Dynamic Museum Experience through Augmented Audio Reality and Adaptive Information Retrieval." *Academia*, 2004. https://www.academia.edu/30012334/Interactive_Audio_Content_An_Approach_to_Audio_Content_for_a_Dynamic_Museum_Experience_through_Augmented_Audio_Reality_and_Adaptive_Information_Retrieval.

Nelson, Noah. "Virtual Reality's Next Hurdle: Overcoming 'Sim Sickness.'" NPR.org, August 10, 2014. http://www.npr.org/sections/alltechconsidered/2014/08/05/338015854/virtual-realitys-next-hurdle-overcoming-sim-sickness.

Noor, Ahmed. "The Hololens Revolution." *Mechanical Engineering* 138, no. 10 (2016): 30–35.

Paaßen, Benjamin, Thekla Morgenroth, and Michelle Stratemeyer. "What Is a True Gamer? The Male Gamer Stereotype and the Marginalization of Women in Video Game Culture." *Sex Roles* 76, nos. 7/8 (2017): 421–35.

Ravipati, Sri. "5 VR Trends to Watch in Education." *Campus Technology*, May 16, 2017. https://campustechnology.com/articles/2017/05/16/5-vr-trends-to-watch-in-education.aspx.

———. "Report: IT Professionals Worldwide Say It's Still Early for AR Adoption." *Campus Technology*, November 15, 2016. https://campustechnology.com/articles/2016/11/15/report-it-professionals-worldwide-say-its-still-early-for-ar-adoption.aspx.

Robinson, Lyn. "Multisensory, Pervasive, Immersive: Towards a New Generation of Documents." *Journal of the Association for Information Science and Technology* 66, no. 8 (2015): 1734–37.

Rossoff, Matt. "Oculus Founder Explains Why Some People Get Sick When Using His Product." *Business Insider*, March 16, 2017. http://www.businessinsider.com/oculus-founder-palmer-luckey-on-vr-sickness-2016-3.

Sanabria, Jorge C. "The Gradual Immersion Method (GIM): Pedagogical Transformation into Mixed Reality." *2015 International Conference Virtual and Augmented Reality in Education* 75 (2015): 369–74.

Schaffhauser, Dian. "Stanford VR Project Shows Students Oceans of the Future." *THE Journal*, October 19, 2016. https://thejournal.com/articles/2016/10/19/stanford-vr-project-shows-students-oceans-of-the-future.aspx.

Siegal, Jacob. "Netflix and HBO Launch Virtual Reality Apps on Google Play." BGR, December 12, 2016. http://bgr.com/2016/12/12/netflix-hbo-vr-android-apps/.

Smith, Frank. "Could HoloLens' Augmented Reality Change How We Study the Human Body?" *EdTech*, April 18, 2016. http://www.edtechmagazine.com/higher/article/2016/04/university-testing-limits-hololens-augmented-reality.

Stansbury, Meris. "5 Ways Virtual Reality Is Being Used in Education Right Now." *eSchool News*, October 17, 2016. http://www.eschoolnews.com/2016/10/17/5-ways-virtual-reality-used-education-right-now/.

Stern, Michael J., Alison E. Adams, and Shaun Elsasser. "Digital Inequality and Place: The Effects of Technological Diffusion on Internet Proficiency and Usage Across Rural, Suburban, and Urban Counties." *Sociological Inquiry* 79, no. 4 (2009): 391–417.

Straight, Ryan. "An Exploratory Study of Augmented Reality and Mobile Games Examining Ingress Player Motivation and Potential Educational Value." PhD Dissertation, Ohio University, 2015. https://etd.ohiolink.edu/pg_10?0::NO:10:P10_ACCESSION_NUM:ohiou1426691458.

Torres-Díaz, Juan-Carlos, Josep M. Duart, Héctor F. Gómez-Alvarado, Isidro Marín-Gutiérrez, and Verónica Segarra-Faggioni. "Internet Use and Academic Success in University Students." *Comunicar* 24, no. 48 (2016): 61–69.

Ulukuz, Huseyin. *Use of Augmented Reality in Museums: The Relationship between Children's Engagement and Immersive Visitor Experience.* PhD dissertation, University of Manchester, 2016.

Vigdor, Jacob L., and Helen F. Ladd. "Scaling the Digital Divide: Home Computer Technology and Student Achievement." *Economic Inquiry* 52, no. 3 (2014): 1103–19.

"Virtual Reality Helping California Students Overcome Learning Barriers." *eSchool News*, June 21, 2016. http://www.eschoolnews.com/2016/06/21/virtual-reality-helping-calif-students-overcome-learning-barriers/.

Yavarkovsky, Jerome. "Editorial Board Thoughts: The Promise of Immersive Libraries." *Information Technology and Libraries* 32, no. 4 (2013): 5–7.

Young, Jeffrey R. "After Frustrations in Second Life, Colleges Look to New Virtual Worlds." *Chronicle of Higher Education* 56, no. 23 (2010): A14.

Zak, Elizabeth. "Do You Believe in Magic? Exploring the Conceptualization of Augmented Reality and Its Implications for the User in the Field of Library and Information Science." *Information Technology and Libraries* 33, no. 4 (2014): 23–50.

Zaki, Mahmoud. "Image Recognition and Augmented Reality Technologies in Libraries, Museums and Bookstores." *Academia*, August 16, 2015. https://www.academia.edu/30377087/Image_Recognition_and_Augmented_Reality_Technologies_in_Libraries_Museums_and_Bookstores.

Zap, Nick, and Jillianne Code. "Virtual and Augmented Reality as Cognitive Tools for Learning." *Proceedings of EdMedia: World Conference on Educational Media and Technology* (2016): 1340–47. https://www.learntechlib.org/p/173128/.

Hyperlinks Used in the Chapter

Adobe CC Suite: http://www.adobe.com/creativecloud.html

BYOD: http://blog.stcloudstate.edu/ims?s=BYOD

Gear Action Director: https://resources.samsungdevelopers.com/Gear_360/02_Download_Gear_360_Action_Director

InforMedia Services Group: http://blog.stcloudstate.edu/ims/free-tech-instruction/

More on virtual reality in the IMS blog: http://blog.stcloudstate.edu/ims?s=virtual+reality

Samsung Gear 360 camera: http://www.samsung.com/us/mobile/virtual-reality/gear-360/sm-c200nzwaxar-sm-c200nzwaxar

Virtualization Lab: https://www.facebook.com/SCSUVizLab

13

Teaching through Experiencing

A Case Study Using 360-degree Video in Library Instruction

Alanna Aiko Moore and Scott McAvoy

The University of California San Diego (UCSD) Library (hereafter referred to as "the Library") plays a critical role in advancing and supporting the research, teaching, and public service missions of the university.[1] One of the ways that the Library supports the campus is by providing a liaison librarian for each academic department, who conducts outreach to faculty and provides specialized instruction, research assistance, and other services through a personalized, one-on-one approach. In addition, the Library is staffed by many "functional" specialists who specialize in offering technological support and expertise to the campus in areas such as GIS,[2] data curation, and digital preservation. These functional specialists and liaison librarians often work together to provide a seamless research experience to Library users.

The Library is also widely recognized as an innovative leader on the cutting edge of technology to support the university's world-class research and instruction. The Library was the first academic library in Southern California to partner with Google in its efforts to build a global digital library, plays a leadership role in HathiTrust,[3] and is also a partner in the university's Research Cyberinfrastucture Initiative (RCI). Continuing the Library's trend of innovation and forward thinking, the technology-equipped Digital Media Lab (DML) was launched in October 2015 to meet the high-demand multimedia needs of UC San Diego faculty and students.

This chapter will discuss DML creation,[4] outline the services it provides, and describe 360-degree video, just one of the many technologies offered by the DML. Through a case study, the authors will outline how 360-degree video has a role in library instruction and describe how a liaison librarian for the Department of Ethnic Studies and a functional specialist—the Digital Media Lab manager—collaborated on a seminar class. Finally, the chapter will examine how the technology was deployed in the class and discuss challenges and next steps.

CREATING THE DIGITAL MEDIA LAB

The DML in the Library was originally conceived as a post-production lab with video-editing software, image manipulation programs, and sound editing tools. However, an environmental scan and service gap analysis of campus technology resources showed that traditional media services and video editing were in the process of quickly being expanded campus wide. It became clear that the real need on campus was for equipment and services centered on new 3D visualization technologies, which were evolving quickly in industry and research areas but remained largely unsupported by university resources. DML planners used this knowledge to create a unique, niche space in the Library that served the entire campus community. In addition to 3D visualization technology, the DML currently offers free 3D printing, video editing, image manipulation, sound editing, media-rich website creation, and support for app development. The DML is open to all UCSD faculty, staff, and students.

Academic libraries have an opportunity to engage with new technology in ways that "serve the education and research interests of our organizations" and can also "represent a central unit within the university to act as a gateway to this technology."[5] The DML built on the novelty and promise of new consumer-grade 3D technology, and transformed the DML into a full-service, high-traffic "gateway" staffed 12 hours a day by skilled student assistants and overseen by the Digital Media Lab manager. The Library was on trend with the DML and continued to prioritize student learning, access, and media literacy by providing "information resources and technologies that students may not otherwise be able to afford; many [libraries] are now expanding their offerings to include cutting-edge tools such as virtual reality equipment, advanced digital editing software, and 3D printers which can enhance student learning while teaching media literacy concepts."[6]

In building the DML services, library staff placed enormous time and effort into identifying technology that met the following criteria: (1) provided high-impact experiences for most new users, (2) allowed content to be created with easily accessible tools such as free software and less expensive equipment, and (3) was easily incorporated into the Library's existing infrastructure. One of the newest technologies featured in the DML that fulfilled the requirements was 360-degree photography and video, which incorporates elements of 3D and virtual reality.

360-DEGREE VIDEO CONCEPTS

Many of us are familiar with traditional film, which records its subjects through a narrow frame. In contrast, 360-degree video records in every direction around a camera, giving the user a full "panoramic" field of view. Multiple cameras are often used, and resulting footage is often "stitched" together into a single video. At times, 360-degree videos are also termed "immersive" videos—a virtual space in which the user can view, hear, and move. As the technology and cameras become cheaper and easier to access, the body of 360-degree content has exploded. Tourists record their journeys, putting viewers of their travel adventures literally "in their shoes." Protestors hold the cameras high to capture the crowd and record police activity. Researchers record wildlife, landscapes, and events from unexpected angles, capturing and processing more useful data than they have in the past.

Independent filmmakers are taking 360-degree video very seriously and helping to move it into the mainstream. Since 2014, both the Sundance and Tribeca film festivals have included 360-degree films.[7] The format requires drastically different photography strategies, as directors no longer frame individual shots, but build entire environments and then direct the viewers' attention where they want it. Marvel Studios has released 360-degree trailers that viewers can watch multiple times from different angles, with a different experience each time. Several studios have invested heavily in cinematic 360-degree video startups, but there does not seem to be any commitment to making feature-length 360-degree studio films.[8] While the market for 360-degree video for entertainment is uncertain, the power and usefulness of the medium for documentary film and scholarship is very clear. The technologies "may ultimately transform the ways in which we teach, learn, engage with each other and experience the world writ large. Technologies advance at a steady pace and become embedded in our lives, so we may one day look back with a sense of amazement at students once bound to a physical classroom, campus setting, locale, or even place in time."[9]

The UC San Diego Library determined that offering this technology in the Library was vital to supporting student learning and media literacy. In addition, since 360-degree video can be adopted for instruction and research, and integrated into library digital collections with relatively little effort, it fits in seamlessly with existing services like subject-specific instruction, faculty outreach, and liaison relationship building. With 360-degree photography and video, the Library hoped to build bridges across campus and find and share content that complemented all academic disciplines. In launching this new technology, staff decided to offer 360-degree cameras for users to *film* video content; video-editing software to *create* videos; headsets for users to *view* existing and newly created 360-degree videos; a library of 360-degree videos for users to *browse* and *search;* and, of course, expert assistance to *advise* on using the equipment and software.

DML AND 360-DEGREE VIDEO SERVICES

Equipment for recording 360-degree video has become increasingly more attainable and inexpensive within the past year, with quality cameras beginning in the $250 range. The Digital Media Lab at UC San Diego Library surveyed virtual reality researchers on campus, who recommended specific camera models for purchase that were based on price, ease of use, and video quality. The DML purchased seven 360-degree cameras: five consumer-grade Samsung Gear 360 cameras, one mid-range dual Kodak sp360-degree4k, and one high-end GoPro multicam.[10] The GoPro was mounted on a custom-built 3D rig, printed at the DML.[11]

To begin using 360-degree equipment, users set up an appointment with the Digital Media Lab manager, who introduces them to the camera and teaches them how to use it and care for it. The cameras can be checked out by any UC San Diego student, staff, or faculty member, and loan periods usually range from three days to one week. Patrons who borrow the 360-degree cameras often return to meet with the DML manager to learn how to use video-editing software like Adobe Premiere and Cyberlink Action Director to turn their filmed matter into a video. Some of these completed projects include a capoeira dance documentary with performers placed all around the camera, a recording of an art gallery opening and music festival, wildlife photography, and a graduate student recruitment film showing popular beach-side spots and San Diego cultural centers like Balboa Park and the Wild Animal Park.[12]

The 360-degree videos are played back on a headset containing googles and a screen in front of the eyes that allows the individual to "view" images, sounds, and other stimuli that make the environment seem realistic. The DML offers six head-mounted displays (HMDs) to view 360-degree videos, including two Oculus Touches, two HTC Vives (both higher-end models), and two Samsung Gears (mid-range in pricing). While the DML has invested in expensive headsets to support programming and simulation development, a $10 Google Cardboard headset paired with a high-end smartphone also enables viewing of 360-degree content.[13]

Using collection development techniques, the staff researched the best educational 360-degree videos and offers over 10,000 videos for users to view. They include several curated collections and are captured on a LibGuide.[14] All videos were procured at no cost, and many videos are available for free on

YouTube, Vimeo, Facebook, and through free curated apps by a variety of publishers, like Discovery Channel and Within. High-impact examples showing inaccessible locations, dangerous surroundings, and important events are generally chosen for demonstration. Most videos are between 5 and 7 minutes long.

Although the DML does offer headsets for viewing, the technology was appealing because headsets are not necessarily needed, which helps to close the digital divide. Videos are viewable on every virtual reality (VR) platform, including mobile and desktop systems, and can even be viewed outside of the VR environment. YouTube and Facebook have invested heavily in this new media format and have made content widely available on flat screens without the use of a headset. Current-generation smartphones employ their tilt sensors to show 360-degree content from whatever angle the phone is facing, and photo-stitching software like Google's Photo Sphere app allows users to build 360-degree content by layering pictures from their device's camera.

The DML also supports a pilot 360-degree video wall called the Cavekiosk.[15] This wall consists of six 55-inch 3D televisions arranged in a curve. Users can choose between various 360-degree photographs from at-risk world heritage sites, and rotate the photo spheres with an Xbox controller mounted in front of the screens. All photos were taken by UCSD archaeologists and VR researchers with a special stereoscopic ultra-high-definition photography setup. The Cavekiosk[16] represents an effort to bring immersive VR experiences to larger groups and tours without the use of individual headsets. It has proved to be a highly engaging exhibit that has linked the Library to researchers and programmers across campus, and there are plans to use it in instructional activities in the future.

COLLABORATION: INTEGRATING 360-DEGREE VIDEO INTO INSTRUCTION

In the same way that a subject specialist or liaison librarian prepares to teach a class by learning about the subject area and assignment, the Digital Media Lab instructor generally follows the same methods. When contacted with a request for 360-degree video for a class (by a faculty member or a liaison librarian), DML staff searches for content related to the discipline and the focus of the class. For example, in the fields of history and archeology, 360-degree videos may show important historical locations like the Hagia Sofia, Egyptian ruins, remote Tibetan temples, or other important world heritage sites. Videos in science and technology might show relevant data visualizations on a spherical plane, facilities, and environments; a marine biology class may choose to view underwater dive footage or world-scale temperature data; and students studying aerospace engineering could see inside of a multi-million-dollar jet or spacecraft. The curriculum is then created for the class, with several videos chosen to best reflect the assignment or class focus. This is active learning at its best. After students view the videos, an informal class discussion takes place in the DML to help place their experience in context, tie it into the course assignment, and communicate further applications.

Using 360-degree video makes the content relevant, and students remain engaged with the course material. As the 2017 New Media Consortium (NMC) Horizon report states, "As higher education continues to move away from traditional, lecture based lessons toward more hands-on activities, classrooms are starting to resemble real-world work and social environments that foster organic interactions and cross-disciplinary problem solving."[17] Working in collaboration, faculty, DML staff, and liaison librarians can design a research session that can increase both information and media literacy for students and help them to build strong research strategies to complete assignments. Liaison librarians play important roles in bringing faculty on board with new technology, sharing emerging services with their departments, and working with DML staff to provide background on disciplines, faculty research, and instruction methodologies.

VIEWING DISSENT: 360-DEGREE VIDEO AND A SEMINAR CLASS

Incorporating 360-degree content into undergraduate classes is a new phenomenon for UC San Diego Library, and in fall 2016, the librarian for the Department of Ethnic Studies and the DML manager had a chance to incorporate the technology into a seminar class. A faculty member in Ethnic Studies, who had previous experience using the DML's 3D printing services for a conference presentation, asked for 360-degree video to be included in her practicum-style seminar class entitled "Ethnic Studies 120, Race and Performance: Performing Dissent." The class is described as follows:

> Trump's campaign and election has inspired many public acts of xenophobia, racism, ableism, transphobia, Islamophobia, anti-Semitism, homophobia and sexism. In response to this, people . . . are showing their dissatisfaction through performances of dissent. We will follow and participate in these actions, consider how theories and performances provide insights into understanding race as a social formation and how theories of race provide insights into better understanding performance as social phenomenon.[18]

The description pointedly states that students will "participate in these actions." The prompt for the final project was to engage the concepts covered in the course through an analytical paper or a video or audio performance in which the student participated.

The faculty member requested that students be exposed to "social movement videos," experience "performances of dissent," and watch suggested videos from Black Lives Matter, NODAPL,[19] and recent protests in Korea against president Park Geun-hye.[20] Coordinating with the DML manager, the class was booked for the fifth week of the ten-week quarter.

The Library has a long history of working closely with the Ethnic Studies faculty—the librarian to the Department of Ethnic Studies has built strong relationships over the past decade, and has taught dozens of research methods and instruction classes each year. Several Ethnic Studies classes have made use of primary source material through visits to the Library's Special Collections and Archives, and have viewed primary source material through databases that house digital collections. Through intensive outreach and attendance at departmental events and conferences, the Ethnic Studies librarian has built knowledge of faculty needs and scholarship. She makes a practice of continually highlighting technological services that the Library offers (such as those in the Digital Media Lab) to faculty whenever possible.

Approximately 20 students from "Ethnic Studies 120, Race and Performance: Performing Dissent" attended the 80-minute session at the DML. In preparing for the visit, the DML manager decided it would be appropriate to employ two main videos from award-winning filmmaker Chris Milk's Within collection, "bringing together the best immersive experiences from the world's finest VR creators . . . with the goal of exploring and expanding the potential of immersive storytelling."[21] The first video, entitled "VICE NEWS VR: Millions March"[22] is a news piece captured by a 360-degree camera that was kept in constant motion while following a Black Lives Matter protest down the streets of New York City.[23] The video "takes viewers into the December rally that saw 60,000 protestors descend on the street of New York to demand greater police accountability."[24] The 360-degree film allows the audience to see, hear, and feel the protest; the viewer is swept up in a moving crowd, can gather around speakers to hear their passionate outcries from feet and sometimes inches away, and is surrounded by chanting, signs, and banners. The viewer of "VICE NEWS VR: Millions March" is part of the protest, blocking traffic on Broadway and lying down in the middle of the street in a "die-in" demonstration.

The second piece students viewed was "Clouds Over Sidra,"[25] a virtual reality piece commissioned for the United Nations (UN) World Economic Forum. The video is narrated by a 12-year-old girl and shows the inside of the Za'atari Syrian refugee camp in Jordan in intimate detail. In this video, the 360-degree format is especially effective in communicating a sense of space and scale. Viewers can look around the tiny tent she sleeps in with her entire family, follow her to school, and see the camp that houses over 84,000 Syrian refugees. "Clouds Over Sidra" is the first virtual reality film produced for the UN, which is using the medium to generate greater empathy and new perspectives on people living in conditions of great vulnerability. Gabo Arora, senior advisor at the UN, states: "By leveraging breakthrough technologies, such as virtual reality, we can create solidarity with those who are normally excluded and overlooked, amplifying their voices and explaining their situations."[26]

The emotional impact of the 360-degree videos is considerable. Researchers are finding that a virtual environment can change the way users think about the subject and impact their behavior over time. One 2016 study by Stanford's Virtual Human Interaction Lab[27] found that virtual environments "led to greater feeling of embodiment, perception of being present in the virtual world, and interconnection between the self and nature compared to video."[28] No longer just "watching," a 360-degree video can impart a feeling of presence. Users are there in that moment, in that place, with the people around them. This is a powerful research tool. To empathize with one's subject by sharing their experiences is critical to understanding it.

TEACHING 360-DEGREE TECHNOLOGY

The class began with a brief introduction to the DML and the services that students (and faculty) have access to, free of charge. An overview of the two films followed, with a brief warning that the subject matter and viewing the videos may affect students and/or cause an emotional reaction. Students were then divided into small groups, and headsets were used to view the pre-selected videos. Two headsets were set up to view "VICE NEWS VR: Millions March," two headsets were set up to view "Clouds Over Sidra," and the DML manager used a fifth headset to demonstrate how to navigate the videos. He explained the controls to start, stop, and pause, showed students how to secure the headsets, then assisted them in navigating the environment. The remaining students who were not wearing headsets watched classmates engage with the technology.

The virtual reality headsets worn by the students not only generate realistic images, sounds, and other sensations that replicate a real environment or create an imaginary setting, but also block out all outside distractions. This results in total immersion and engagement. Students interact with the 360-degree videos by controlling movements of their bodies, and can pause or rewind to watch the event from a totally different angle, to take in every detail.

Students share a world with the films' subjects, and even from the safety of the quiet, air-conditioned library, can share the sentiments and experiences of the video's subjects. After each small group of four had a chance to view the 360-degree videos, the class gathered together to discuss, analyze, and share their thoughts about using the technology and viewing the two videos.

In the post-viewing discussion, students talked about how it felt to watch the videos and experience things in 360 degrees, and debated the prevalence of new technologies and the role that they play in individual lives. Several students made referenced to the Netflix *Black Mirror*[29] science fiction series, which features stories about future technologies. The episode "The Entire History of You" explored a technology that allowed users to record their entire day through "grains" implanted behind their ears. The characters watch and rewatch the events they'd just lived through, agonizing over details they might have previously missed, reliving job interviews and relationships. Students felt that the concept of 360-degree video and the ability to record everything you see along with the everything going on around you brings about this same idea—that we might record our own lives and rewatch them later to try to uncover a story that perhaps we had perceived incorrectly. The engagement of the students underlined how, when technology is used correctly in an academic class, it can increase collaborative learning through peer-to-peer and group activities, and supports the theory that learning is a social construct.[30] Finally, students could see the connections between race, environment, and performances of dissent through their interactions with the videos.

CHALLENGES

One of the challenges the Library faces with using 360-degree video in instruction is the size and configuration of the Digital Media Lab. Since the DML houses working computers, a 3D printer, and other technologies, there is a lack of open instruction space to teach students who are wearing the headsets, who must stand and physically engage with the environment. Currently, the DML manager shuts down reservations for the entire lab to accommodate instruction sessions, which means that other users are unable to access the technology or the space. The cramped quarters also make it challenging to have multiple students using the equipment simultaneously, as each student must be a discreet and safe distance from their classmates. For the seminar class, four students at a time viewed the videos. A separate instruction space will allow for larger class sizes and more fluid co-teaching between the DML manager and liaison librarians. The space would also be more conducive for students to discuss and debrief at the end of a class.

There are other challenges to integrating 360-degree video technology into library instruction. In regard to the technology itself, the main limitation of 360-degree video is picture quality, as even when cameras shoot at a 4k resolution (3840 × 1920 pixels), the image is stretched over a spherical canvas and can be degraded when viewed through a headset. While this is a current concern, improvements rapidly taking place in the field will soon resolve this drawback. Motion sickness is another important consideration, as a small percentage of users experience some discomfort almost instantly; this can often be remedied by remaining seated while viewing.[31] The best strategy for mitigating motion sickness without compromising the range of movement visually is to utilize an office chair. The swivel of an office chair will allow users to rotate, and the fixed position will help them to feel grounded. It is important for instructors using the equipment to warn of the possibility of motion sickness, and then to be vigilant about spotting it and supporting the user if they are uncomfortable.

Since using 360-degree video in library instruction classes has only been done a few times so far in the Library, the authors have not yet developed formal methods of assessment. For future classes, a simple "one-minute paper"[32] will be used to ascertain student learning ("What did you enjoy about using the technology?"), the content of the videos ("Summarize one thing you learned from the video"), and how/if the 360-degree video experience will inform students' assignments ("How will you apply what you experienced today to your assignment?"). The authors also want to ask students what they would like to learn more about, and what concepts were unclear or difficult to comprehend in the instruction session. The authors plan to work with the instructional design librarian in the next year to create learning outcomes for each incoming class. It is important to assess whether students and faculty find the technology useful in achieving assignment goals, to discover what works well and what could be improved to enhance student learning.

Finally, strengthening communication between the DML staff and the liaison librarians who work directly with the faculty in the various disciplines and departments will ensure that faculty and students have a seamless research experience at the Library. DML staff have felt that it is a struggle to get librarians aware of and involved with the resources that they offer, and liaison librarians have often been left out of communication, discovering that faculty and students from departments they support have utilized DML services after the fact.

Both liaison librarians and DML staff are working to try to overcome these barriers by making commitments to share information and learn more about the scope of their positions and how each does their work. Finally, being open to working together and giving each other feedback is key to the future success of integrating DML technology into subject-specific library instruction.

CONCLUSION

By engaging with 360-degree content, the UC San Diego Library supports the mission of the university by providing access to technology, skilled instructors, and a variety of ways to apply the technology to the academic environment. Experimenting with the technology generates different approaches in how it can be applied to both education and research.

According to the New Media Consortium, virtual reality and 360-degree photography and film have "the potential to connect us with the world and each other in ways not previously realized. Our classroom buildings, libraries and shared academic spaces may someday provide physical grids or open sound stages designed for virtual interaction, where groups of students may take guided field trips to remote sites, interface with other cultures, or travel in time. . . . [S]tudents with physical disabilities or financial disadvantages might have access to places and experiences like never before."[33] While virtual reality and 360-degree content have value in the education sector, primarily in data visualization,[34] there remains much to explore in how the technology is used in subject-specific library instruction. By engaging students in materials that make the world literally "come alive," libraries can integrate this technology into classes and strengthen collaboration with faculty while showing students unique video content. The 360-degree video technology has the potential to reshape and enhance existing library instructional services, is an unparalleled opportunity for outreach, and illustrates how technology can be used to support many academic fields. With limited investment in hardware, students can don a headset and immediately interact with content. High-quality videos are freely available for almost any subject matter, and the number and range of titles expand weekly. The novelty and impact of this technology, and its relative scarcity in other campus teaching environments, can be leveraged toward greater engagement with academic partners.

By working together, liaison librarians and Digital Media Lab staff can provide seamless service to faculty members who engage with the Library in a myriad of ways, while demonstrating how the Library is evolving to meet the changing needs of students in the digital age. Further plans to upgrade and renovate the interior public spaces of the Geisel Library building are currently in the works, which may include multiple new active learning areas to more effectively support the current approaches to study, research, and learning of today's students and scholars.

NOTES

1. UC San Diego Library, "2015–18 Strategic Plan."

2. A short explanation of GIS can be found in the National Geographic Society encyclopedia: "GIS (geographic information system)."

3. HathiTrust is an international partnership of 52 academic and research libraries committed to long-term digital preservation; see "HathiTrust Digital Library: Millions of Books Online."

4. UC San Diego Library, "Digital Media Lab."

5. Ben Weatherall, "Experimenting with Virtual Reality," 8

6. S. Adams Becker et al., *NMC Horizon Report: 2017 Higher Education Edition*, 16.

7. Deniz Ergurel, "The International Film Festivals to Submit Virtual Reality Movies in 2016"; Sundance Institute, "Sundance Institute Announces Films and Installations for 2014 Edition of New Frontier at the Sundance Film Festival."

8. Aaron Tilley, "Disney Invests $65 Million into Virtual Reality Startup Jaunt."

9. Bryan Sinclair and Glenn Gunhouse, "The Promise of Virtual Reality in Higher Education."

10. Higher-end cameras like the GoPro use more than one camera, which creates higher resolution video with less distortion in the final product.

11. By using open source models and existing DML 3D printers and GoPro cameras, staff created a six-camera, 360-degree video rig comparable to GoPro's $5,000 Omni rig; see Raymond Hopk, "[Ver2] 360 Spherical Video Mount for GoPro Hero3/4."

12. Christopher Murphy, "UC San Diego: SACNAS 2016."

13. Google, "Google Cardboard."

14. Scott McAvoy, "360 Video."

15. UC San Diego Library, "CAVEcam Virtual Reality Photography Collection"; Dolores Davies, "New 3D CAVEkiosk at UC San Diego Brings Cyber-Archaeology to Geisel Library."

16. The UC San Diego Library's CAVEkiosk was funded by the UC Office of the President through a President's Research Catalyst Award for At-Risk Cultural Heritage and the Digital Humanities (Grant ID Number CA-16-376911).

17. Adams Becker et al., *NMC Horizon Report*, 16.

18. Roshanek Kheshti, "Ethnic Studies 120, Race and Performance: Performing Dissent."

19. NODAPL is an acronym and hashtag for protests against the Dakota Access Pipeline construction that cuts through Native American land.

20. There were numerous NODAPL and Korean protest videos, so the DML manager showed a large search list to illustrate the breadth and general quality of this type of content. Due to time constraints, only two students viewed videos on these topics.

21. Within, "About Within."

22. Within, "VICE NEWS VR: Millions March NYC 12.13.14."

23. VICE News, "Chris Milk, Spike Jonze, and VICE News Bring the First-Ever Virtual Reality Newscast to Sundance."

24. "VICE NEWS VR: Millions March"

25. Chris Milk, "The United Nations: Clouds Over Sidra,."
26. Ibid.
27. Virtual Human Interaction Lab, "Empathy/Diversity."
28. Sun Joo Ahn et al., "Experiencing Nature: Embodying Animals in Immersive Virtual Environments Increases Inclusion of Nature in Self and Involvement with Nature."
29. *Black Mirror*, Internet Movie Database.
30. Adams Becker et al., *NMC Horizon Report*, 20.
31. Betsy Mason, "Virtual Reality Has a Motion Sickness Problem."
32. Students are given a few minutes at the end of a class to write answer(s) to one or two specific questions given to them by the instructor. Answers can be collected and analyzed to inform curricula and to see if the main points the instructor is making are being synthesized by the students.
33. Sinclair and Gunhouse, "The Promise of Virtual Reality."
34. Weatherall, "Experimenting with Virtual Reality," 15.

BIBLIOGRAPHY

Adams Becker, S., Cummins, M., Davis, A., Freeman, A., Hall Giesinger, C., and Ananthanarayanan, V. *NMC Horizon Report: 2017 Higher Education Edition.* Austin, Texas: The New Media Consortium, 2017. http://cdn.nmc.org/media/2017-nmc-horizon-report-he-EN.pdf.

Ahn, Sun Joo, Joshua Bostick, Elise Ogle, Kristine L. Nowak, Kara T. McGillicuddy, and Jeremy N. Bailenson. "Experiencing Nature: Embodying Animals in Immersive Virtual Environments Increases Inclusion of Nature in Self and Involvement with Nature." *Journal of Computer-Mediated Communication* 21, no. 6 (2016): 399–419. doi:10.1111/jcc4.12173.

Black Mirror (TV Series, 2011–). Internet Movie Database, 2017. http://www.imdb.com/title/tt2085059/.

Davies, Dolores. "New 3D CAVEkiosk at UC San Diego Brings Cyber-Archaeology to Geisel Library." UC San Diego News Center, October 31, 2016. http://ucsdnews.ucsd.edu/pressrelease/new_3_d_cavekiosk_at_uc_san_diego_brings_cyber_archaeology_to_geisel.

Ergurel, Deniz. "The International Film Festivals to Submit Virtual Reality Movies in 2016." PBS.org, August 22, 2016. http://www.pbs.org/pov/blog/news/2016/08/film-festivals-to-submit-virtual-reality-films-360-video/.

Google. "Google Cardboard." Accessed July 28, 2017. https://vr.google.com/cardboard/.

HathiTrust. "HathiTrust Digital Library: Millions of Books Online." Accessed May 12, 2017. https://www.hathitrust.org.

Hopk, Raymond. "[Ver2] 360 Spherical Video Mount for GoPro Hero3/4." Thingiverse, October 7, 2015. https://www.thingiverse.com/thing:1057740.

Kheshti, Roshanek. "Ethnic Studies 120, Race and Performance: Performing Dissent." Syllabus, UC San Diego, La Jolla, CA, 2017.

Mason, Betsy. "Virtual Reality Has a Motion Sickness Problem." *ScienceNews*, March 7, 2017. https://www.sciencenews.org/article/virtual-reality-has-motion-sickness-problem.

McAvoy, Scott. "360 Video." UC San Diego Library LibGuides, July 13, 2017. http://ucsd.libguides.com/c.php?g=696979.

Milk, Chris. "The United Nations: Clouds Over Sidra." Here Be Dragons, Accessed May 2, 2017. http://dragons.org/creators/chris-milk/work/the-united-nations-clouds-over-sidra/.

Murphy, Christopher. "UC San Diego: SACNAS 2016." YouTube, September 12, 2016. https://youtu.be/-t4TfMaEXSc?list=PLtcuNHWW3NTnN-ZFsUQPvjeU0nAa3vCRd.

National Geographic Society. "GIS (geographic information system)." *National Geographic Society*, October 9, 2012. https://www.nationalgeographic.org/encyclopedia/geographic-information-system-gis/.

Sinclair, Bryan, and Glenn Gunhouse. "The Promise of Virtual Reality in Higher Education." *EDUCAUSE Review*, March 7, 2016. http://er.educause.edu/articles/2016/3/the-promise-of-virtual-reality-in-higher-education.

Steel, Emily. "Vice Uses Virtual Reality to Immerse Viewers in News." *The New York Times*, January 23, 2015. https://www.nytimes.com/2015/01/23/business/media/vice-uses-virtual-reality-to-immerse-viewers-in-news.html

Sundance Institute. "Sundance Institute Announces Films and Installations for 2014 Edition of New Frontier at the Sundance Film Festival." December 5, 2013. https://www.sundance.org/blogs/news/2014-festival-new-frontier-projects-announced.

Tilley, Aaron. "Disney Invests $65 Million into Virtual Reality Startup Jaunt." *Forbes*, September 21, 2015. https://www.forbes.com/sites/aarontilley/2015/09/21/disney-invests-65-million-into-cinematic-virtual-reality-startup-jaunt/#2b6d9764227a.

UC San Diego Library. "2015–18 Strategic Plan." Accessed July 28, 2017. https://libraries.ucsd.edu/_files/about/documents/ucsd-library-strategic-plan-2015-2018.pdf.

———. "CAVEcam Virtual Reality Photography Collection." Library Digital Collections, 2016. https://library.ucsd.edu/dc/collection/bb0309246g.

———. "Digital Media Lab." 2017. https://library.ucsd.edu/computing-and-technology/digital-media-lab/.

———. "Digital Media Lab Open in Geisel Library." 2017. https://libraries.ucsd.edu/blogs/blog/digital-media-lab-opens-in-geisel-library/.

VICE News. "Chris Milk, Spike Jonze, and VICE News Bring the First-Ever Virtual Reality Newscast to Sundance." *VICE News*, January 22, 2015. https://news.vice.com/article/chris-milk-spike-jonze-and-vice-news-bring-the-first-ever-virtual-reality-newscast-to-sundance.

Virtual Human Interaction Lab. "Empathy/Diversity." Stanford University. Accessed May 16, 2017. https://vhil.stanford.edu/topics/empathy-diversity/.

Weatherall, Ben. "Experimenting with Virtual Reality in a University Library." *Annual Australian Library and Information Association National Conference,* Adelaide, South Australia, August 29–September 2, 2016. https://nationalconference.alia.org.au/sites/default/files/Ben_Weatherall.pdf.

Within. "About Within." Accessed May 2, 2017. https://with.in/about/.

Within. "VICE NEWS VR: Millions March NYC 12.13.14." YouTube, November 5, 2015. https://www.youtube.com/watch?v=N9cZRfp6mOA.

Index

About the Editors and Contributors

Jolanda-Pieta van Arnhem is the studio librarian at the College of Charleston Libraries. She contributes her expertise researching emerging technologies and providing instruction for faculty, staff, and students regarding information technology utilization and digital scholarship tools for research and classroom use in the arts and humanities. She also teaches for the Department of Studio Art as part of the First Year Experience program at the College of Charleston. Jolanda is a member of the American Library Association, is on the editorial board for the *Charleston Advisor*, and contributes advisor reports from the field in her column, "Mobile Apps in Libraries." Jolanda's most recent publication is a chapter titled "The Intersections of Art and Librarianship, Issue 1: Filling in the Gaps," in *The Self as Subject: Autoethnography Research into Identity, Culture, and Academic Librarianship*, edited by Anne-Marie Deitering, Rick Stoddart, and Bob Schroeder (2017). (vanarnhemj@cofc.edu)

Christine Elliott is an information services librarian at The Citadel, The Military College of South Carolina. Elliott has been utilizing her interest and expertise in technology and innovative teaching methods to enhance library instruction. She has integrated experimental technologies and applications in face-to-face and online interactions with patrons and students. She has presented on augmented reality at Summer ALA 2016 and at the 2017 South Carolina Conference on Innovations in Teaching and Learning in Charleston, with Jolanda-Pieta van Arnhem and Marie Rose. Christine has published reviews for ARLIS/NA and chapters in *The Discovery Tool Cookbook* (2016) and *Teaching Technology in Libraries: Creative Ideas for Training Staff, Patrons, and Students* (2017). (celliot1@citadel.edu)

Marie Rose is an information services librarian at The Citadel, The Military College of South Carolina. She provides expertise in systems and technology at her library, and led efforts to create The Citadel's first makerspace. Through this initiative, Marie has been introducing emerging technologies, such as AR/VR, to students and faculty. With an undergraduate degree in art and design, she is also interested in how good design will shape the future of AR/VR. (mrose5@citadel.edu)

* * *

Phillip Ballo is a library assistant at Southwestern College and a DIY hobbyist who likes to dabble in technology. His hobbies include 3D printing, 3D modeling, 2D art, video game design, virtual reality, computer programming, and other tech-related interests. He has written reviews, guides, and presented on the tools and use of technology, makerspaces, and the library. He is currently working on a job simulator type application using the Unity game engine. (pballo@swccd.edu)

Raven Bishop, NBCT, is an instructional technologist at Washington College. She is also National Board Certified Visual Arts Educator and Creative Consultant working with the area of community arts programming. (rbishop3@washcoll.edu)

Heather Calloway is the archivist and special collections librarian and an assistant professor at Washington College. Prior to this position, she served as museum curator and managing director of digital and social media for 14 years with the headquarters of the Scottish Rite Freemasons in Washington, D.C. She earned her doctorate from the University of Pennsylvania, and her passion is preserving fraternal and religious ephemera. (hcalloway2@washcoll.edu)

Gabri Christa is assistant professor of professional practice in the Department of Dance, Barnard College at Columbia University, where she teaches screendance, technique, and composition. Christa makes original works for stage and screen, hails from Curaçao, Dutch Caribbean, and lives in New York. Awards include the Guggenheim Award for Choreography, an ABC Television award for creative excellence for her short film "High School," and Pangea Day Festival's One World's 100 Most Promising Filmmakers distinction. Her films have won several prizes and her latest documentary, "One Day at a Time" (2016), about yoga Master Leo Floridas, won best short documentary at the Harlem International Film Festival, among others.

She has two new films in the works, a feature film and a short dance film. (gchrista@barnard.edu)

Art Gutierrez is an assistant professor and head of technical services at Emporia State University. He received his MLS from Emporia State. His research interest areas include technology in the library, leadership, and information literacy. (agutierr@emporia.edu)

Cynthia Hart has been a public librarian for almost 30 years. For more than a decade, she managed Virginia Beach Public Library's intranet and Internet sites. Among her accomplishments include establishing the library's social media, coordinating gaming and multimedia projects across the system, and developing and implementing technology tools and training, including coding classes for everyone from preschoolers to adults. She also facilitated VBPL's partnership with Tagwhat, making the library the first in the nation to be included in the mobile app, using augmented reality for rich, location-based storytelling and showcasing local history collections. She is a trend watcher, identifying and writing about emerging technologies. (chart@vbgov.com)

Melanie Hibbert is the director of instructional media at Barnard College, Columbia University. Her career has focused on education and media, including teaching in rural Alaska for two years and working as a media producer in New York City. She holds a doctorate in education from Teachers College, Columbia University; her research focuses on learning from technology and media. Her video work screened at places including the Harlem International Film Festival, FLEX Fest, and the Center for Documentary Studies. (mch2145@tc.columbia.edu)

Julie N. Hornick is an instructional services librarian at Florida Southern College's Roux Library, where she recently moved after 13 years as a school librarian in South Carolina. She earned her MA in French from Penn State and her MLIS from the University of South Carolina's School of Library and Information Science. She liaises with the art, art history, and all science departments, as well as the School of Education and School of Nursing and Health Sciences. Her research interests include incorporating new technologies into instruction, instructional design, and the impact that embedded librarians can have on student achievement and retention. (jhornick@flsouthern.edu)

Paul R. Hottinger is the subject librarian for the College of Education at Cal Poly Pomona. (prhottinger@cpp.edu)

Abby Lee, a New York native, is the instructional media specialist at Barnard College's Instructional Media and Technology Services. At IMATS, Abby wears many hats and whether it is managing the equipment room, editing the latest event video recordings, or teaching video-making workshops, she is constantly on the move. Previously, she was a freelance editor for several independent film companies, nonprofit organizations such as Japan Society, as well as a sizzle reel editor for HGTV. Abby is working on a master's degree in instructional technology at Teacher's College, Columbia University. In her free time, she is also a film editor, artist, and photographer. (aglee@barnard.edu)

Scott McAvoy is an educational technologist and head of UC San Diego Library's Digital Media Lab. He has built a number of innovative library services around 3D visualization, including 3D modeling, animation, 3D printing, and AR/VR. He routinely collaborates with researchers and faculty from a wide variety of backgrounds to integrate these technologies into instruction and research. (smcavoy@ucsd.edu)

Katie Mills is the library manager (Arts, Business, Law, and Education) at the University of Western Australia. Katie's expertise and interests include digital media and scholarship, marketing and engagement, VR/AR, and 3D printing. (katie.mills@uwa.edu.au)

Plamen Miltenoff is an information specialist and professor at St. Cloud State University. His education includes graduate degrees in history and in library and information science, and terminal degrees in education and psychology. Dr. Miltenoff teaches various classes, from undergraduate to doctoral, as well as instructional sessions in educational technology. His professional interests encompass new technologies in education, social media, multimedia, web development and design, gaming and gamification, learning environments (LEs), online education, and virtual solutions. (pmiltenoff@stcloudstate.edu)

Alanna Aiko Moore is the sociology, ethnic studies, and gender studies librarian for UC San Diego Library. She is passionate about helping students learn through information literacy initiatives, underserved populations, and first-generation college students. She works with faculty to integrate digital storytelling methods into their instruction and research. (aamoore@ucsd.edu)

Bethanie O'Dell is an assistant professor and virtual learning librarian at Emporia State University. She received her MLS from Emporia State University, and her MS in instructional design and technology from Emporia State. Her research interest areas include web tools and education, game-based learning, and active learning in online learning. (bodell1@emporia.edu)

Michael Ovens is an early career researcher and an active VR/AR developer at the University of Western Australia whose research seeks to make tangible the subjective sensory experiences associated with reading literature in the past and present. (michael.robert.ovens@gmail.com)

Alexis Seeley is currently the associate dean of online education at Columbia University. Alexis holds a BA in communications with a concentration in film and media studies, and an MA in education with a concentration in curriculum design, both from Adelphi University. (lexseeley@gmail.com)

Kai Alexis Smith is the subject librarian for the College of Environmental Design, Performing Arts, and Ethnic and Women's Studies at Cal Poly Pomona. (kasmith@cpp.edu)

Brian Sutherland is a lecturer in biomedical communications at the University of Toronto, a UX design professional in scientific communications and e-learning. He is currently a PhD student at the school's Faculty of Information, studying pervasive computing and Internet of Things (IoT). (b.sutherland@utoronto.ca)

Steven Wade has been working with college students since 2011, first as a tutor of math and English at West Kentucky Community and Technical College, then as a graduate assistant in the School of Library and Information Science at Louisiana State University. He earned his MLIS at LSU in 2015, and began working at Florida Southern College in September of that year. At FSC, Steven provides information literacy instruction and manages the library's electronic resources. (swade@flsouthern.edu)

Markus Wust is the Digital Research and Scholarship librarian at North Carolina State University Libraries. Together with several colleagues, he released WolfWalk, a mobile historic walking tour of the NC State Campus, an early example of simple augmented reality. He has taught numerous workshops on augmented reality, including weeklong workshops at the Digital Humanities Summer Institute at the University of Victoria, and has given presentations on the topic. (mgwust@ncsu.edu)